W9-BRO-691

Contents

THE BOOK OF
Jewish Books
A Reader's Guide to Judaism

Ruth S. Frank & William Wollheim

1817

Harper & Row, Publishers, San Francisco

Cambridge, Hagerstown, New York, Philadelphia, Washington
London, Mexico City, São Paulo, Singapore, Sydney

To My Martins

—R. S. F.

To Judy

—W. W.

Title page drawing by Mark Podwal, author and illustrator, New York. © 1978

"Introduction" © 1986 by Blu Greenberg; "A Celebration of Jewish Children's Books" © 1986 by Marcia Posner; "New Perspectives on the Jewish Past" © 1986 by Robert Chazan; "American Jewish Historiography" © 1986 by Jeffrey Gurock; "Holocaust" © 1986 by Judith Herschlag Muffs; "Israel and the People of the Book" © 1986 by David C. Gross; "Hands On" © 1986 by Mae Shafter Rockland; "Holidays as Memory Makers" © 1986 by Lydia Kukoff; "Text, Tradition, and Reason: The Dynamics of Medieval Jewish Thought" © 1986 by David Shatz; "Diversity and Dissent: Competing Trends in Modern Jewish Thought" © 1986 Charles M. Raffel; "The Literature of the Jewish Idea" © 1986 by Joseph Lowin; "The Modern Experience in Hebrew and Yiddish Literature" © by Jacob Kabakoff; "Renaissance in the Arts" © 1986 by Esther Nussbaum; "Women and the Jewish Literary Tradition" © 1986 by Roselyn Bell.

FIRST EDITION

Designed by Donald Hatch

Library of Congress Cataloging-in-Publication Data

The Book of Jewish books.

   Includes indexes.
   1. Jews—Bibliography.   2. Judaism—Bibliography.
I. Frank, Ruth S.   II. Wollheim, William.
Z6366.B66   1986   [BM561]   016.296   86-45014
ISBN 0-06-063008-6
ISBN 0-06-063009-4 (pbk.)

86 87 88 89 90 HC 10 9 8 7 6 5 4 3 2 1

Preface

The Book of Jewish Books has been written to serve as a guide—
and an invitation—to Jewish knowledge. It is meant for the
general reader, for both Jews and non-Jews who wish to learn
more about Jewish religion, thought, and history. Behind it
lies a deep love for the Jewish heritage and a conviction that
books are one of the best ways to help perpetuate this heritage.
The books listed in it come from many different sources, and
we hope that gathering information about them in one place
will help readers find what they are looking for. Although this
guide is written from a Jewish perspective, the needs of non-
Jewish readers have also been kept in mind.

Some understanding of how books were selected for inclusion in this guide might be helpful to you. We began by
drawing up a tentative list of suggested titles. That list was
circulated to scholars, educators, and other people knowledgeable about Jewish books. The initial response was largely one
of horror that *this* book had been omitted or *that* book included. Those suggestions that fit in with our purposes were
used to create a new list. This second list was circulated for
additional responses, and then used as the basis of this book.
Although many people looked at our list, criticized it, and
commented on it, the decisions about what to include are solely
our own. It must be emphasized that the authors of the chapter introductions are not responsible for the other parts of the
book.

Scholars and experts in every field have protested that the
list of titles in their subject area is "thin." We will admit as
much, and can only plead that to have listed more titles in
each area would have resulted in a book too costly to have
been published. There are already several excellent specialized
bibliographies available, and some of them are listed in the
REFERENCE section. There is no point in duplicating those

efforts. The goal here is to cover, even if only in an introductory manner, the entire body of Jewish knowledge, to provide a starting point for anyone beginning to study. Anyone who wants to become truly expert in a given area will have to go far beyond what we can discuss, but we believe we have provided some useful guidance to those beginning the process. As much as possible, technical terms have been avoided, and when they are used, they are defined. A glossary on page 295 is included for the reader's convenience. The first time a word that is defined in the glossary appears, it is set in **boldface** type.

Just what were our criteria for including a book? The principal one was excellence. That was not, however, our only guideline. We have also included books that, while flawed, are especially useful to beginners, or are the only ones to cover a subject. This criterion is particularly true of the FICTION section, where we have included titles that are more notable for their educational value than for their literary merit. For the most part, we have tried to avoid duplication, but in some areas several similar books are listed, because any of them will serve the purpose and whichever one of them is most readily available can be recommended. All the major viewpoints, secular and religious, are represented. For examples, prayer books from the Conservative, Orthodox, Reconstructionist, and Reform movements are included.

The basic structure of the book is simple. Each chapter begins with an introduction to the subject written by an authority in the field. This introduction is followed by a brief survey suggesting which books are best for beginners, which might be good for further study, and so on. Next come the book descriptions. These listings are intended to point to each book's special strengths and to let you know who might find each book particularly useful.

The categories into which this guide is divided are, admittedly, arbitrary. The Holocaust is given a separate chapter, rather than being included as part of MODERN HISTORY, not because it had to be that way, but because the large number of books on the subject made it most useful to use that arrangement. The dividing lines between the various age groups for children's books also reflect a sense of what is most useful. Several books in the "adult" sections are suitable for younger readers, and we have tried to let you know when that is the case. Certain books could have been included in more than one chapter. The final decision on where to put each book was based on where a reader was most likely to look for it. In the case of anthologies, the category that covered the largest part of each book's contents was chosen.

In the course of preparing this book, we became aware of the sad lack of large-type books of Jewish interest. The number of visually impaired and elderly readers is growing and there is very, very little available for them to read. There is no Jewish Bible in large-type. There are no cookbooks, no how-to books, no Jewish philosophy, and virtually no fiction. All told, we found barely thirty books of Jewish interest available in large-type editions. As bad as this is, the situation with large-type Jewish children's books is even worse. The JWB Jewish Book Council has recently published an annotated list of large-type books of Jewish interest. Readers who are interested should contact that organization.

A few details need to be mentioned here. In keeping with Jewish usage, **B.C.E.** and **C.E.** are used (which stand for Before the Common Era, and Common Era), not B.C. or A.D., both of which have Christological implications. We have made an effort to assure that all the books listed were in print, with a few exceptions. The exceptions are books of such merit or importance that it would have been wrong to leave them out. The publication date of each book is given, where available. However, some publishers do not include the publication date in their books. In those cases, we have used the copyright date, which is usually the same as the publication date or a year earlier. The dates given are of the particular edition listed, which is *not* necessarily the original appearance of a book.

And then there is the problem of spelling. No one "official" system represents Hebrew or Yiddish words in English. Even if there were such a system, many book titles use variant spellings. Book titles are always given as they actually appear on the book. Our listings use the most generally accepted transliteration. In cases of doubt, the *Encyclopaedia Judaica* has been our guide. So, if you see "Chanukah" and "**Hanukkah**," don't blame our poor, overworked copyeditor—it's just the inconsistencies caused by spelling a word in an alphabet different from that of the original language.

Acknowledgments

Many people have contributed to the making of this book, offering suggestions, encouragement, and constructive criticism. We would like to offer our thanks to all of them, especially Eugene Borowitz, Yaffa Eliach, Mark Friedman, Paula Gottlieb, Meyer Katzper, Adaire Klein, Monty Noam Penkower, Howard Sachar, Marlene Schiffman, Barry ("Nostradamus") Sher, and the staffs of the Jewish Division of the 42nd Street Library and the Library of the 92nd Street Y. For contributing their words to this book, we want to thank Roselyn Bell, Robert Chazan, Robert Gordis, Blu Greenberg, David C. Gross, Jeffrey Gurock, Jacob Kabakoff, Lydia Kukoff, Joseph Lowin, Judith Muffs, Esther Nussbaum, Marcia Posner, Charles M. Raffel, Mae Shafter Rockland, and David Shatz. Thanks are also due to Avrum I. Ashery, Giora Carmi, Tamar Fishman, Naomi Hordes, Linda Katzper, Mark Podwal, Betsy Platkin Teutsch, and Tsirl Waletzky for the artwork. R.S.F. appreciates the support of Blu Greenberg as mentor and devoted friend. W.W. also wishes to express his appreciation to J. S. Bach and W. A. Mozart.

Introduction

Blu Greenberg

Two verities about scholarship seem appropriate to mention here. First, half the task of scholarship lies in tracking, that is, in searching and sorting out work related to the scholar's own area of interest. This winnowing process prepares the stage for creative work. Second, the superior teacher is one who not only shares knowledge but also points the student in the direction of independent study. In both regards—in collecting, assessing, and narrowing relevant materials and in the enterprise of self-study—annotated bibliographies are of inestimable value. Student, scholar, librarian, and researcher alike have long appreciated such works. This volume, then, takes its rightful honored place alongside other annotated bibliographies.

Yet there is something else, something quite unique, about this particular work. It makes a statement larger than itself. More than a well-organized and generously summarized listing of books, more than a useful guide to further study, this bibliography testifies to a remarkable new phenomenon in Jewish life today—the democratization and popularization of Jewish culture and scholarship. It is a phenomenon to be observed in this generation as perhaps in no other generation of Jews before ours.

Now, one might demur; one might reasonably argue with this thesis of novelty. After all, were not the Jews always characterized as the People of the Book? Did we not pioneer, since the days of Ezra the Scribe, in a system of universal education? Yes, but the focus was on sacred texts. Torah, Talmud, Codes— for most of our history, these tomes were the essence of study,

Blu Greenberg is president of the Jewish Book Council and author of *On Women and Judaism* and *How to Run a Traditional Jewish Household.* She lectures widely on contemporary Jewish issues.

the cornerstone of both formal and informal educational enterprises. In every generation, broader and more intense scholarship lay in the hands of an elite few.

Moreover, even the claim of universal familiarity with the central sacred texts could not be made in recent centuries of Jewish life. During the last two hundred years, as Jews increasingly embraced modernism and a growing secular culture, they abandoned study of particularist Jewish texts. The more universalist Jews became, the more Jewishly uneducated. As we entered the second half of the twentieth century, there was likely more widespread Jewish ignorance than in any previous generation. An observer of contemporary Jewish culture remarked not long ago that "Jews have become the people of the unopened book." In the overall Jewish community, a relatively small number were routinely educated in Jewish texts; and there was a great dearth of serious Jewish scholars.

Third, the classic association of Jews with book study overlooked one simple fact: it applied to only half the Jewish population. With some minor exceptions, females were not part of the great enterprise of study of sacred texts. They appreciated, and enabled others to study, but they did not actively participate.

Today, however, a virtual explosion of Jewish culture and learning has taken place. This blossoming includes study of sacred texts, yet extends much beyond it, encompassing many other realms of study such as those indexed in this volume. It is an egalitarian practice, not only in that women are also included, but that Jewish scholarship is no longer the exclusive purview of the elite few. Rather, it reaches into the broader community.

What does it look like, this democratization and popularization of Jewish culture? It has many faces. A doctor, whose book on *kabbalah* rests beside the lounge chair in his elegant office, frayed bookmark one-third of the way through; a homemaker, sitting on her front steps waiting for a carpool dropoff, reading a book on Jewish medical ethics ("Why?" I ask. "I just wanted to know," she replies with a gentle shrug, as if to say, "And why not?") A promising young artist, immersed in a sociological review of Jewish life in America; a Fortune 500 president, taking a year's leave from his multimillion-dollar toy company to study about medieval Spanish Jewry; and my sister, director of social services of a large metropolitan hospital, preparing extensively for her monthly Jewish book club meeting. Add to these the hundreds of formal programs of Jewish studies in universities and institutes of higher learning; the abundance of classes for leaders in federations and other secular service organizations; the thousands of graduate students in intensive Jewish scholarship. Add again the packed shelves of the Jewish bookstores; the expansion of university presses in the field of Judaica; the receptivity of popular publishers, so much so that an author of a book with Jewish content has a slight edge; the window display of a Fifth Avenue bookstore featuring six books of Jewish interest out of a total of sixteen; the growth of private home Judaica libraries—and a picture begins to emerge.

Perforce, one is brought to the next question: why is all this happening now? Several factors prevail, not the least of which are changes in the publishing field itself, particularly the accessible paperback. (The reader will note that the majority of books annotated here appear in paperback.) The expansion of leisure time, the general rise in socioeconomic status of the Jewish community, the new celebration of ethnicity all contribute to more book writing, book buying, and book reading by the Jewish public. For many contemporary Jews, it was precisely the lack of formal Jewish education in their youth and the compounded ignorance of recent past generations that prompted them to begin to compensate in their adult lives.

Perhaps more than anything else, the watershed events of our times have contributed to the growing cultural responsiveness of Jews as Jews. An ever-expanding Holocaust consciousness and a heightened awareness of the centrality of Israel has impacted powerfully on the self-identity of Jews—secular, marginal, and religious alike.

So Jews everywhere are in the process of discovering themselves, of finding out about their roots and their heritage. For many, it is a first step; for others, it means a deepening of knowledge. Some have sought teachers through every stage; others are primarily autodidacts; yet others have dedicated their lives to Jewish culture and scholarship. In one way or another, the books annotated here touch the lives of hundreds of thousands of Jews at every point along the communal spectrum.

This book, then, is more than a bibliography. It is a celebration of this cultural renaissance. To be sure, the democratization process is not complete, nor will it likely ever encompass every Jew. Nevertheless, it is well under way, and, more important, it is a process that will not be reversed but rather will gather momentum as time goes on.

Some will say it is all superficial, insubstantial, "popular." And the gloom-and-doomers will point to learned scholars of the past and say how relatively few giants we have in this generation. I believe they miss the point of what Jewish life is all about today. To me, this bibliography represents the flowering of Jewish culture among the learned elite and the laity. It is a sign of our cultural growth, not our dissolution. That more books on Jewish subjects have been published in the last ten years than in any previous decade in the last two centuries is a fact of great significance and great promise.

A book such as this, with its broad scope, could only have come from one who is at the very heart of the Jewish cultural enterprise, one whose life and work have centered around the Jewish book. After an initial career as a librarian, Ms. Frank served as executive director of the JWB Jewish Book Council for many years and was deeply involved in every aspect of the Jewish book enterprise. Thus it was most fortuitous that the editors at Harper & Row, who clearly recognized the signs of this new phenomenon, approached Ruth Frank to take up the task of compiling this bibliography. She and her able coauthor, William Wollheim, have produced a most valuable tool that will be used by many in the years to come. To them and to the fine scholars they gathered to write the introductions, we all owe a large debt of gratitude.

1
<u>Bible</u>

Yad. When reading the Torah scroll, which is written with a quill on parchment, a *yad* pointer is used to follow the text. Drawing by Mark Podwal, © 1978.

Invitation to the Bible
Robert Gordis

The Bible towers over the human landscape like Mount Everest over the plain. It remains the fountainhead of the two major faiths of the Western world, Judaism and Christianity, and has had a profound effect on Islam. The modern world, for all its secularism, continues to look to the Bible as the source of the fundamental ethical ideals on which the survival of the human species depends.

In our long and difficult climb from savagery to civilization, which must constantly be defended anew, the Bible has been a standard to which men and women have repaired, as they have sought to attain to true humanity. If our age appears spiritually lost, adrift on uncharted seas, it is due in no slight measure to the fact that Voltaire's sarcastic epigram, spoken two hundred years ago, is truer today than when he first uttered it: *"La Bible est plus célèbre que connue,"* "the Bible is more celebrated than known."

Moreover, the Bible is a collection of supreme masterpieces in every literary genre. Beyond its own intrinsic greatness, the Bible has been a never-failing fountain of inspiration for creative achievement in literature, music, and art, by people of all faiths and cultures.

It is no wonder, therefore, that earnest men and women, actuated by the highest of motives, often undertake "to read the Bible through from cover to cover." At the beginning, they encounter the majestic account of creation, followed by the simple but profound narrative of Adam and Eve in the Garden,

Dr. Robert Gordis is professor emeritus in Bible and the philosophies of religion at the Jewish Theological Seminary of America and editor of the quarterly journal *Judaism*. He is author of over twenty books in biblical scholarship, Jewish thought, and contemporary issues.

and all is well with the project. But as they persevere, they find long genealogical tables, detailed descriptions of building and design, technical instructions on animal sacrifices, long lists of animals forbidden for food, and directions for diagnosing contagious diseases. This material occurs cheek by jowl with fascinating historical narratives, powerful ethical and religious exhortations, and deeply moving poetry of every type. Moreover, many of its references are difficult for the modern reader to understand. Before too long, the project of Bible reading tends to break down, unless the reader surrenders to some cult whose adulation of the Bible is matched only by its total misunderstanding of its contents.

The reasons why Bible reading proves so unrewarding are not far to seek. To tell the truth, the Bible cannot be read; it must be studied, or rather, it must be studied in order to be read. It is an ancient book reflecting conditions and events far removed from our modern experience. Unless we become familiar with the background from which it sprang, it remains incomprehensible to us, or what may be even worse, we are led to misunderstand and distort its meaning, albeit from the highest motives.

In fact, the Bible is not a book at all. The word is derived from the Greek *biblia*, which means "books." It is a vast collection of Hebrew literature written over a period of fourteen centuries. Taking the Bible in one's hand is like picking up a volume of English literature containing selections from Shakespeare, Milton, Shaw, and O'Neill, not arranged either chronologically or by author!

A true appreciation of the Bible, whether as literature or as religion or as a cultural monument, is predicated on recognizing that it is not an anthology of sacred texts or a collection of edifying tracts written by the like-minded believers of a religious sect. It is, in the words of an acute twentieth-century scholar, "a national literature upon a religious foundation."

The Hebrew name for the Bible, **Tanakh**, is an acronym of the names of its three parts: *Torah*, the Teaching; *Nebiim*, the Prophets; and *Ketubim*, the **Sacred Writings**. This tripartite arrangement, which is very ancient, reflects the three principal cultural elements in ancient Israel, the priest, the prophet, and the sage.

Judaism assigns the highest level of sanctity and authority to the Torah, revealed to Moses at Sinai. The term Torah, mistranslated for centuries as "law," means "teaching, guidance." Actually it contains two elements, narrative and law, including the great ethical injunctions of the Decalogue and the Golden Rule. The biblical narratives were the seed-bed of the **Aggadah**, the vast body of rabbinic ethics, wisdom, and legend. Biblical law served as the basis for the three-thousand-year-old development of the **Halakhah**, the corpus of rabbinic law.

The Torah was the special province of the priests. They preserved the narratives of creation, Adam and Eve, Noah and the Flood, the lives of the Patriarchs, the enslavement in Egypt, the liberation of the Israelites under Moses, the Revelation at Sinai, the wandering in the desert, and the entrance into the Promised Land. Together with these traditions, the Torah contained the authoritative laws, ethics, ritual, civil, and criminal, regulating the life of the individuals and society. This material the priests employed in adjudicating lawsuits between litigants, deciding issues of contagion and ritual impurities, and above all officiating at the sacrifices at the Temple and lesser sites.

The second great division of the Bible is called the Prophets. The first four books, Joshua, Judges, Samuel, and Kings contain the history of the Jewish people from the conquest of the Holy Land under Joshua until the destruction of the First Temple. The entire account is narrated from the prophetic perspective; that is to say, all the figures and events in Jewish history are evaluated in terms of Israel's obedience or disobedience to the Divine will. The biblical historian accepted wholeheartedly the basic teaching of the Torah and the prophets that well-doing leads to well-being and wrong-doing to disaster.

This outlook did not prevent the biblical historians from investing their account with all the vividness and excitement of a great narrative, peopled by unforgettable characters like Samuel and Saul, David and Solomon, Elijah, Hezekiah, and many others.

Following the historical books, which Jewish tradition calls the Earlier Prophets, come the four books of Isaiah, Jeremiah, Ezekiel, and the Twelve, containing the words spoken by the prophets, incomparably the greatest moral teachers of the human species.

While the powers and prerogatives of the priests derived from the Torah of Moses, of which they were the custodians, the authority of the prophets was not mediated, but came from their personal experience, the overmastering conviction that God had spoken to them ("Thus says the Lord"). They passionately believed that their task was to proclaim his Word and transmit their vision of life to an imperfect, even sinful, people before it was overtaken by catastrophe.

The last of these four books, the Twelve, is sometimes—and unfortunately—called the Minor Prophets. They are minor only in point of length, being smaller, and therefore were put together, as the Talmud indicates, "so that they might not be lost." Several of the Twelve are major prophetic figures, like Amos, Hosea, Micah, and the author of Jonah, who stand on the same exalted level as Isaiah, Jeremiah, Ezekiel, and Deutero-Isaiah.

Collectively, the Hebrew prophets have been the driving power for ethical aspiration and the struggle for a world of justice, freedom and peace that remains the most significant activity of the human race.

The third section of the Bible, called *Ketubim*, literally "Writings," is the repository of the third strand in the intellectual and spiritual life of ancient Israel, that of *Hokhmah*, "Wisdom."

The connotations of the Hebrew *hokhmah* are far wider than the English rendering "wisdom" would imply. *Hokhmah* may be defined as a realistic approach to the problems of life, including all the practical skills and technical arts of civilization.

The term *hakham*, "sage, wise man," is accordingly applied to the artist and craftsman. Bezalel, who built the Tabernacle and its appointments in the wilderness, as well as all of his associates, are called "wise of heart," as are goldsmiths, farmers, and sailors. The midwife, for whom practical skill was obviously important, is called *hakhamah*. Ability in the conduct of war and in the administration of the state are also an integral aspect of wisdom. So too is skill in managing one's estate and handling slaves, as well as treating one's spouse and raising one's children well.

Above all, the term *wisdom* is applied to the arts of poetry and song, vocal and instrumental. The song in ancient Israel was coextensive with life itself. Harvest and vintage, the royal coronation and the conqueror's return, courtship and marriage, were all accompanied by song and dance. The earliest traditions dealing with the exploits of tribal and national heroes were embodied in song. The guilds of singers in the Temple, the women skilled in lamentation at funerals, the magicians and soothsayers with all their occult arts, are described by the same epithet, "wise."

All these aspects of ancient Hebrew civilization have disappeared with the destruction of its material substratum. What has remained of Wisdom is its literary incarnation, concerned not so much with the arts of living as with developing a sane, workable attitude toward life. To convey its truths, Wisdom created an educational method and a literature generally couched in the form of the *mashal*, a term meaning "resemblance, comparison," and applied to the proverb, parable, fable, and allegory as well as to poetry. Unlike Torah and prophecy, which set the nation and its destiny at the center of their concern, Wisdom was primarily interested in the individual as a human being. *Hokhmah* may be defined as the cultivation of all the skills and techniques as well as the personal qualities required for success in life. For the Wisdom teachers—sane, practical, and realistic—morality was the best policy.

What is today often called "the Protestant work ethic" is actually the ethic of practical Wisdom, embodied in the Book of Proverbs and the Book of Ben Sirah (which was not admitted into the canon of Scripture) and carried further in the teaching of the rabbis.

Among the many preceptors of Wisdom, however, were some whose restless minds refused to be satisfied with the practical goals of what may be termed the lower Wisdom. They sought to penetrate to the great abiding issues, the meaning of life, the purpose of creation, the nature of death, the mystery of evil. In grappling with these ultimate problems, they insisted on using the same instruments of observation and common sense that they applied to daily concerns, rather than relying on religious authority and conventional doctrines. Like so many rationalist minds since their day, however, they found unaided human reason incapable of solving these issues. Some finally made their peace with the traditional religion of their day. But others, more tough-minded, refused to take on faith what their reason could not demonstrate. Hence their writings reveal various degrees and types of skepticism and heterodoxy.

Several of these devotees of the higher or speculative Wisdom were highly fortunate, for they were able to transmute the frustration and pain of their quest into some of the world's greatest masterpieces, notably the Books of Job and Kohelet (Ecclesiastes). Job is the immortal protest of humanity against the mystery of suffering. Kohelet expresses the tragic recognition that the basic truth of the universe is beyond human ken, so that all that remains in life is the achievement of happiness. Job is basically concerned with justice, Kohelet with the problem of truth. Thus, Wisdom, which began with practical and down-to-earth matters, ended by grappling with the profoundest and most abiding issues of life.

It is now clear that this third section of the Bible, called *Ketubim*, Sacred Writings or Hagiographa, is not a miscellaneous collection, but, on the contrary, has an underlying unity. Basically, it is the repository of Wisdom, to which each book in this section belongs, either by virtue of its form or its content. The Book of Psalms is a great collection of religious poetry, most of which was chanted at the temple service with musical accompaniment. Both the composition and the rendition of the Psalms required a high degree of that technical skill that is *hokhmah*. Moreover, in point of content, many Psalms (such as 37, 49, 112, 128) have close affinities with the proverbial lore of the Wisdom teachers.

Three other books, Proverbs, Job, and Ecclesiastes, obviously belong in a Wisdom collection. So does Ben Sirah, or Ecclesiasticus, which was not included in the canon of Scripture, because it clearly betrayed its late origin. Lamentations is a product of *hokhmah* in its technical sense. The Song of Songs is included, not merely because it is traditionally ascribed to King Solomon, the symbol and traditional source of Hebrew Wisdom, but because these songs, whether sung at weddings or at other celebrations, were also a branch of technical song.

Moreover, the Song of Songs may have entered the Wisdom collection because it was regarded as a *mashal*, an allegory of the relationship of love existing between God and Israel. The Book of Daniel, the wise interpreter of dreams, obviously is in place among the Wisdom books.

The Books of Ruth and Esther were included here, because both reveal practical sagacity, Esther in saving her people from destruction and Ruth in securing a desirable husband! The three closing books of the Bible, which survey history from Adam to the Persian period, are really parts of one larger work, Chronicles-Ezra-Nehemiah. It is possible that they have been included in the Wisdom section merely because they were placed at the end, as an appendix to the Bible as a whole. The place of these last-named books in *Ketubim* has also been explained differently. It has been suggested that Chronicles (with its adjuncts) is really an appendix to Psalms, since one of its principal concerns is to describe in detail the establishment of the Temple ritual. Ruth may then have been a supplement to the Psalms, since it concludes with the genealogy of David, who is the traditional author of the Psalter. Esther may be an appendix to Chronicles, the style of which it seeks to imitate. These suggested links, however tenuous they may appear to the Western mind, will not seem farfetched to anyone familiar with the Semitic logic of association, evidence for which is plentiful in the redaction of the Bible and in the organization of the **Mishnah** and the **Talmud**.

It is clear that the Bible is inexhaustible in the wealth and variety of its contents. Yet it possesses a unity fashioned out of every current of Hebrew thought and action. Priest, prophet, historian, poet, and sage rub shoulders with one another within its covers, as they actually did in their own lifetimes, differing, arguing, and influencing one another and unconsciously collaborating in producing the greatest spiritual force in the history of humanity.

It is a striking paradox—and a saving grace—that in spite of the antiquity, the variety, and the profundity of the Bible, it is in large measure accessible even to an uninstructed reader. But to understand the Bible fully, we must remember that during the two thousand years after its composition, it had a long and eventful history. It has had a powerful impact on human events in general, and on religion and ethics in particular. A true appreciation of the Bible requires that we approach it on three distinct levels: (1) *what it meant originally,* (2) *what it meant subsequently,* and (3) *what it means for us today.*

It cannot be emphasized too strongly how important it is to take into account all three stages in the history of the Jewish and human encounter with the Bible.

First, we must seek to discover what the Bible meant to its original speakers-writers and its listeners-readers. It is here that the disciplines of archeology, philology, comparative religion and law, anthropology, ancient history, and literary criticism make their contribution. All must be drawn on to help us ascertain what the words of the Bible meant when first spoken or written. It must be remembered that it was the *original* meaning of the text that impressed its contemporaries as vital and true so that it was first preserved, then recognized as holy, and was ultimately admitted into the canon of Scripture.

Moreover, if we disregard the first stage and make no effort to discover the "plain meaning" of the text, we shall be defenseless against all the vagaries and inanities that different individuals and groups have read into the Bible. It is a sad fact of history that many passages have been distorted in order to subvert the ideals of justice and truth to which the Bible is dedicated.

The original sense of the Bible, which can generally be discovered with the aid of modern scholarship, is fundamental. But if we stop short at the first stage, there is the danger that the Bible will emerge as an antiquarian document, a relic of the Jewish past, of interest to specialists rather than to the generality of humankind.

We must, therefore, move on to the second stage and determine what the Bible has signified through the ages, as reflected in the vast literature of Judaism and its daughter religions. We must examine the religious and moral content of the aggadah and the legal-ethical structure of the *halakhah,* as embodied in the Talmud and the *midrash,* both of which based themselves on the Bible. We must reckon with the vast philosophic, mystical, and homiletic literature of medieval and modern times, which also saw itself as derived from the Bible.

This vast and variegated literature, which extends from the Dead Sea scrolls and Philo to our day, has its own independent life and its own intrinsic value, without which we would be immeasurably poorer. This material is the key to understanding what earlier generations found in the Bible and derived from it, and by that token, helps us understand its central role in human history.

If we disregard this second stage, the history of biblical interpretation through time, we shall be unable to understand the true character and nature of Judaism, which may be described with little exaggeration as an extended, many-faceted commentary on the Bible.

Moreover, if we do not reckon with the second stage, a vast gap will be created in our understanding of Western civilization in which the Bible played a major role for centuries, its impact being far from spent even today.

Finally, we must move on to the third stage and discover how the Bible speaks to us and how it illumines our condition today. Its insight into human nature and its comprehension of human history remain perpetually valid and relevant, because the eternal is always contemporary.

To omit the third stage and refrain from asking what the Bible says to us today, must lead to an impoverishment of spirit in our times. It would deprive us of the courage and the vision that the Bible can offer us in a difficult age, as we face the perils and perplexities of the human condition.

In sum, the full understanding of the Bible rests on two pillars—(1) *exegesis*, seeking to discover what may legitimately be read *out* of the biblical text, and (2) *eisegesis*, reckoning with what has been read *into* the Bible by the later generations that have revered it.

The Bible is not merely one more great book, or even the greatest of books that has come down to us from antiquity. It is the fountainhead of our faith in the capacity of the human race—even when threatened by nuclear annihilation—to move toward the fulfillment of its God-given duty and destiny. In inspiring the human race to make the establishment of God's kingdom on earth the goal of human striving, it presents a blueprint for the future of the world.

The exalted content of the Bible is matched by its literary

greatness. Virtually every genre is represented within its pages by at least one masterpiece. Its prose exhibits the storyteller's art, the skill of the historian, the stirring orations of the prophet, and the realistic understanding of the sage. The poetry of the Bible, which permeates its prose sections as well, illuminates the human yearning and love for God and the love of man and woman, which also serve as a paradigm of the Divine-human relationship. Poetry is the vehicle for the Prophet's call for justice, the sage's realistic counsel to his disciples, and the supreme pathos of Job's encounter with God on the ultimate issues of human existence.

The Bible is not great because it is holy; it is holy because it is great. Perhaps it is best for the reader at the outset to forget both these qualities; it may then be easier to recognize that the Bible is fascinating in its energy and vitality and its deep understanding of human nature. To be sure, the first stage is primary—all else is commentary. But—as Hillel told the would-be convert, whom he informed that the Golden Rule was the essence of Judaism and that the rest is commentary—"Go and study."

If we follow his injunction, we shall then recognize the truth of the words of the sages, "Turn it over and over, for everything is in it. Grow gray and old in it, and do not swerve from it, for there is no better portion than this." (*Ethics of the Fathers*, Chapter 5:22.)

BIBLES AND BOOKS ABOUT THE BIBLE

To Jews, the word "Bible" means something different from what non-Jews mean by "Old Testament" or "Bible." For one thing, "Old Testament" carries the implication that it has in some way been outdated or supplanted. Even more than that is involved, though. The very understanding of what the Bible says is different. A long Jewish tradition deals with the trans-mission and meaning of the Bible text. Only a translation that takes that tradition into account can be fully acceptable to Jewish readers. A "Jewish translation" is also of value to non-Jews, and we would encourage non-Jews to study one. There are many different editions of the Bible in print. For someone wanting to buy a Bible, the new translation published by the Jewish Publication Society is the edition of choice. It reflects the latest scholarship and is regarded as the most accurate translation available. Readers looking for a bilingual (Hebrew and English) Bible can consider the two-volume Jewish Publication Society edition, or the multivolume *Soncino Books of the Bible*, edited by Cohen. For an edition of the Torah, the Kaplan, which is Orthodox, and the Plaut, which is Reform, can both be recommended. Rosenbaum and Silbermann's *Pentateuch with Rashi* includes the Torah plus the commentaries of Rashi, one of the greatest scholars in Jewish history.

The Bible is a difficult book to understand without help, and if there are many Bibles in print, there are almost countless Bible commentaries. The two books by Sandmel described hereafter are both very good introductions: *The Enjoyment of Scripture* is shorter and simpler than *The Hebrew Scriptures*. For lengthier and more detailed commentaries, there is a wide choice. The Anchor Bible, edited by Albright and Freedman, is scholarly and not specifically Jewish in its approach. It does not yet include volumes on all the biblical books. The *Soncino Books of the Bible* includes a representative selection of traditional commentaries. The ArtScroll Bible Series, edited by Zlotowitz and Scherman, offers a fundamentalist Orthodox approach to the Bible. The scope of its commentaries can be understood by knowing that *Genesis* alone comprises six volumes. And, although it deals only with selected topics, the six volumes of commentary on Torah by Leibowitz are highly regarded and an excellent value.

When it comes to commentaries on specific books of the Bible, we have limited ourselves to mentioning only a few, representing a spectrum of approaches from traditional (Malbim) to innovative (Graves and Patai's *Hebrew Myths*). Between religious, textual, and historical commentaries, the choice runs into the thousands. By the time you have read even a few of the books described here, you will be equipped to make selections on your own.

The REFERENCE BOOKS section includes some books useful to students of the Bible, including a Hebrew-English dictionary, an atlas, and a Bible dictionary. Aharoni's *Archaeology of the Land of Israel* and Bright's *History of Israel*, both in the ANCIENT HISTORY AND ARCHEOLOGY section, are also valuable adjuncts to Bible study. —R. S. F. & W. W

Albright, William Foxwell, and David Noel Freedman, eds.

Anchor Bible, Doubleday, 1964–1985.

An ad for the Anchor Bible once asked whether it was "too much Bible?" The answer is no, but the series *is* massive. Of the forty volumes scheduled to cover the Hebrew Bible, twenty-two have appeared. Several volumes of the Apocrypha have also been published, and the series also includes the Christian New Testament. All the books provide translations that emphasize accuracy over linguistic beauty, plus extremely detailed commentaries on the text, and historical and archeological information. Some of the volumes, such as E. A. Speiser's on Genesis are extraordinarily readable and informative. Others, such as Mitchell Dahood's on the Psalms, concentrate on details of translation and, while excellent, are of value primarily to scholars. In between are such treasures as Marvin Pope's volume on the Song of Songs, which in its 700-plus pages summarizes virtually everything relevant ever said about this biblical book.

The commentaries are written by a variety of scholars, only some of whom are Jewish, and the emphasis throughout the series is on a secular approach to Bible study. If you are looking for a specifically Jewish approach to the Bible, look elsewhere.

The titles published so far are *Genesis*, by E. A. Speiser, $16. *Joshua*, by Robert G. Boling, $18. *Judges*, by Robert G. Boling, $16. *Ruth*, by Edward F. Campbell, Jr., $14. *Lamentations*, by Delbert R. Hillers, $14. *Esther*, by Carey A. Moore, $14. *Song of Songs*, by Marvin H. Pope, $18. *1 Samuel* and *2 Samuel*, by P. Kyle McCarter, Jr., $18 each. *1 Chronicles* and *2 Chronicles*, by Jacob M. Myers, $14 each. *Ezra-Nehemiah*, by Jacob M. Myers, $16. *Job*, by Marvin H. Pope, $18. *Psalms 1–50, Psalms 51–100,* and *Psalms 101–150*, by Mitchell Dahood, $16, $16, and $18. *Proverbs-Ecclesiastes*, by R. B .Y. Scott, $14. *Second Isaiah*, by John L. McKenzie, $14. *Jeremiah*, by John Bright, $18. *Ezekiel, 1–20*, by Moshe Greenberg, $16. *Book of Daniel*, by Louis F. Hartman, $16.

Hosea, by Francis I. Andersen and David Noel Freedman, $18.

Apocrypha:

Judith, by Carey A. Moore, $14.

1 Maccabees and *2 Maccabees,* by Jonathan Goldstein, $18 each.

I & II Esdras, by Jacob M. Myers, $16.

The Wisdom of Solomon, by David Winston, $16.

Daniel, Esther, and Jeremiah: The Additions, by Carey A. Moore, $16.

Alter, Robert

The Art of Biblical Narrative. Basic Books, 1981, $14.95 hc, $7.95 pb.

An intelligent and stimulating reading of the Bible as a work of literature, this book analyzes literary techniques such as the interplay between narrative and dialogue and the use of interior monologue. Alter takes a modern, secular approach to the Bible, viewing it as a collection of works written by men over a stretch of several centuries, offering "splendid illustrations of the possibilities of narrative." He writes with clarity, avoids obscure or jargonish terms, and shows how the literary mastery of the Bible enhances its profound religious message. The book won the National Jewish Book Award.

The Art of Biblical Poetry. Basic Books, 1985, $17.95.

A sequel to Alter's study of biblical narrative, this volume is an analysis of biblical poetry that is both a work of literary criticism and an attempt to provide greater understanding of the ways in which the poetry conveys a religious message.

Ashkenazi, Jacob ben Isaac

Tz'enah Ur'enah. Translated from the Yiddish by Miriam Stark Zakon. Mesorah, 1983–1984, Vol. 1, $13.95 hc, $10.95 pb; Vol. 2, $13.95 hc, $10.95 pb; Vol. 3, $14.95 hc, $11.95 pb.

Originally written in the early seventeenth century, **Tz'enah Ur'enah** is an anthology of Torah interpretation and lore. Written in Yiddish, its principal readership was women, who at that time did not receive an education in Hebrew, and it was one of the few books considered suitable for women readers. It was immensely popular. Ashkenazi, an itinerant preacher from Poland, drew on traditional commentators such as Rashi and Rambam and added legends, embellishments, and his own moralistic commentary. Volume 1 includes Genesis; Volume 2, Exodus and Leviticus; Volume 3, Numbers and Deuteronomy. Mesorah's edition, the first complete English translation, is illustrated with woodcuts from the 1726 Frankfurt edition. The title *Tz'enah Ur'enah,* meaning "Go forth," is derived from the words of the Song of Songs: "Go forth, O ye daughters of Zion, and behold."

Asimov, Isaac
Asimov's Guide to the Bible. Volume 1: The Old Testament. Avon Books, 1971, $8.95 pb.

This guide to secular aspects of the Bible discusses people, places, events, and their historical background. Asimov speculates about the real nature of the Flood, the date when Abraham entered Canaan, what a cherub might have looked like, and other items. He sees the Bible as an important source of historical information and attempts to link it with what is known from other sources. Some familiarity with the Bible is needed to make the best use of this book.

Bialik, Hayyim Nachman
And It Came to Pass: Legends and Stories about King David and King Solomon. Translated from the Hebrew by Herbert Danby. Hebrew Publishing, 1938, $6.95.

Most of the stories in this book were adapted from Hebrew and Arabic sources; others were the fruits of Bialik's own fertile imagination. It is a book filled with delights and surprises, and the old-fashioned design and woodcuts add to its charm. Suitable for younger readers. (For more on Solomon, Frederic Thieberger's *King Solomon* is a biography based on substantial research, placing Solomon in historical perspective and analyzing the biblical writings attributed to him. Hebrew Publishing, 1947, $6.95 pb.)

Birnbaum, Philip, trans.
The Torah and the Haftarot. Hebrew Publishing, 1983, $19.50.

This handsomely produced edition of the Torah and weekly readings from the Prophets (**Haftarot**) gives the English and the Hebrew on facing pages. The translation groups the verses into larger paragraph-like units, adding to the readability. Birnbaum's commentaries are concise and draw primarily on traditional sources, yet do not totally ignore modern biblical scholarship.

Bronstein, Herbert N., and Albert H. Friedlander
The Five Scrolls. Illustrated by Leonard Baskin. Central Conference of American Rabbis, $12 congregational edition, $60 art edition.

Published by the organization of Reform rabbis, this is a translation of and commentary on Ecclesiastes, Esther, Song of Songs, Ruth, and Lamentations—the biblical books called **the Five Scrolls**. The congregational edition includes liturgies, making it suitable for use as a self-contained prayer book. Both editions contain informative introductions to each of the scrolls, poetic and readable translations, legible Hebrew texts, and dramatic, often grim watercolor illustrations by Leonard Baskin. The oversized art edition is unusually well produced and is a bargain for lovers of Baskin's work.

Buber, Martin

On the Bible: Eighteen Studies. Translated from the German and Hebrew by Olga Marx et al. Schocken Books, 1982, $17.95 hc, $7.95 pb.

Best known for his philosophical writings and retellings of **Hasidic** tales, Martin Buber was also a profound student of the Bible. Working with Franz Rosenzweig, he began a Bible translation in 1925 that was finally completed in Jerusalem in 1961. (It is the basis for the Everett Fox translation of Genesis listed later.) *On the Bible* comprises essays by Buber on a variety of topics and, as always with Buber, the work is filled with insights—and occasional obscurities.

Cohen, A., ed.

The Soncino Books of the Bible. Soncino Press, 1946–1984, 14 vols., $149.95.

Including both the Hebrew text and the 1917 Jewish Publication Society English translation (described later), this is one of the best sets of Bible commentaries. Each book has a lengthy introduction, and there are extensive excerpts from the works of the classical Jewish commentators, including Rashi, Gersonides, Nachmanides, and Abraham Ibn Ezra. The five books of the Torah are contained in the one-volume **Chumash** (a word meaning "five" in Hebrew). It is an excellent compact introduction to the traditional viewpoint on the Torah.

The volumes and their individual prices are
Chumash. $22.50.
Joshua and Judges. $10.95.
Samuel 1 and 2. $10.95.
Kings 1 and 2. $10.95.
Isaiah. $10.95.
Jeremiah. $10.95.
Ezekiel. $10.95.
The Twelve Prophets. $10.95.
The Psalms. $10.95.
Proverbs. $10.95.
Job. $10.95.
The Five Megilloth. $10.95.
Daniel, Ezra, Nehemiah. $10.95.
Chronicles 1 and 2. $10.95.

Fox, Everett, trans.

In the Beginning: A New English Rendition of the Book of Genesis. Schocken Books, 1983, $14.95.

Based on the approach espoused by Martin Buber and Franz Rosenzweig in the 1920s, this version of Genesis is guided by the principle that the Bible originated as a spoken literature and, therefore, should be translated with special attention to rhythm and sound. It reads extremely well. The commentaries are relatively brief and address literary issues more than religious ones.

Freehof, Solomon

Ezekiel: A Commentary, 1979, $15; *The Book of Isaiah,* 1972, $15; *The Book of Jeremiah,* 1977, $15. Union of American Hebrew Congregations.

Produced by the Reform movement, these attractive volumes are solid introductions to three prophetic books, combining the 1966 Jewish Publication Society translation with a selection of mostly traditional Jewish commentaries. Among the many major authorities cited are Rashi, David Kimchi, Malbim, Isaac Abravanel, Samuel David Luzzato, and Abraham Ibn Ezra. There is also historical background, and some references to the work of modern Israeli scholars. The commentaries are generally short but consistently illuminating.

Ginzberg, Louis
The Legends of the Jews. Translated from the German by Henrietta Szold. Jewish Publication Society, 1968, 7 vols., $80; individual volumes, $11.95 each.

Originally published in 1909, this is a magnificent collection of Jewish folklore, tales, and legends dealing with biblical personages and events. Ginzberg gathered the material from a vast number of sources, including the Talmud and rabbinic commentaries dating from the second through the fourteenth centuries, and synthesized it into a continuous narrative. It is a work filled with emotional wonder and intellectual riches. A one-volume abridgement, *The Legends of the Bible*, is also available. It sells for $14.95, but if you can afford the time to read it and the money to buy it, the seven-volume set is greatly preferable.

Gordis, Robert
The Book of God and Man: A Study of Job. University of Chicago Press, 1978, $8.95 pb.

The existence of evil in the world is one of the key issues with which a religion must deal. The Book of Job is the place in the Bible where this problem is confronted most directly, and the result is a book that is powerful, enigmatic, and psychologically astute. Gordis, a leading scholar of Conservative Judaism, provides in this book an introduction to Job, clear and direct commentaries, and his own, readable translation.

Koheleth: The Man and His World. Schocken Books, 1968, $10.95 pb.

This is a study of the book of Ecclesiastes, called Koheleth in Hebrew. Ecclesiastes is an interesting and unusual book, with a pessimistic tone and skeptical attitude that contrasts with other parts of the Bible. Gordis includes the Hebrew text of the original and his own translation, and writes of Koheleth's authorship and place in the canon, its relationship to Greek and Egyptian thought, its author's world view, the transmission of the text, and other aspects of the book.

Graves, Robert, and Raphael Patai
Hebrew Myths: The Book of Genesis. McGraw-Hill, 1966, $5.95 pb.

Here the authors look at the book of Genesis and the traces it contains of ancient accounts of gods and goddesses. Graves and Patai blend anthropology and mythology in their analysis of Genesis, and explore the historical implications of its myths and the ways in which they laid the basis for Western ethics. Much of the book is speculative and conjectural.

Hertz, J. H., ed.
The Pentateuch and Haftorahs.
Soncino Press, 1978, $25.

This book gives the Hebrew text of the Torah and Haftarot (the selections from the prophets that are read during the Sabbath service and other occasions after the Torah reading). The English text is the 1917 Jewish Publication Society translation. Compared to the Soncino Press *Chumash*, the commentaries come from a wider variety of sources— Jewish and non-Jewish, ancient, medieval, and modern, and include Rashi and Maimonides, but also Samson Raphael Hirsch, R. Travers Herford, and Marcus Jastrow. Possibly the best choice for the general reader looking for a one-volume Torah with commentaries despite its somewhat old-fashioned—even dated— qualities. (One critic referred to Hertz as bombastic and stodgy, which seems overly harsh to us.)

Heschel, Abraham J.
The Prophets. Harper & Row, 2 vols., $5.95 each pb.

One of the leading Jewish theologians of the twentieth century here examines the nature of prophetic inspiration and the message of the biblical prophets. Heschel is not always easy to understand, but he always rewards his reader.

Jewish Publication Society

The Jewish Publication Society (JPS) has two different Bible translations, available in a number of editions. *The Holy Scriptures* is a translation originally published in 1917. It has been criticized for being too like the Christian King James translation, but it remains an excellent translation with unusually poetic language. It is available in a clothbound edition for $10.95, in both black and white Leatherette editions for $16.95, and in a two-volume edition with Hebrew and English in parallel columns for $25.

Beginning in 1962, JPS began issuing a new translation by publishing an edition of the Torah. This was followed in 1978 by *The Prophets* and was completed in 1982 with the publication of *The Writings.* The translation takes into account the latest findings of archeology and linguistic research and is considered to be the most accurate and precise Jewish translation so far. The language is modern and direct—there are no archaic words like "thou" or "thee"—and is notable for its clarity. The three volumes are available separately, *The Torah* for

$7.95, *The Prophets* for $9, and *The Writings* for $10.95. A one-volume edition of the new translation called *Tanakh* was published in 1985 and is available for $19.95.

Kaplan, Aryeh
The Living Torah. Maznaim, 1981, $30.

When Rabbi Aryeh Kaplan died recently at the age of forty-eight, the Orthodox Jewish community lost one of its most incisive writers and thinkers. *The Living Torah* is a translation that is clear, idiomatic, modern, and readable. Rather than having commentaries explaining the traditional Orthodox understanding of the text, the translation itself reflects that point of view. What notes there are, are largely limited to brief clarifications of the text. The Hebrew type, on pages facing the English text, is large and clear. Supplemental materials include maps, illustrations, diagrams, charts, and an extensive bibliography. If any criticism can be offered, it is that 1,400 pages make an unwieldy book. But these pages are well produced and attractive, and make an excellent gift.

Keller, Werner
The Bible as History. Translated from the German by William Neil and B. H. Rasmussen. Morrow, 1981, $14.95.

This study of the archeological evidence describes the ways in which the evidence supports the accuracy of the Bible's account of events. Keller is a journalist, not a scholar, and his book both gains and loses from that. It is highly readable, at times even entertaining, but it has been criticized for sometimes reaching conclusions beyond those justified by the facts. The hardcover book is a second edition; the first edition is available in paperback from Bantam Books for $4.95.

Kohlenberger, John R., III, ed.
The NIV Interlinear Hebrew-English Old Testament. Vol. 1, *Genesis–Deuteronomy*, 1979, $24.95; vol. 2, *Joshua–2 Kings*, 1980, $24.95; vol. 3, *1 Chronicles–Song of Songs*, 1982, $21.95; vol. 4, *Isaiah–Malachi*, 1986, $24.95. Regency Reference Library/Zondervan.

A very useful series of books for students of biblical Hebrew, these interlinear editions alternate lines of Hebrew text from the Bible, with lines of a grammatically exact, literal word-for-word English translation. A readable English translation, that of the New International Version, is given in the margins. Commentaries are held to a minimum, but there are occasional explanatory footnotes.

Leibowitz, Nehama
Studies in Bereshit (Genesis). $11.50.
Studies in Shemot (Exodus). Two vols., $17.50.
Studies in Vayikra (Leviticus). $9.

Studies in Bemidbar (Numbers).
$11.
Studies in Devarim (Deuteronomy).
$11.
  Translated from the Hebrew by
Aryeh Newman.
  All published by the World Zionist Organization, 1981.

Leibowitz is a professor of Bible at Tel Aviv University. These outstanding books are based on a series of lessons she prepared, one for each of the fifty-four weekly synagogue Torah readings (known as *sidrot*). (How fifty-four readings fit into a fifty-two-week year we leave to you to discover.) Leibowitz draws on a broad range of both traditional and modern Bible commentaries, and writes in a down-to-earth style. The books are crammed full with information, and both beginning and more advanced students will find much material of value. The books provide a solid introduction to the classical commentaries and how to study them further on your own. Each lesson deals with just one or two aspects of the weekly reading rather than attempting to cover all the issues involved. Because of that, beginning students might find Leibowitz's works most useful as a supplement to more comprehensive surveys. Each chapter ends with questions for further study, something teachers are likely to find useful. A knowledge of Hebrew is helpful, but isn't nec-

essary. Unfortunately, the typography and binding are mediocre.

Malbim, Meir Leibush
Malbim on Mishley. Adapted and translated from the Hebrew by Charles Wengrov and Avivah Gottleib Zornberg. Feldheim, 1982, $10.95 hc, $7.95 pb.

  This book is a commentary on the Book of Proverbs, known in Hebrew as Mishley. Malbim (an acronym for Meir Loeb ben Jehiel Michael, 1809–1879) was an uncompromising opponent of Reform Judaism—a stand that at one point even led to his arrest on charges that he had "preached against the idea of progress and freedom." His Bible commentaries were written to counter Reform interpretations that ignored the traditional talmudic understanding of the text. He looks at both the literal and the symbolic meanings and his remarks are to the point and understandable. This edition is abridged from a longer Hebrew original, and includes the Hebrew and English texts on facing pages.

Metzger, Bruce M., ed.
The Oxford Annotated Apocrypha. Oxford University Press, 1977, $9.95.

  The Apocrypha are a series of books that were not accepted as part of the canon of the Hebrew Bible but that did appear in the Greek translation of the Bible known as the Septuagint, produced in the second and third centuries B.C.E. It includes some well-known works, among them Judith, Tobit, the Wisdom of Solomon, and Ecclesiasticus, also called the Wisdom of Ben Sirah. This elegantly produced volume includes all the generally accepted apocryphal books plus Third and Fourth Maccabees and Psalm 151. There is an introduction to the Apocrypha in general, and each of the books has a brief introduction detailing its composition, date, and contents. Annotations explain historical, geographical, literary, and religious matters in the text, and provide cross references to the other books.

Pearlman, Moshe

In the Footsteps of Moses and *In the Footsteps of the Prophets*. Out of print.

These volumes retell the Bible stories of Moses and the Prophets, adding some analysis and historical information, but mostly staying with the biblical account. What makes them of interest is their extensive illustrations, many in color, reproducing works of art—most of them ancient—and photographs of locales associated with the events. Pearlman's prose can be leaden—for example, "In a flash, everything fell into place in Moses' mind"—but he is informative and knowledgeable. The books are suitable for young adult readers.

Plaut, W. Gunther, and Bernard J. Bamberger

The Torah: A Modern Commentary. Union of American Hebrew Congregations, 1981, $30.

One of the outstanding works of Reform Judaism, this edition of the Torah includes the 1962 Jewish Publication Society English translation and a cantillated version of the Hebrew. (The term *cantillation* refers to the intonations used while reading the Torah during a synagogue service.) The special value of this edition comes from its extensive commentaries and explanatory materials. Textual notes help clarify the translation and the original Hebrew text; brief essays accompany each section of the text, explaining how Jewish tradition sees its meaning and its contemporary relevance; and "gleanings" from world literature, ancient and modern, supplement the text and expand on it. The Haftorahs are included, and both English- and Hebrew-opening editions are available.

Rosenbaum, M., and A. M. Silbermann, eds.

Pentateuch with Rashi. Feldheim, 5 vols., 1973, $44.95.

Rashi (which is an acronym for *Rabbi Shlomo Yitzaki*, 1040–1105) is considered to have been one of the most lucid and precise commentators ever on the Bible and Talmud. His work is the basis for almost all later commentaries. Rashi's writing is clear and to the point, and emphasizes the plain meaning of the text, although it does also include material drawn from older traditional Jewish commentaries (**midrash**). Students wishing to delve deeply into the Jewish understanding of the Bible *must* read Rashi. This edition includes the Hebrew original and English translation of his complete commentary, plus the text of the Torah and Haftorahs. Rashi's commentaries are given in modern, vocalized Hebrew, not the traditional "Rashi script" that is harder for most modern readers.

Samuel, Maurice

Certain People of the Book. Union of American Hebrew Congregations, 1977, $7.50 pb.

A highly personal and imaginative exploration of the Bible and some of the people in it. Samuel is especially astute in his character analysis and offers many psychological insights.

Sandmel, Samuel

The Enjoyment of Scripture: The Law, the Prophets, and the Writings. Oxford University Press, 1978, $7.95 pb.

This accessible but scholarly introduction to the Scriptures emphasizes their literary aspects. Sandmel also provides some background on the redaction of the Bible and accepts as fact that it was written by humans rather than God—an approach unacceptable to many Orthodox Jews.

The Hebrew Scriptures: An Introduction to the Literature and Religious Ideas. Oxford University Press, 1978, $15.95 pb.

Considerably more detailed than *The Enjoyment of Scripture* but every bit as accessible and almost as readable, this book summarizes all the biblical books, placing them in historical context and relating them to each other. Textual questions are discussed, but the focus is meaning, purpose, and origins of the writings. Extensive quotations are included. Although the approach is nontechnical and does not require any special expertise, Sandmel is not superficial. This is a good introductory text.

Sarna, Nahum M.

Exploring Exodus: The Heritage of Biblical Israel. Schocken Books, 1986, $17.95.

Sarna sees the Exodus from Egypt as the pivotal event in the Bible—not just a historical event, but a permanent and central symbol in Jewish life. This book, intended for the general reader, takes into account modern research into the Bible and the civilizations of the ancient Near East; however, Sarna always keeps in mind that Exodus is not important primarily as history, but for the spiritual and moral values it conveys.

Understanding Genesis: The Heritage of Biblical Israel. Schocken Books, 1970, $6.95 pb.

This study of Genesis was written to revitalize awareness of it not as a collection of "children's tales" such as "Noah and the Ark," but as a volume dealing with such profound problems as the presence of evil in the world and the nature of the good life. Sarna bases his study both on traditional Jewish sources and on such extra-biblical sources as modern philosophy, science, and archeology. He examines such questions as the historicity of the Flood, the chronology of the patriarchs, and human sacrifice in the ancient Near East as it relates to the binding of Isaac. It's a stimulating book.

Steinsaltz, Adin
Biblical Images: Men and Women of the Book. Translated from the Hebrew by Yehuda Hanegbi and Yehudit Keshet. Basic Books, 1984, $16.95.

This is not one of Steinsaltz's best books, but his learning is so profound and his writing so clear that anything by him is worth reading. In this book, he explores the characters and spiritual experiences of twenty-five biblical characters, both the well-known and respected (Eve, Isaac, Joseph) and the obscure or despised (Leah, Michal, Jezebel). Steinsaltz sees them as reflecting enduring traits of human nature with qualities we should emulate or condemn—men and women we can learn from by studying the way they related to others and to God. Interestingly, the chapters in this book are based on programs by Steinsaltz originally commissioned for broadcast over the Israeli Army radio.

Wiesel, Elie
Messengers of God: Biblical Portraits and Legends. Translated from the French by Marion Wiesel. Summit Books, 1976, $16.95 hc, $6.95 pb.

These studies are not so much portraits of as meditations on some of the major figures in the Bible: Adam, Cain and Abel, Isaac, Jacob, Joseph, Moses, and Job. If Steinsaltz aims to educate in *Biblical Images*, in his book Wiesel aims to inspire, and he writes in dramatic and intense language. Like Steinsaltz, he draws on traditional Jewish sources—Mishnah, Talmud, Midrash—but the effect is very different. Parables and stories between the chapters provide an additional dimension.

Zlotowitz, Meir, and Nosson Scherman, eds.
The ArtScroll Bible Series. Mesorah, 1976–1985.

Like the Anchor Bible, the ArtScroll Bible is a massive undertaking. It has, however, a totally different perspective. In addition to a translation based on an Orthodox Jewish view of the text, the series provides extensive commentaries drawn exclusively from traditional Jewish sources. It is strictly Orthodox in its approach. For example, the translation of the Song of Songs reflects only the allegorical interpretation of the text, completely ignoring literal meaning. It unquestionably provides the best access in English to a traditional Orthodox understanding of the Bible. The volumes available so far are

Genesis. Six volumes, $16.95 each, hc, $13.95 each, pb.

Joshua. $16.95 hc, $13.95 pb.

Ezekiel. Three volumes, $16.95 each, hc, $13.95 each, pb.

Jonah. $11.95 hc, $8.95 pb.

Psalms. Five volumes. $15.95 each, hc, $12.95 each pb.

Song of Songs. $11.95 hc, $8.95 pb.

Ruth. $11.95 hc, $8.95 pb.

Lamentations. $11.95 hc, $8.95 pb.

Ecclesiastes. $11.95 hc, $8.95 pb.

Esther. $11.95 hc, $8.95 pb.

Daniel. $16.95 hc, $13.95 pb.

Ezra. $11.95 hc, $8.95 pb.

11

Children's Books

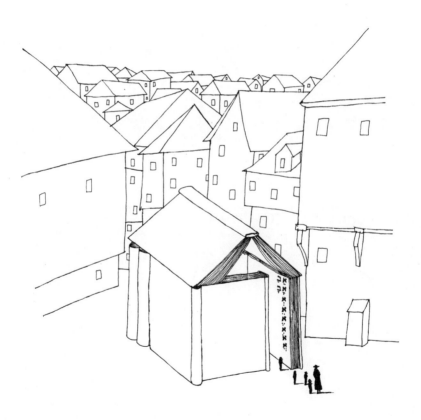

Heder. In the *Heder* (elementary school) of Eastern Europe, children were introduced to Hebrew letters, the sacred books, and formal schooling at a very early age. Drawing by Mark Podwal, © 1978.

A Celebration of Jewish Children's Books

Marcia Posner

The Edwardian period is known as the Golden Age of children's literature because educators and psychologists then learned that children were not smaller editions of adults, and authors began—at last—to write for children. Today, we are witnessing another type of Golden Age—one of Jewish children's literature—as general trade publishers and Jewish publishers are producing books intended to convey Jewish content only incidentally and also books specifically meant to teach about Jewish holidays, the Holocaust, and life cycle events.

Jewish educators were the first to commission children's books. From the late 1920s to the 1940s, fine histories, collections of legends and Bible stories for children were written by Hyman and Alice Chanover, Lily Edelman, Hyman Goldin, Elma Levinger, and Abraham Burstein. These were intended for use in the classroom, to teach Judaism.

An important step towards creative Jewish children's literature was taken more than 40 years ago by Sadie Rose Weilerstein, the creator of K'tonton, a mischievous thumbling who is saved from disaster by remembering and making use of Jewish teaching. These stories and others written by the author (now over 90) are still enjoyed by children today.

During the 1950s and 1960s, Sydney Taylor wrote the winning *All-of-a-Kind* family series, the first books with Jewish

Dr. Marcia Posner is a library educator and library consultant for the Federation of Jewish Philanthropies of New York and the JWB Jewish Book Council. Dr. Posner is the author of "Selected Jewish Children's Books" published by the council, and *Jewish Children's Books: How to Choose Them, How to Use Them.*

content written purely for children's recreational reading. The Jewish values learned are secondary to the story. The strong characterizations and universal appeal have brought this series a broad readership, including non-Jews. These were followed by Bea Stadtler's *Adventures of Gluckel of Hameln* and *The Holocaust: A History of Courage and Resistance*, the first book about the Holocaust for children; and Ruth Brin's Bible stories and craft books.

Contemporary Authors and Illustrators

The books by the talented authors and artists who are writing and illustrating today merit a place in the Jewish home and library. Like Sydney Taylor, many of these authors and artists have wide appeal far beyond the Jewish marketplace. Authors such as David Adler, Chaya Burstein, Miriam Chaikin, Barbara Cohen, Malka Drucker, Howard Greenfeld and Carol Snyder are writing children's books that reflect the American Jewish experience and that teach Judaism. Non-Jewish children also enjoy their books and also learn about Judaism.

A Parent's Responsibility to Teach: Leading the Child to Jewish Children's Books

Historically, the Jewish family has been central to the transmission of the teachings of Judaism; but more recently, the task of "teaching (them) diligently to our children" (Deut. 6:7) has been relegated by the family to Jewish day schools and supplementary schools, or to no one at all. One way for parents to pass on Jewish tradition is to study together with their children; if not to teach children, then to learn with them. And one way of doing this together is by reading, discussing, and enjoying Jewish children's books.

The Importance of Establishing a Healthy Concept of Self

In order to function effectively in adult life, a person needs a strong sense of self. An ethnic and religious identity is part of the sum of what we are. Children from assimilated families have little ethnic or religious identity and may use borrowed role models and identities. Children of minority groups often see themselves through the eyes of the majority culture. Even a child with a strong Jewish identity is under stress from the ideas and influences of the majority culture. It is therefore all the more important for Jewish children to read about Jewish children and their families, to read books that will give them a sense of pride in their religion and traditions and a feeling of oneness with the Jewish people.

DIFFERENT TYPES OF BOOKS

Books come in different shapes and sizes and genres, or types. I have attempted to provide an overview of the varieties of children's books.

Picture Books

Most Jewish children's picture books are about Jewish holidays, Bible stories, or adaptations of folktales that reflect Jewish values and the Jewish historical experience. There are many Bible stories. Most recently, the UAHC, or Union of American Hebrew Congregations (Reform), and Merkos (Orthodox), two denominational publishers, have issued picture books that reflect basic teachings of Judaism, Jewish symbols, and rituals on levels appropriate for young children and that involve feelings (affective learning), in addition to facts (cognitive learning).

Fiction

As in most good literature with child appeal, the plot structure is (1) a problem; (2) meeting and overcoming the challenge presented by the problem; and (3) a satisfying resolution of the problem or manifestation of growth by the protagonist. We have Jewish fiction when the subject of the book is a Jewish problem or concern and when the characters are identifiable as Jews. If the reader identifies with the characters and enters the story—then we have good Jewish fiction!

Nonfiction

The scholarship and meticulous research done by many current authors of children's nonfiction inspire confidence. Their writing is clear and often assumes little or no prior knowledge about Judaism. Today, therefore, if a family begins on a program of reading the nonfiction noted here, they will have made a good beginning in the *mitzvah* of "teaching them (the Commandments) diligently to your children."

Current books of this genre include books about Jewish life cycle events, the derivation and meaning of holidays, and how to observe them in the family.

There are also books about Jewish personalities and history, the State of Israel, and Jewish social, civil, and religious concerns.

HOW TO SELECT BOOKS FOR CHILDREN

Books speak to us. What is over our head at one age, has new meaning for us at another. A good book read at the wrong age will never have the same impact it would have had when the child was ripe for it. Notice I don't say "ready" for it. Even though, according to some reading formula, such as chronological age, a child may not be "ready" for a particular book, a prior life experience or developmental need may very well make him or her ripe for it.

Because they extend us, books are wonderful. They help us move from one plateau to another, from one level of understanding to a new one. They offer new concepts, new attitudes. Finding and matching the right book for a child is an art. There are adequate matches where books entertain and inform a child, but the "chemical" match has been made when the experience of the book moves from what is printed on the page—and becomes a part of the reader. It is almost a mystical experience!

Although books are here graded (ages 4–8, 8–12, 10–14, and 12–up), these are only guidelines and may not help in selecting books for your child. The best judge, therefore, is the child. The parent may direct a child to a general age range, but should never try to dissuade a child from reading a book below or above his or her chronological grouping.

AGE-LEVEL RELEVANCE OF CHILDREN'S LITERATURE

Here are some common age-level characteristics of children, which you will no doubt recognize, and some developmental needs of the different age levels that may help in selecting a book:

Age 2–4

Children at this age are fidgety. They like repetition and rhythm, familiar objects and animal stories where the animals assume the role of small children. They like to join in on repeated phrases. Large single-concept picture books are most suitable.

Ages 4–8

A longer attention span appears toward the upper level of this age range. Children are now more social, being more outward directed and ready for books about the community, children playing together, and family tales. At the lower level of the age range, they still are fond of animal stories; at the upper, they begin to like stories of children interacting with others in longer picture storybooks. They have a linear sense of time and no historical sense at all until age six or seven.

Ages 8–12

If children don't read at this time in their development, they may never read! This is the prime reading age. They love stories about children getting the better of adults, family stories, and humorous stories. Boys love sport and adventure tales. All like hero tales and legends.

Ages 10–14

A sense of fantasy, time lapse, and historical time begins to develop around age ten. By eleven, children are beginning to challenge the authority of parents, a phase that may continue with a vengeance in the next stage. They are cliquish, and stories involving compassion, friendship, the handicapped and aged, anti-Semitism or any kind of bigotry (or its opposite, brotherhood) will be received well at this age. Family tales are still the most popular.

12–up

It is no longer difficult to find good books of Jewish interest that speak to this age range. Children of this age range are experimenting with identity, lifestyles, and self-assertion, among other concerns. They don't feel the way they used to. Sometimes they are sure that they will do a better job than their parents and look forward to adult life. And some of the time they fall prey to doubts and insecurities and need reassurance.

Literature for this age group should be about learning to make responsible decisions. Literature helps teens experiment safely. It also provides teens with role models. These models are important because teens look for role models other than their parents. One way parents can provide teens with positive models is through their reading.

The books included in the following list can serve as a guide and provide hours of pleasure for you and your family and enrich the children who read them.

BOOKS FOR CHILDREN

There are books for children on virtually any subject you can think of. Rather than pointing to a few specific titles, it is probably more helpful to mention some of the writers and publishers who have been most active in producing children's books on Jewish themes.

Not all writers will appeal to all tastes, but all of the following have created a body of work that is respected and substantial. Barbara Cohen, one of the best and most active writers for children, has written books for all age levels. In addition to other works, Miriam Chaikin and Malka Drucker have each produced a series of books on the Jewish holidays. Isaac Bashevis Singer, renowned for his adult books, is also the author of some wonderful children's books. Some other contemporary children's authors to look for are David Adler, Chaya Burstein, and Marilyn Hirsh.

Several Jewish publishers are particularly active in children's literature. These include the Jewish Publication Society, Kar-Ben Copies, and the Union of American Hebrew Congregations, which is the organization of Reform Jewish congregations. Among general publishers who have a record of issuing quality books of Jewish interest for children, Adama, Clarion,

Holiday House, and Lothrop, Lee and Shepard are all well represented in this chapter.

To help people who enjoy reading aloud, we have indicated in the listings when a book is especially suitable for this purpose. Two writers whose books can be mentioned in this context are Isaac Bashevis Singer, author of *Stories for Children* and *Zlateh the Goat*, among many others, and Solomon Simon, who has produced two collections of stories about the fools of Chelm.

It is important to realize that the age levels into which the following books are divided are somewhat arbitrary and are meant to serve as guidelines, not hard-and-fast rules. Some books described in other parts of this guide also are suitable for younger readers. Their listings mention this fact. For additional information on children's books, Enid Davis's *Comprehensive Guide to Children's Literature with a Jewish Theme* (see REFERENCE section) is a valuable resource.—R. S. F. & W. W.

PRESCHOOL TO AGE EIGHT

Abells, Chana Byers
The Children We Remember. Greenwillow Books, 1986, $9.95.

This photographic essay focuses on children during the Holocaust. The pictures are from the archives of Yad Vashem, the Holocaust memorial in Israel, where Abells is director of the Photo and Film Division. There is very little text, and the pictures are not intended to shock, merely to make us remember. However, the disturbing nature of the material means that parents should use discretion and be sure their children are emotionally equipped to deal with it.

Adler, David
In addition to being the author of a number of books for children, Adler is the children's book editor at the Jewish Publication Society.

A Picture Book of Hanukkah. Illustrated by Linda Heller. Holiday House, 1982, $9.95 hc, $5.95 pb.

This book discusses how the celebration of Hanukkah came about, what it signifies, and the ways in which it is celebrated today. The story of the **Maccabees** and their war for religious freedom is narrated simply, and Adler links it to the presentday struggle by Soviet Jews and others who still are persecuted for their religious beliefs. The illustrations are bright and cheerful.

Among Adler's other books are *A Picture Book of Jewish Holidays* (Holiday House, 1981, $9.95), a survey of the major Jewish holidays, and *A Picture Book of Passover* (Holiday House, 1982, $9.95

hc, $5.95 pb), which tells the **Passover** story and describes a modern Passover *seder*. Both books are illustrated by Linda Heller.

The House on the Roof: A Sukkot Story. Illustrated by Marilyn Hirsh. Kar-Ben Copies, 1984, $9.95.

When a grandfather builds a **sukkah** on his roof, it leads to a dispute with his Christian landlord. This is the story of how that dispute is settled. The lesson about the need for cooperation between Jews and non-Jews is conveyed without heavy-handedness.

Cashman, Greer Fay

Jewish Days and Holidays. Illustrated by Alona Frankel. SBS Publishing, 1979, $9.95.

The outstanding feature of this book is its intensely colored illustrations. The text is very short and less informative than the Adler book just described, but the pictures are energetic and pleasing.

Chanover, Hyman, ed.

Home Start. Behrman House, 1985, six holiday packages plus parents' handbook for $12.95 + $3.00 postage.

Home Start is a series of six packages mailed to children over the course of a year, each one arriving in time for a major Jewish holiday. Each package includes an activity book, with recipes, crafts, and so on, and a storybook. There is also a mailing for parents including a handbook that offers advice on how to teach children about the holidays, a storybook, and a cassette. The material is aimed primarily at Reform and Conservative Jews, and is best suited to children from age four to six.

Cohen, Barbara

Cohen has written a succession of books for younger readers, from preschoolers to young adults. She has shown a consistent ability to understand the world as children see it and to present Jewish values in a way that is easy to understand and positive. She has received several awards, and her authorship of a book virtually guarantees its quality.

The Carp in the Bathtub. Illustrated by Joan Halpern. Lothrop, Lee & Shepard, 1972, $11.25.

In this amusing story a grandmother recalls how, as a child, she and her brother Harry tried to save a live carp that had become their pet from being turned into gefilte fish for Passover.

Here Come the Purim Players. Illustrated by Beverly Brodsky. Lothrop, Lee & Shepard, 1984, $12.

Here Cohen combines the atmosphere of the Prague Ghetto, with its overtones of persecution, with the **Purim** story. The residents of the Ghetto watch and listen to a Purim *shpiel* (play) that portrays the characters from the Bible story who had to fight anti-Semitism in their own day. The contrast between the gloom of the Ghetto and the gaiety of the players is effectively communicated by Brodsky's watercolor illustrations.

Yussel's Prayer: A Yom Kippur Story. Illustrated by Michael J. Deraney. Lothrop, Lee & Shepard, 1981, $11.25.

Based on a traditional rabbinic tale, this story tells of a congregation whose **Yom Kippur** prayers are delivered by rote, and of the orphan boy Yussel, who doesn't know how to read or write—but who does know how to play his pipe with all his heart, soul, and mind. The book design and Deraney's illustrations add to the book's appeal; it won the National Jewish Book Award in 1983.

Friedman, Audrey Marcus, and Raymond Zwerin

But This Night Is Different: A Seder Experience. Illustrated by Judith Gwyn Brown. Union of American Hebrew Congregations, 1981, $7.95.

The authors describe Passover, focusing on a family *seder* and its meaning. The book explains how familiar events of daily life are changed on the **Seder** night.

Shabbat Can Be. Illustrated by Yuri Salzman. Union of American Hebrew Congregations, 1979, $7.95 pb.

This picture book about the joys of the Sabbath tells about the Friday night **kiddush**, and the observance of **Shabbat** at home and in the synagogue.

Heller, Linda

The Castle on Hester Street. Illustrated by the author. Jewish Publication Society, 1982, $8.95.

In this warm and humorous book, Julie's grandpa regales her with tall tales about his journey to America and early days as an immigrant. Meanwhile Grandma Rose—a more pragmatic soul—presents a version of the past that includes an overcrowded boat, inspectors on Ellis Island, and a tenement apartment.

Hirsh, Marilyn

Hirsh has illustrated many Jewish children's books, both written by herself and by others. Her work is imbued with an awareness of Jewish tradition and has an appealing sense of humor and childlike quality.

I Love Hanukkah. Holiday House, 1984, $11.95.

A young boy learns all about the history and celebration of Hanukkah, and describes the things he especially likes about the holiday.

I Love Passover. Holiday House, 1985, $11.95.

In this companion volume to *I Love Hanukkah*, Sarah's mother tells her how the various elements of the Passover *seder* commemorate the escape of the Jews from slavery in Egypt.

Hutton, Warwick

Jonah and the Great Fish. Illustrated by the author. Atheneum, 1984, $12.95.

Hutton retells the Bible story of Jonah, using simple and conversational text. The prose is good; the watercolor illustrations are better than that, beautifully enhancing the story. This is an outstanding picture book. (Beverly Brodsky's *Jonah*—Lippincott, 1977, out of print—is also good, with excellent pictures.)

Kitman, Carol

One Mezuzah: A Jewish Counting Book. Photos by Ann Hurwitz. Rossel Books, 1984, $9.95 hc, $6.95 pb.

This book successfully ties the concept of counting and numbers to themes in Jewish life—tradition, ritual, holidays, and values. Each number from 1 to 13 is presented as a word in both English and Hebrew, as an Arabic number, and as a Jewish object or concept, from one **mezuzah** and four questions on Passover to eight nights of Hanukkah and the all-important age of thirteen. All the numbers are illustrated with black-and-white photos, and the authors resist sexual stereotyping. This is an enjoyable book that is also educationally effective.

Meshi, Ita, illus.

A Child's Picture Hebrew Dictionary. Adama Books, 1985, $9.95.

This bright and colorful word book is laid out with each two-page spread illustrating ten or eleven Hebrew words. The letter is shown in a large size, and the words are given in Hebrew, English translation, and English transliteration. Even preschoolers who can't read will like the cheerful pictures.

Pessin, Deborah

The Aleph-Bet Storybook. Illustrated by Howard Simon. Jewish Publication Society, 1946, $6.95.

Pessin draws on Jewish legends to tell stories about each of the Hebrew letters. The layout of the book is slightly dated, but the stories are charming, even for adults. This is a fine book to read aloud to the family.

Pomerantz, Barbara

Bubby, Me, and Memories. Photos by Leon Lurie. Union of American Hebrew Congregations, 1983, $6.95.

Written from a child's point of view, *Bubby* tells of a young girl's relationship with her grandmother and how she learns to deal with her grandmother's death. The girl describes the period of sitting **shivah**, the saying of *Kaddish*, and the purpose these customs serve. The writing and the photos are warm and sensitive, making this a book useful to anyone helping a child through the period of loss after the death of a grandparent. A similar book is *Zeydeh* by Moshe Halevi Spero with illustrations by Marilyn Hirsh (Simcha Books, 1984, $9.95). It also is about the death of a grandparent, but is more concerned with Jewish traditions and practice, and less with the child's emotions.

Saypol, Judyth, and Madeline Wikler

My Very Own Jewish Library. Kar-Ben Copies.

Saypol and Wikler are more than authors, they are also the founders of Kar-Ben Copies, a company specializing in Jewish children's books. They started it out of dissatisfaction with the Jewish books available for their own children—after whom the company is named. My Very Own Jewish Library is a popular series of paperback books, eight of them about the Jewish holidays, six about other aspects of Jewish life. The books include information, prayers, songs, crafts, and activities. They run in length from 24 to 80 pages and are available individually or in boxed sets. The holiday titles and their prices are
My Very Own Chanukah Book, $2.95.
My Very Own Haggadah, $2.95.
My Very Own Megillah, $2.95.
My Very Own Rosh Hashanah, $2.95.
My Very Own Shavuot, $2.95.
My Very Own Simchat Torah, $2.95.
My Very Own Sukkot Book, $2.95.
My Very Own Yom Kippur, $2.95.

The eight titles of the Holiday Library are sold as a group for $24.

The other titles in the series are
Come, Let Us Welcome Shabbat, $2.95.
Let's Celebrate, $4.95.
Let's Have a Party, $4.95.
My Very Own Jewish Community, $4.95.
My Very Own Jewish Home, $3.95.
What's an Israel? $2.95.

The six titles of the Year-Round Library sell as a set for $24.

Schwartz, Amy

Mrs. Moskowitz and the Sabbath Candlesticks. Illustrated by the author. Jewish Publication Society, 1984, $8.95.

Mrs. Moskowitz has moved from the house where she raised her family into a new apartment, a place that doesn't feel at all like a home. When her son drops by with a box she had left behind, she finds a pair of old tarnished Sabbath candlesticks. Seeing them unleashes a flood of memories of Sabbaths past and sets in motion a process that will soon turn the barren apartment into a real home. The message that culture and tradition infuse life with value and meaning is conveyed gently but effectively. The pencil drawings are filled with little details and enhance the story. National Jewish Book Award winner, 1985.

Taubes, Hella

The Bible Speaks. Translated from the Hebrew by Lolla Bloch; illustrated by Dan Bar-Giora. Soncino Press, 1974, 3-vol. set, $14.95.

More than fifty popular Bible stories are here retold for young children. The illustrations are stylized and attractive and the writing is clear and simple. The stories are especially good for reading aloud.

Waskow, Arthur, David Waskow, and Shoshanna Waskow

Before There Was a Before. Illustrated by Amnon Danziger. Adama Books, 1984, $8.95.

This imaginative retelling of the story of creation is enhanced by powerful and stark black-and-white illustrations. In this version, God is seen as learning as he goes along, a God engaged in dialogue with his creation. The language is clear and suitable for very young children and the book is elegantly and attractively produced.

Weilerstein, Sadie Rose

The Best of K'tonton. Illustrated by Marilyn Hirsh. Jewish Publication Society, 1980, $6.95 pb.

An entire generation of Jewish children has grown up on the stories of K'tonton, the "Jewish Tom Thumb." He has appeared in three books, the first published more than fifty years ago, and this book offers a selection of sixteen of his adventures—and getting stuck inside a **shofar** is just one example of his knack for getting into trouble. The stories all offer lessons on Jewish tradition in an appealing manner. Weilerstein, now in her nineties, was a pioneer in the writing of Jewish books for children. She has written more than the K'tonton books, and readers should look for her books.

Zemach, Margot

It Could Always Be Worse: A Yiddish Folktale. Illustrated by the author. Farrar, Straus & Giroux, 1977, $10.95 hc; Scholastic, 1986, $2.95 pb.

A man living in a one-room hut can no longer bear the crowded conditions of his home and goes to the rabbi for help—only to be given some very strange advice. A silly story with a serious message, drawn from Yiddish folklore. There is also a version of the story, as told and illustrated by Marilyn Hirsh, called *Could Anything Be Worse?* (Holiday House, 1974, $9.95).

AGES EIGHT TO TWELVE

Adler, David

A Picture Book of Israel. Holiday House, 1984, $10.95.

This loving introduction to Israel has a well-written text that covers a lot of ground in a few words. Adler presents Israel's variety and contrasts—ancient and modern, desert and city, land and sea, and, of course, its diverse people. The photos are not as well reproduced as could be desired, but the overall result is good.

Our Golda. Viking/Penguin, 1984, $10.95.

This captivating biography of Golda Meir emphasizes her younger years, allowing children to identify more easily with her. Her life is presented in anecdotes, and Adler vividly conveys Golda's lifelong commitment to Zionism. The story is told simply and without complexities, but is filled with historical information.

Aleichem, Sholom. *See* Sholom Aleichem.

Asch, Sholem
In the Beginning: Stories from the Bible. Translated by Caroline Cunningham; illustrated by Eleanor Klemm. Schocken Books, 1966, $3.95 pb.

These are retellings of Bible stories, from Adam and Eve, through Noah, and Abraham, to Joseph, and Jacob. Asch has enriched the stories by drawing on traditional *midrashim* (rabbinic legends and explanations). The stories have been simplified enough to be understandable by younger readers, without being oversimplified.

Ashabranner, Brent
Gavriel and Jemal: Two Boys of Jerusalem. Photographs by Paul Conklin. Dodd, Mead, 1984, $10.95.

This plea for brotherhood takes the form of a photo essay about two boys living in Jerusalem, one an Arab, the other a Jew. Their families, neighborhoods, and daily routines are described, showing the many ways in which they are alike. Yet, despite their similarities, the distance between them is shown as being "almost unbridgeable." The photographs are especially expressive.

Burstein, Chaya M.
The Jewish Kids Catalog. Illustrated by the author. Jewish Publication Society, 1984, $10.95 pb.

Encyclopedic in scope, entertaining, and educational, *The Jewish Kids Catalog* combines history, Bible stories, folklore, recipes, music, crafts, party and game ideas, book recommendations, information on Jewish names, travel advice, fiction, and more. The illustrations are profuse and lighthearted, and the layout is uncluttered and clear. This book won a National Jewish Book Award in 1984, and makes a fine gift.

Joseph and Anna's Time Capsule: A Legacy from Old Prague. Illustrated by Nancy Edwards Calder. Summit Books, 1984, $8.95.

This beautiful book re-creates the life of two Jewish children in nineteenth-century Prague. The illustrations include lovely full-color paintings of great warmth and photographs of objects from the Czechoslovak State Collections, also shown in Altshuler's *Precious Legacy* (see ARTS section). In addition to showing what Jewish life was like, this book encourages children to make a time capsule of their own for future generations, using similar objects from today. The illustrations are unusually well reproduced for so affordable a book.

Chaikin, Miriam

The Seventh Day: The Story of the Jewish Sabbath. Illustrated by David Frampton. Schocken Books, 1983, $4.95 pb.

A lyrical retelling of the origin and development of the Sabbath through biblical passages. Frampton's woodcut illustrations are striking and evocative.

In addition to the book on the Sabbath just described, Miriam Chaikin has done a series on the Jewish holidays. Four titles have appeared so far, with more scheduled to appear. Each book includes a glossary, an index, and suggestions for further reading. The emphasis is on the significance and meaning of holidays, with some information included on how they are celebrated today. The currently available titles are (all published by Clarion Books): *Ask Another Question: The Story and Meaning of Passover.* Illustrated by Marvin Friedman. 1985, $13.95.

Light Another Candle: The Story and Meaning of Chanukah. Illustrated by Demi. 1981, $9.95 hc, $3.95 pb.

Make Noise, Make Merry: The Story and Meaning of Purim. Illustrated by Demi. 1983, $10.95.

Shake a Palm Branch: The Story and Meaning of Sukkot. Illustrated by Marvin Friedman. 1984, $12.95.

Cohen, Barbara

King of the Seventh Grade. Lothrop, Lee & Shepard, 1982, $11.

Vic is a boy with problems—he hates Hebrew school, hangs out at the mall with his pals, shoplifts occasionally for kicks, and shuttles between his divorced parents, feeling fully at home with neither. However, when he suddenly finds there may be an obstacle to his **Bar Mitzvah** (his Christian mother had never converted), his reactions aren't what he would have expected. An exceptional novel about a boy struggling to learn what it is to be a Jew and a **mensch**. National Jewish Book Award, 1983.

Molly's Pilgrim. Illustrated by Michael J. Deraney. Lothrop, Lee & Shepard, 1983, $10.

Molly is a new immigrant from Russia, attending public school in a small town at the turn of the century. She is subject to taunts and jeers because she is Jewish and ignorant of such American customs as Thanksgiving. With the help of her compassionate teacher and her mother, Molly shows her classmates the similarity between herself as a modern-day immigrant and the Pilgrims of early American history. The historical connections between Sukkot and Thanksgiving are also described. Deraney's illustrations are soft and evoke the era in which the story is set.

Drucker, Malka

There are two noteworthy series of children's books about the

Jewish holidays: the books of Miriam Chaikin just described, and those of Malka Drucker. Drucker writes from a Conservative Jewish perspective and emphasizes the customs and celebrations of the holidays. She provides a wealth of information on the holidays' origins and evolution, their observance in other parts of the world, and the Jewish values inherent in them. Most suitable for readers over the age of ten. All are illustrated by Bram Hoban, and all are published by Holiday House. Currently available are

Hanukkah: Eight Nights, Eight Lights. 1980, $9.95.
Passover: A Season of Freedom. 1981, $9.95.
Rosh Hashanah and Yom Kippur: Sweet Beginnings. 1981, $8.95.
Shabbat: A Peaceful Island. 1983, $11.95.
Sukkot: A Time to Rejoice. 1982, $10.95.

Gaines, M. C.
Picture Stories from the Bible. Scarf Press, 1980, $9.95.

There are not enough books of Bible stories available for younger readers. This one, a reissue of a book originally published in the 1940s, presents a selection of Bible stories in comic book form. It is a lot of fun to look at, to read, and to learn from.

Ganz, Yaffa
Savta Simcha and the Cinnamon Tree. Illustrated by Bina Gewirtz. Feldheim, 1984, $8.95.

Savta Simcha is a sort of Jewish Mary Poppins who manages to have an unending series of adventures, each illustrating some Jewish custom or belief. Marred by a tendency to didacticism, it is still a pleasing book that presents an Orthodox Jewish viewpoint in an entertaining manner. This is a sequel to *Savta Simcha and the Incredible Shabbos Bag* (Feldheim, 1980, $7.95).

Hurwitz, Johanna
Once I Was a Plum Tree. Morrow, 1980, $9.95.

Ten-year-old Gerry Flam feels confused and foolish when she must stay home for the High Holy Days, a confusion caused in part by her assimilated parents' ambivalence toward their own Jewishness. When refugees from the Holocaust move in next door, she has the opportunity of learning about Jewish customs and values—and about their importance to her.

Ish-Kishor, Shulamith
A Boy of Old Prague. Pantheon, 1963, $6.95 hc; Scholastic, $1.75 pb.

This historical novel says a great deal about Jewish-Christian relations. It tells the story of a Christian boy, raised to distrust and dislike Jews, who is sentenced to serve a Jewish family and becomes devoted to them and other Jews in the ghetto. Winner of a National Jewish Book Award, 1964.

Levine, Gemma
We Live in Israel. Franklin Watts, 1984, $10.90.

This book is composed of interviews with Israelis from every walk of life: sabra and immigrant, Jew and Arab, kibbutznik and rabbi, student and politician, and so on. Each first-person interview is accompanied by photos, including one of the speaker, and the voices are natural, straightforward, and varied. Some knowledge of Israel and Jewish history is useful.

Levoy, Myron
Alan and Naomi. Harper & Row, 1977, $9.95.

A touching and powerfully told story of a young girl attempting to put her life together again after the Holocaust. It is a good choice for introducing the subject of the Holocaust to children, especially as it is told from the perspective of an American child.

The Hanukkah of Great-Uncle Otto. Illustrated by Donna Ruff. Jewish Publication Society, 1984, $10.95.

Great-uncle Otto has become a shaky and dependent old man in the home of Joshua's parents, with whom he lives. His growing infirmity alarms Joshua, and when Otto's plan to make a **menorah** like the one he had in pre-Hitler Germany doesn't work out, Joshua must make a courageous and risky choice to try and save the situation. This story of a special relationship across the generations is told with great sensitivity.

Meir, Mira
Alina: A Russian Girl Comes to Israel. Translated from the Hebrew by Zeva Shapiro; photos by Yael Rosen. Jewish Publication Society, 1982, $7.95.

This fictionalized photo essay examines the difficulties a nine-year-old Russian Jewish girl faces adjusting to life as an immigrant in Israel—she doesn't speak Hebrew well, she misses the familiar sights of Russia, and has trouble making friends. In the end, she makes the adjustment and befriends an even newer immigrant, helping her to solve the problems she must face.

Metter, Bert
Bar Mitzvah, Bat Mitzvah: How Jewish Boys and Girls Come of Age. Illustrated by Marvin Friedman. Clarion Books, 1984, $10.95 hc, $3.95 pb.

Metter describes the ceremonies of **Bar** and **Bat Mitzvah**, and discusses their history and significance. This book is a good introduction to the subject, reassuring in tone but not especially deep and of most use to those with little Jewish education. A useful supplement is Jacob Neusner's *Mitzvah: Basic Jewish Ideas* (Rossel Books, 1981, $3.95 pb), which deals with the concept of **mitzvah** from its rabbinic origins to its implications for a boy's or girl's life today.

Ofek, Uriel
Smoke over Golan. Translated from the Hebrew by Trina

Schart Hyman; illustrated by Lloyd Bloom. Harper & Row, 1979, $9.89.

An adventure story about a nine-year-old boy who finds himself alone in the path of advancing Syrian soldiers during the **Yom Kippur War.** The author is particularly successful in conveying a sense of excitement.

Orlev, Uri
The Island on Bird Street. Translated from the Hebrew by Hillel Halkin. Houghton Mifflin, 1984, $10.95.

The winner of Israeli and American literary prizes, this beautifully written novel is based on its author's experiences hiding in the Warsaw Ghetto with his mother and brother. It tells about Alex, a young boy suddenly on his own in the ghetto who must find ways to survive physically and mentally.

Peretz, I. L.
The Seven Good Years and Other Stories of I. L. Peretz. Translated from the Yiddish and adapted by Esther Hautzig; illustrated by Deborah Kogan Ray. Jewish Publication Society, 1984, $10.95.

Obviously a labor of love, this book includes ten tales by I. L. Peretz, including the touching "Bontche Schweig." The stories have been simplified for younger readers, but retain the nuance and pith of the original versions. Ray's soft pencil drawings communicate a sense of dreaminess, and

the layout, design, and binding are all first-rate.

Posner, Raphael
Junior Judaica: The Encyclopaedia Judaica for Youth. Keter, 1983, 6 vols., $95.

Using material drawn from the authoritative *Encyclopaedia Judaica, Junior Judaica* is written in a clear and understandable style and is well organized. It gives a detailed description of Jewish life in the past and present, covering concepts and ideas of Judaism, important events of Jewish history, Jewish festivals, and the heritage of the Jewish people. The type is legible, and the set has a comprehensive index, as well as plenty of maps, photos, charts, and illustrations. The volumes make a useful reference set for a library, and a very nice Bar or Bat Mitzvah gift. Although published in 1983, much of the material in this set is drawn from an earlier edition published in the 1970s.

Ribalow, Harold U., and Meir Z. Ribalow

Harold Ribalow published the first edition of *The Jew in American Sports* in the late 1940s. Recently, his son Meir undertook the job of updating the book and turned up so much additional information that he divided it into the two books listed here. Both tell the stories of prominent Jewish athletes, many of whom had to overcome poverty or discrimination to achieve their successes.

The Jew in American Sports.
Hippocrene Books, 1985, $16.95.

This book presents profiles of twenty-nine American Jewish athletes. The sports covered include baseball, boxing, basketball, football, tennis, and bullfighting. Among the athletes included are Sandy Koufax, Benny Leonard, Nancy Lieberman, Sid Luckman, Harold Solomon, and Sidney Franklin, who is probably the only Jewish bullfighter from Brooklyn.

Jewish Baseball Stars. Hippocrene Books, 1984, $12.95.

The authors have collected eighteen short biographical essays on noted Jewish baseball players, including Hank Greenberg, Al Rosen, Moe Berg (more noted for his career as a U.S. government spy before World War II than for his hitting), Sandy Koufax, and Steve Stone. Not all of the players were really "stars," but plenty of young baseball enthusiasts will read this with pleasure.

Rossel, Seymour

Israel: Covenant People, Covenant Land. Union of American Hebrew Congregations, 1985, $8.95 pb.

This history of Israel—the land, the people, and the Jewish religion—covers biblical times to the present. Written for use in the classroom, it includes questions for discussion at the end of each chapter. There are lots of pictures and maps, and the writing is simple.

Ruby, Lois

Two Truths in My Pocket. Viking/Penguin, 1982, $9.95 hc; Fawcett Books, 1983, $1.95 pb.

These six short stories are about Jewish teenagers trying to find their own identity in an adult, mostly non-Jewish world.

Sholom Aleichem

Holiday Tales of Sholom Aleichem. Edited and translated by Aliza Shevrin; illustrated by Thomas di Grazia. Aladdin/Atheneum, 1985, $4.95 pb.

This anthology of seven humorous stories, all with holiday themes, is by the master Yiddish writer Sholom Aleichem. An excellent introduction to Aleichem's work, with its loving portrayal of fools and families, the holidays, and **Yiddishkeit**. The stories are suitable for older readers as well, and good for reading aloud.

Singer, I. B. (Isaac Bashevis)

Known primarily for his adult fiction, Singer has also written for children with a special and obvious affection and love. He draws frequently on the Yiddish folklore of Eastern Europe and a delightful sense of wonder and magic.

The Power of Light: Eight Stories for Hanukkah. Illustrated by Irene Lieblich. Farrar, Straus & Giroux, 1980, $10.95.

Of these captivating stories for the holiday celebrations, some are remembered from Singer's childhood, some are the product of his imagination. Lieblich's pictures perfectly complement the text.

Zlateh the Goat: And Other Stories. Translated from the Yiddish by the author and Elizabeth Shub; illustrated by Maurice Sendak. Harper & Row, 1966, $13.95.

A gem of a book. The stories are set in the lost world of Eastern European Jewry, and include several superbly silly ones about the fools of Chelm. The others have a creepy, Grimm Brothers quality, and Sendak's illustrations are a perfect match for the stories. The book makes a lovely gift and is a pleasure to read aloud.

Snyder, Carol

The Ike and Mama books are a series of humorous books about the trials and tribulations of Ike Greenberg, a young boy who sometimes has trouble telling the truth. Set in the Bronx in the 1920s, they are filled with authentic details and appealing people who are portrayed in an understandable way. The titles in the series, all published by Coward, McCann & Geaghegan, are *Ike and Mama and the Block Wedding.* 1980, $7.95.
Ike and Mama and the Once-a-Year Suit. 1978, out of print.
Ike and Mama and the Once-in-a-Lifetime Movie. 1981, $7.95.
Ike and Mama and Trouble at School. 1983, $9.95.

Simon, Solomon
The Wise Men of Helm. Translated from the Yiddish by Ben Bengal and David Simon; illustrated by Lillian Fischel. Behrman House, 1945, $4.95 pb.
More Wise Men of Helm. Illustrated by Stephen Kraft. Behrman House, 1965, $4.95 pb.

These two books constitute the best and most comprehensive collection of tales about the "Wise Men" of Chelm, whose deepest thinker, Gimpel, explains that summer days are long and winter days short since "in the summer, the days expand because of the heat, and in the winter, they contract because of the cold." The prose style is a bit dated, but the inspired silliness of the stories remains ever fresh. Both books are illustrated throughout.

Stadtler, Bea
The Holocaust: A History of Courage and Resistance. Behrman House, 1975, $5.50 pb.

Each chapter of this book closes with questions for the reader intended to generate thought and introspection. A National Jewish Book Award winner in 1975, Stadtler's book is best suited to children older than age ten or eleven.

Sussman, Susan
There's No Such Things as a Chanukah Bush, Sandy Goldstein. Illustrated by Charles Robinson. Whitman, 1983, $7.95.

This story deals with the touchy problem of Jewish children not being a part of Christmas, with its fun and gifts, when so many other people are enjoying the celebration. In it, Sandy's grandfather finally shows her how she can enjoy other people's holidays without making them her own. Of value more for its subject than for the way it is treated.

Taylor, Sydney
A pioneer author for children, Sydney Taylor produced a series of books about a close-knit family living in New York's Lower East Side at the turn of the century, their subsequent move uptown, and their lives up to the American entry into World War I. The books are warm and full of atmosphere, with a pleasing touch of humor. Taylor was one of the first authors to write about Jewish life for children. The Association of Jewish Libraries has named an award in recognition of her contribution.

The titles in this Dell Books series in chronological order are *All-of-a-Kind Family.* 1966, $2.50 pb.
More All-of-a-Kind Family. Out of print.
All-of-a-Kind Family Uptown. 1968, $1.95 pb.
All-of-a-Kind Family Downtown. 1973, $1.75 pb.

Volavkova, Hana, ed.
I Never Saw Another Butterfly: Children's Drawings and Poems from Terezin. Schocken Books, 1983, $6.95.
Terezin, also known as Theresienstadt, was a ghetto set up in Czechoslovakia by the Nazis as a "model" ghetto in which prominent people could be interned. Of the roughly 140,000 Jews sent to Terezin, more than 30,000 died there and 87,000 were eventually sent to the death camps. *I Never Saw Another Butterfly* is a collection of drawings and poems by some of the 18,000 children who passed through Terezin and is a profoundly sad book. It is a book of interest to older readers also.

AGES TWELVE AND UP

A Page From . . . Out of print.
Each two-page spread of this book shows a sample page from one of the classic Jewish religious works with a clear explanation of what each part means. The historical background and religious significance of the Torah, Talmud, Midrash, Maimonides' *Mishneh Torah*, and **Shulkhan Arukh** are given and supplemental information is provided. Although published for young adult readers, this publication is also very useful for adults. The Union of American Hebrew Congregations informs us that they plan to issue a new edition of this book soon.

Atkinson, Linda
In Kindling Flame: The Story of Hannah Senesh, 1921–1944. Lothrop, Lee & Shepard, $13.50.
Born in 1921, Hannah Senesh came from an upper-class, assimilated Hungarian Jewish family. As a young woman, she emigrated to Palestine. Eventually,

troubled by events in Europe and worried about the safety of her family and other Hungarian Jews, she volunteered for a British mission into occupied Europe. She was shortly afterward captured by the Nazis, tortured, and executed. Atkinson has combined Senesh's diaries and poems with photographs and historical background to trace Senesh's growth into a committed Zionist. She has obvious admiration and respect for her subject, but writes without undue reverence. This is a splendid biography of a very special woman.

Ben-Asher, Naomi, and Hayim Leaf, eds.

The Junior Jewish Encyclopedia: 10th Edition. Shengold, 1984, $19.95.

This comprehensive and up-to-date reference covers Jewish history, customs, communal life, and biography from biblical times to modern Israel. The material is presented clearly for younger readers without undue oversimplification, and there are many photos and illustrations. The book is a good value, and very suitable as a Bar or Bat Mitzvah gift.

Bialik, Hayyim Nachman

Knight of Onions and Knight of Garlic. Translated from the Hebrew by Herbert Danby; illustrated by Emanuel Romano. Hebrew Publishing, 1939, $4.95.

Based on an Eastern European Jewish story on the foibles of society. It tells of a prince who comes to an island where only the lowly onion is missing from their idyllic life. He presents the onion to the island, and is rewarded by being treated as royalty. However, when a second prince decides to seek fame and fortune by bringing them garlic, he is greeted with disdain and rejection. The black-and-white illustrations are beautiful and delicate.

Bridger, David, and Samuel Wolk

The New Jewish Encyclopedia. Behrman House, 1976, $14.95.

This is a solid reference work. The pages are attractive, with large, easy-to-read type and ample illustrations. The only drawback is that an updated edition is needed.

Butwin, Frances

The Jews in America. Lerner, 1969, $7.95 pb.

Part of a series on American groups, their background, experiences in America, and the contributions of outstanding individuals, this book covers the early history of Jews in America, the two major waves of immigration in the nineteenth and early twentieth centuries, and twentieth-century life. It discusses art and literature, business, government, science, sports, among other subjects. Butwin has written a biography and done translations of Sholom Aleichem; she writes well.

Cohn, Emil Bernhard
This Immortal People: A Short History of the Jewish People. Revised, expanded, and translated from the German by Hayim Goren Perelmuter. Paulist Press, 1985, $5.95.

This concise history of the Jewish people was originally published in Germany in 1936; it was first published in English by Behrman Jewish Book House in 1945. It has recently been revised and updated. Although written for adult readers, it is an excellent choice for younger readers. In its 160 pages, it surveys the major events and periods of Jewish history, avoiding footnotes and complexities.

Cowen, Ida, and Irene Gunther
A Spy for Freedom: The Story of Sarah Aaronsohn. Lodestar/Dutton, 1984, $11.95.

Sarah Aaronsohn was the daughter of settlers in Palestine at the turn of the century. She rejected the traditional woman's role of homemaker for the rather more dangerous one of spy. She and her brother were part of an espionage group, NILI, established to pass information to the British so that they might capture Palestine and free the Jews from Turkish rule. Sarah was captured and tortured to gain information. She resisted the torture and committed suicide rather than inform on her comrades.

The authors did considerable research in preparing this excellent book.

Drucker, Malka
Celebrating Life: Jewish Rites of Passage. Holiday House, 1984, $11.95.

Drucker is the author of a popular series of books on the Jewish holidays, described earlier. In this book, she provides an energetic and clear account of the life cycle events in Jewish tradition. A description of each ceremony, its variations and historical background, is accompanied by interesting black-and-white photos and illustrations. Drucker's approach, which includes a belief in the equality of women and the development of new forms of worship, is probably not acceptable to the Orthodox.

Epstein, Isidore
Step by Step in the Jewish Religion. Soncino Press, 1968, $4.95.

Emphasizing simplicity and directness, this is a guide to the essential teachings and practices of Judaism. The book deals with such topics as justice, righteousness, love, and holiness. A number of quotations from the Bible and Talmud are given, and their Hebrew texts supplied in an appendix. Although written from an Orthodox point of view, there is useful material for people from all branches of Judaism.

Fisher, Leonard Everett
A Russian Farewell. Illustrated by the author. Four Winds Press/ Scholastic, 1980, $9.95.

A National Jewish Book Award winner, this book is the story of the Shapiro family's emigration from tsarist Russia at the turn of the century and of the religious persecution that led to their decision to leave for America. The author's illustrations are effective.

Flinker, Moshe
Young Moshe's Diary: The Spiritual Torment of a Jewish Boy in Nazi Germany. Board of Jewish Education, $5.95. This diary of a pious Orthodox Jew who was killed in the Holocaust is of interest especially for the deep and steadfast religious faith it reflects in the face of the horrors of those times.

Frank, Anne
Anne Frank: The Diary of a Young Girl. Doubleday, 1967, $15.95; Modern Library, $5.95.

Great tragedies can numb us through their sheer overwhelming size; smaller tragedies can reawaken and resensitize us. This book, with its account of one young teenage girl's experiences, forces us to come to grips with what the Holocaust means on an individual level. For two years, while in hiding with her family from the Nazis in occupied Holland, Anne Frank kept a diary recording the tensions—and occasional pleasures—of life under extraordinary stress. Discovered after she died in the Bergen-Belsen concentration camp, the diary has justifiably become one of the most famous accounts of Jewish life during the war. Its psychological insight, faith in the essential goodness of humanity, and hope for a better future are extraordinarily moving.

Geras, Adele
Voyage. Atheneum, 1983, $10.95.

Solidly researched, gripping entertainment, deftly plotted, romantic yet realistic, this novel provides insight into the lives— and dreams—of the generation of immigrants who came to America early this century. It is a story with a large cast of characters: a shipload of people, some young, some old, all speaking with their own voices. Geras conveys the cramped and smelly trip in steerage and convincingly expresses the immigrants' hopes of what awaits them in their new home.

Gross, David C.
Pride of Our People: The Stories of One Hundred Outstanding Jewish Men and Women. Illustrated by William D. Bramhall, Jr. Doubleday, 1979, $14.95.

These stories are brief biographical portraits of Jewish men and women who have made significant contributions to their people and to the world. Many of these Jews are famous—Nobel Prize winners, diplomats, writers—and some are comparatively obscure. All have been chosen based on their suitability as role models for young people.

Jackson, Livia E. Britten
Elli: Coming of Age in the Holocaust. Times Books, 1983, $6.95 pb.

Forced to leave her Hungarian village, the author recalls her experiences in Auschwitz—beginning with her introduction to the notorious Dr. Mengele and his hideous medical "experiments."

Kresh, Paul
Isaac Bashevis Singer: The Story of a Storyteller. Illustrated by Penrod Scofield. Lodestar/Dutton, 1984, $11.95.

The author of a biography of Isaac Bashevis Singer for adults, Kresh has also produced this one for younger readers. Lovingly written, it presents Singer's interesting life in colorful fashion, from his birth in Leoncin, Poland, to his present life as a world-renowned and financially successful author.

Meltzer, Milton
Meltzer is the highly regarded author of a number of children's books, including several on Jewish history. His books are all carefully researched, and he uses original documents to add interest and impact to his work.

The Jewish American: A History in Their Own Words. Crowell/Harper & Row, 1982, $10.50.

This collection of documents describes the personal experiences of Jewish Americans.

Meltzer has selected his materials from a variety of sources: letters, journals, diaries, autobiographies, speeches, petitions, and interviews. The arrangement is excellent. Meltzer introduces each document, explaining who is speaking and clarifying the background. Photos and facsimiles appear every few pages.

Never to Forget: The Jews of the Holocaust. Dell Books, 1977, $2.50 pb. This moving and factually detailed history of the Holocaust draws on eyewitness accounts such as diaries and letters. It won a National Jewish Book Award in 1978. One section of the book is devoted to "The Spirit of Resistance."

Siegal, Aranka
Upon the Head of a Goat: A Childhood in Hungary, 1939–1944. Farrar, Straus & Giroux, 1981, $9.95.

An award-winning autobiographical novel of the Holocaust. It focuses on a close-knit Hungarian family that, even as it is being torn apart by the Nazi persecution, struggles to maintain its dignity and Jewish traditions. The mother is a particularly strong and impressive figure, determined to hold the family together under extreme conditions.

Siegel, Beatrice
Lillian Wald of Henry Street. Macmillan, 1983, $12.95.

Lillian Wald's compassion and concern for social justice led her to leave her pampered, sheltered life and study to be a nurse. In 1893 she founded the Henry Street Settlement House in New York (she served as its head until 1933), and she organized the Visiting Nurse Service. She was also a leader in the establishment of public school nursing services. This biography is well crafted and captures the reader's interest.

Singer, I. B.
Stories for Children. Farrar, Straus & Giroux, 1984, $13.95.

If he had written not a single word for adults, Singer's stories for children would be enough to establish his reputation. He shows enormous respect for the intelligence of children, believing that they are in many ways more astute critics than adults—less impressed by good reviews and more concerned with such basics as stories with a beginning, middle, and end. The thirty-odd stories in this book are collected from a variety of sources and represent much of Singer's output for children. Most draw on his Eastern European background. If you don't have children, buy this one for yourself. If you do have children, read it aloud to them.

Slater, Robert
Great Jews in Sports. Jonathan David, 1983, $14.95.

This book is a collection of biographies of major Jewish sports figures, thumbnail sketches of less important ones, and a section on Israeli sports stars. Photos, information on each athlete, and a section on the **Maccabiah Games** are included.

III

<u>History</u>

Golem. According to Jewish folklore, during the sixteenth century, Rabbi Judah Loew of Prague fashioned a *golem* (robot) to protect the Jewish community. Drawing by Mark Podwal, © 1978.

New Perspectives on the Jewish Past

Robert Chazan

One hallmark of recent Jewish experience has been an un-precedented concern with the Jewish past. Judaism has, since its earliest stages, emphasized key historical events, embellish-ing them with a rich body of folklore and recalling them regularly in central rituals. The disruption occasioned by emancipation—the dismantling of premodern restrictions on Jewish life—triggered unparalleled interest in the history of the Jewish people and an altered style of reconstructing that history. New aspects of Jewish experience have become the focus of the historian's curiosity; fresh sources have been sought and found; innovative patterns of interpretation have been invoked. The result of all this is a virtual rewriting of the Jewish past—ancient, medieval, and modern. The enterprise, to be sure, is still in its earliest stages, and valuable new studies are produced regularly, in the two large research centers of North America and Israel and in smaller research enclaves as well.

What were some of the factors that contributed to the inten-sified interest in the Jewish past, the search for untapped source materials, and the new styles of interpretation of prior Jewish experience? The emergence of the Jews into modern society occasioned a substantial non-Jewish concern with the Jews, their characteristics, and the history that had fashioned such alleged characteristics. Jews and sympathetic non-Jews as well, in their desire to combat harmful stereotypes, began to

Dr. Robert Chazan is professor of history, Queens College, New York and director of the Center for Jewish Studies at the City University of New York Graduate Center.

investigate past patterns of Jewish economic activity, of Jewish political behavior, of Jewish social relations to the non-Jewish world, and of Jewish cultural and spiritual creativity. As emancipation and the altered position of the Jew in the non-Jewish world began to erode traditional Jewish identity, Jewish history was further reexamined to reveal its grandeur and appeal. The hope was that a reinvestigation of the Jewish past would uncover a legacy sufficiently rich and diversified to warrant preserving and maintaining. Innovative movements within the Jewish world—particularly the reforming religious movements and the powerful Zionist movement—inevitably brought in their wake a reinterpretation of earlier patterns of Jewish living, ranging from emphasis on an unremitting dynamism and change in religious creativity to a stress on the underlying political and national identity of Jews throughout the ages. More recently, as Jewish studies have found a surprisingly hospitable haven in general universities, particularly in the United States and Canada, the broad humanistic and social science orientation of these universities has had a discernible impact on research into the Jewish past. Increasingly less particularistic in orientation, students of the Jewish experience tend to observe patterns of Jewish behavior in broader and more generalized terms, seeking to identify problems and responses observable in other human groups and alert to the interaction between Jewish communities of the past and the general ambiance in which they found themselves. The result of these disruptive but stimulating influences has been a spate of new and creative reconstructions of aspects of the Jewish past.

For the ancient period, Jews have been joined by non-Jewish scholars in reinvestigating an era that constitutes sacred history in both the Jewish and Christian traditions. Important new materials have come to light, perhaps most strikingly the Dead Sea Scrolls. This valuable treasure trove is, however, only the best known of a series of finds that reflect a profound commitment to ongoing archeological research. Beyond untapped sources, new fields of interest have emerged as well; for example, Jewish economic history in antiquity, Jewish military affairs, the political stances of the Jewries of the ancient world, the structures of political authority within the Jewish fold, and the striking variety of Jewish religious creativity. The reconstruction of this vital period in the Jewish past has been further enhanced by the development and use of innovative techniques for evaluating and interpreting the often meager sources transmitted from the ancient period. Out of all this activity has emerged a series of new perspectives on the Jewish experience in antiquity.

Understanding of Jewish life in the medieval world, in both the Muslim and Christian spheres, has been significantly enhanced. A number of factors—not the least of which has been the altered relations between Jews and Muslims in the contemporary Middle East—has given rise to powerful new concern with earlier contacts between these two civilizations. Once again new source materials have come to the fore, particularly the rich repository of the Cairo Genizah. These recently discovered materials have allowed fuller knowledge of some of the great intellectual creativity of the eleventh and twelfth centuries, as well as remarkable reconstruction of aspects of everyday Jewish living. The multivolume study by S. D. Gotein, *A Mediterranean Society*, represents a landmark in the depiction of medieval Jewish life. For Jewish life in medieval Christendom substantial progress has also been made in historical research. Fuller portraits of major individuals and important communities appear regularly, often based on new archival materials and a surer sense of the Jewish place in larger society.

Not surprisingly, contemporary research has heavily emphasized the early modern and more recent periods. There has been a profound commitment to depicting the prior existence of European Jewish communities that were all but obliterated during the Holocaust. Some of this commitment flows from a desire to understand the calamitous end of these communities; in other cases, the focus has been an effort to capture the life of these centers in their heyday. The Zionist movement and the eventual establishment of the State of Israel have served as yet another major force in modern Jewish historiography. Likewise, the maturation of American Jewry and its central role on the world Jewish scene have occasioned intensified research into the development of this young but vital Jewry.

Efforts to synthesize the findings of this productive new research have not been lacking. One-volume summaries of Jewish history or major segments thereof appear recurrently. The monumental effort at synthesis is undoubtedly that of Salo W. Baron. Now a nonagenarian, Baron continues to push forward with his unrivaled *Social and Religious History of the Jews*. It is abundantly clear that future attempts at such grand synthesis will be made by groups of scholars working in tandem, rather than by individual researchers. The corporate *World History of the Jewish People* already points in this new direction. The necessity of such group efforts is in part a tribute to the rich flowering of a vast new literature of the history of the Jews. For interested Jews and non-Jews, new horizons have been opened on important facets of historic Jewish experience. Some fruits of this remarkable new literature are highlighted in the following bibliography.

HISTORICAL SURVEYS

The title of this section, "Historical Surveys," is a somewhat broad term encompassing one-volume introductory surveys as well as multivolume scholarly studies. Although both types of book are described here, most readers will be primarily interested in just one or the other. For people just beginning to study Jewish history, the surveys written by Grayzel and Roth are reliable and comprehensive; it is not really possible to state a preference for one over the other. Dimont's *Jews, God and History* is the most readable of the surveys, but it is almost unanimously criticized by scholars for its Jewish chauvinism and unconventional theories. Read it, but do not rely on it. For a more scholarly history than any of these three, there is *A History of the Jewish People* by Ben-Sasson, a volume that is more demanding to read but remains accessible to nonscholars. The major work of Jewish history is Baron's eighteen-volume series, which spans the period from antiquity to the seventeenth century. Only the most serious student would wish to read it from cover to cover, but it is an indispensable reference work.

The histories of specific countries and regions listed here are not meant to be inclusive. Some, such as Weinryb's study of Poland, are included because of the importance of Polish Jewry. Others, such as Pollak's history of the Jews of China, are included because they spotlight little-known corners of Jewish life. There are, however, many books on important aspects of Jewish history that we have not attempted to mention. A bibliography that did no more than cover the histories of Jews in England, Russia, Czechoslovakia, Germany, Austria, Hungary, and France would be large. And it would have done no more than scratch the surface, since it would have omitted Romania, Italy, Bulgaria, and so on. The Jewish Publication Society has an excellent series of histories of the **Diaspora** that can be recommended, and you should consult a copy of their catalogue. Beyond that, we must, somewhat apologetically, leave you on your own. —R. S. F. & W. W.

Ausubel, Nathan, and David C. Gross
Pictorial History of the Jewish People. Crown, 1984, $19.95.

First published in 1953 and recently updated by David C. Gross, former editor of the *New York Jewish Week,* this one-volume encyclopedia-style history of the Jews has more than 1,200 pictures and lots of headings to guide you to the section of the text you want. It covers every aspect of Jewish life and history, and the updating is thorough and careful. The inclusion of a bibliography and index is a substantial plus. The easy readability and the profusion of pictures make this especially suitable for younger readers, and a good gift.

Bamberger, Bernard J.
The Story of Judaism. Schocken Books, 1964, $9.95 pb.

Not so much a history of the Jews as a history of the Jewish religion emphasizing the inner content of Jewish life. Bamberger, a Reform rabbi, focuses on the religious ideas, observances, and institutions. He writes well, and this is a good introduction to the subject. (See also Silver and Martin's *A History of Judaism,* described later.)

Baron, Salo W., Arcadius Kahan, et al.
Economic History of the Jews. Schocken Books, 1976, $5.50 pb.

Following a general survey of Jewish economic history from the First Temple Period to modern times, the articles in this comprehensive book deal with such specific topics as agriculture, goldsmithing, the diamond trade, department stores, money lending, peddling, and textiles. The material all originally appeared in the *Encyclopaedia Judaica.*

Baron, Salo W.
A Social and Religious History of the Jews. Columbia University Press, 1952 to 1973, 18 vols., $40 each.

Unquestionably the major Jewish historical work of our time, Salo Baron's monumental history of the Jews from ancient times to the late Middle Ages is a work of profound scholarship and intelligence. Its sheer size makes it more suitable for libraries and institutions than for individuals, but no Jewish library can consider itself a major library without this work.

Ben-Sasson, H. H., ed.
A History of the Jewish People. Harvard University Press, 1976, $60 hc, $18.95 pb.

Written by six scholars from the Hebrew University, Jerusalem, this massive (1,100-plus pages) history looks at the Jewish experience from religious, political, social, and economic perspectives. The writing is scholarly but not ponderous, and it is arguably the most comprehensive single-volume Jewish history available.

Dimont, Max I.
Jews, God and History. New American Library, 1962, $3.95 pb.

This is a lively survey of Jewish history. Dimont writes with great enthusiasm, arguing that the spiritual, moral, ethical, and ideological roots of Western civilization are all Jewish. His focus is on those aspects unique to Judaism that have enabled the Jewish

people to survive for 4,000 years. Some of Dimont's ideas are controversial—he suggests that Moses was an Egyptian, not a Hebrew—but this remains an entertaining introduction to Jewish history.

Eban, Abba
Heritage: Civilization and the Jews. Summit Books, 1984, $30.

Based on Eban's 1985 Public Broadcasting Corporation television series, this history concentrates on cultural symbiosis—the interaction between Jews and the world around them. A major reason for buying this book is its many color photographs and illustrations.

My People: The Story of the Jews. Random House, 1984, $14.95 pb.

This book is stronger on the Middle Ages and the modern era than on life in biblical times. Not surprisingly, given Eban's role as an Israeli diplomat, the sections of his book dealing with Zionism and the founding of Israel are the best and most detailed. Eban is a fluent and elegant stylist.

Grayzel, Solomon
A History of the Jews. New American Library, 1968, $4.95 pb.

This book offers a solid popular history that is both readable and reliable. Grayzel begins his history with the destruction of Judah in 586 B.C.E., believing that earlier events are meaningful mostly for the ways they have been interpreted since. His emphasis is on those historical aspects of Jewish life, institutions, and problems that help us understand Jewish life today. (See also Cecil Roth's *History of the Jews.*)

Kedourie, Elie, ed.
The Jewish World: History and Culture of the Jewish People. Harry Abrams, 1979, $45.

This survey of Jewish history includes the "inner" history—the Bible, Talmud, and Jewish philosophy, mysticism, and literature. The chapters are written by outstanding authorities: Hyam Maccoby on the Bible, Jacob Neusner on Talmud, S. D. Goitein on the Jews under Islam, T. Carmi on poetry, David Vital on Zionism, and so on. As good as the text is, though, what really sets this book apart is its many illustrations. There are more than four hundred, more than a hundred of those in color, and they have been skillfully selected and reproduced. It wouldn't be fair to call this a "coffee table" book, but it is as beautiful as one and makes a fine gift.

Kobler, Franz, ed.
Letters of Jews Through the Ages: A Self-Portrait of the Jewish People. Hebrew Publishing, 1978, 2 vols., $7.95 each, pb.
Vol. 1: *From Biblical Times to the Renaissance.*
Vol. 2: *From the Renaissance to the Emancipation.*

Is there anything more interesting than reading other people's mail? These two volumes are filled with other people's mail, and they're great fun. Letters of historical importance are included along with those which flesh out the portrait provided by more conventional histories and give a more intimate and human sense of what life was like. The editor's introductions are models of clear and informative scholarship.

Lewis, Bernard
The Jews of Islam. Princeton University Press, 1984, $17.50.

This is not so much a history (for that, see Ashtor in the MEDIEVAL AND MODERN HISTORY section) as an analysis of the cultural relationship Lewis calls the Judaeo-Islamic tradition, in theology and law, in theory and practice. He traces it from its origins in the Middle Ages to its ending with the emigration of most Jews of Arab lands to the new State of Israel. Lewis is scholarly, and this book is definitely not a starting point for study of the subject.

Poliakov, Leon
History of Anti-Semitism. Vanguard Press, 3 vols., $17.50 each.
Vol. 1: *From the Time of Christ to the Court Jews.* Translated from the French by Richard Howard. 1965.
Vol. 2: *From Mohammed to the Marranos.* Translated by Natalie Gerardi. 1974.
Vol. 3: *From Voltaire to Wagner.* Translated by Miriam Kochan, 1975.

This set is generally regarded

as the best and most detailed history of anti-Semitism. Poliakov searches for the reasons behind the origins and persistence of anti-Semitism, in the process looking at economic, theological, political, psychological, and social factors. This is a work of impressive scholarship, assembling and explaining a massive amount of information. Poliakov's prose is undistinguished but sufficient to the task.

Pollak, Michael
Mandarins, Jews, and Missionaries: The Jewish Experience in the Chinese Empire. Jewish Publication Society, 1980, $10.95 pb.

It is ironic that despite the often strained relations between Jews and members of Judaism's "daughter" religions—Christianity and Islam—Diaspora Jewish communities have never flourished in a non-Christian or non-Islamic country. One lesser-known Jewish community that was eventually absorbed by its surrounding culture was that of China. Jews first came to China approximately a thousand years ago. With time, they blended both physically and psychologically with the general population. As recently as the mid-1800s, the community of Kaifeng had preserved a Jewish identity and maintained a still-functioning synagogue. The community has since disappeared. This book tells of this historical footnote and also discusses the interesting story of European reaction to the "discovery" of the community by Father Matteo Ricci in the sixteenth century.

Roth, Cecil
A History of the Jews: From Earliest Times to the Six-Day War. Schocken Books, 1970, $8.95 pb.

Like Grayzel's history, this one offers only limited discussion of the earliest period of Jewish history. It does have more about the time between the establishment of the monarchy (twelfth century B.C.E.) and the Babylonian Exile in 586 B.C.E. Roth's book is shorter than Grayzel's and, perhaps, easier to read. Either is a good introduction to the subject.

Schwarz, Leo W., ed.
Great Ages and Ideas of the Jewish People. Modern Library/Random House, 1956, $7.95.

The contributors to this book are all first-rate historians. Included are Salo W. Baron, Gerson D. Cohen, Abraham S. Halkin, Yehezkel Kaufmann, Ralph Marcus, and Cecil Roth. Kaufmann's section on the "Biblical Age" is outstanding although demanding, and of all the one-volume historical surveys, this one covers that period most thoroughly. It also covers the "Talmudic Age" in more detail than either Grayzel or Roth, although it is not as accessible to beginners as either of those works.

Silver, Daniel Jeremy, and Bernard Martin

A History of Judaism. Basic Books, 1974, out of print.

It's a shame that this two-volume history is out of print. Its focus is the spiritual history of the Jewish people, and it covers social and political events only to the extent needed to make the religious developments understandable. The writing is nontechnical, and the authors avoid obscure material that would be more useful in impressing us with their knowledge than in teaching us what we want to know. Glossaries and substantial annotated bibliographies are included. Look for this one in libraries and used-book stores.

Weinryb, Bernard D.

The Jews of Poland: A Social and Economic History of the Jewish Community in Poland from 1100 to 1800. Jewish Publication Society, 1976, $10.

This book is part of a Jewish Publication Society series of historical works covering Jewish life in the Diaspora. The special importance of the Polish Jewish community makes this volume more than usually interesting. Jews first settled in Poland in the twelfth century, and the community eventually numbered in the millions. Although this history concentrates on the community's socioeconomic life, religious life is not neglected. In fact, the last section of the book deals with the birth of Hasidism and with its practices and doctrines.

Weisbrot, Robert

The Jews of Argentina: From the Inquisition to Peron. Jewish Publication Society, 1979, $12.50.

Another in the Jewish Publication Society histories, this one dealing with a Latin America community that (you may be surprised to learn) is the fifth largest Jewish population in the world.

Yerushalmi, Yosef Hayim

Zakhor: Jewish History and Jewish Memory. University of Washington Press, 1982, $17.50.

Judaism is a religion in which knowledge of God is derived from what he has done in history. One of the central religious injunctions is to remember (which is what *zakhor* means). Much of the Jewish scripture is, in fact, a history of the Jewish people. Yerushalmi's perceptive study begins by pointing out the paradoxical state of affairs that with the close of the biblical canon, Jews virtually ceased writing history: that while the memory of the past was central to Judaism, historians were not. He proceeds to examine the role of the modern Jewish historian, a role he sees as remaining problematic and ambiguous. This is a work of intelligence and astute observation. It deservedly won a National Jewish Book Award.

ANCIENT HISTORY AND ARCHEOLOGY BOOKS

The early period of Jewish history is a fascinating one. It is also one that is not as well covered in historical surveys as are some other periods. Fortunately, certain books do a splendid job of introducing the reader to the subject. Bright's *History of Israel* is an outstanding work of scholarship. Grant's *History of Ancient Israel* is also first-rate and is somewhat easier for readers who do not have much background in Jewish history.

For readers especially interested in archeology, there are many books of interest, but the single best survey is probably Aharoni's *Archaeology of the Land of Israel.* Two of the most readable books on specific archeological sites are Yadin's *Hazor* (Random House, 1975) and *Masada,* both regrettably out of print.

In addition to the books in this section, readers should refer to Keller's *The Bible as History* in the BIBLE section, a book for general readers describing how archeological research has supported the accuracy of the Bible. *The Macmillan Bible Atlas* by Aharoni (in the REFERENCE BOOKS section) is also valuable.

—R. S. F. & W. W.

Aharoni, Yohanan
The Archaeology of the Land of Israel: From the Prehistoric Beginnings to the End of the First Temple Period. Translated from the Hebrew by Anson F. Rainey. Westminster Press, 1982, $27.50 hc, $18.50 pb.

This good introductory text surveys Israelite life from its prehistoric origins to the destruction of the First Temple in the sixth century B.C.E. Aharoni was an active practicing archeologist, the founder of the Institute of Archeology at Tel Aviv University. The book includes more than a hundred diagrams and illustrations, and over fifty photographs. Not exciting reading, but clear, understandable, and informative. Aharoni is also the author of *The Land of the Bible: A Historical Geography* (Westminster Press, 1980, $19.95 pb), one of the best books available on the historical geography of Israel.

Avigad, Nahman
Discovering Jerusalem. Translated from the Hebrew. Nelson, 1983, $24.95.

One of the world's leading archeologists, Avigad takes the reader along with him as he describes the first decade of his excavation of the Jewish Quarter in the Upper City of Jerusalem. He tells how the work was carried out and what was found, and includes many photos and illustrations.

Ben-Dov, Meir
In the Shadow of the Temple: The Discovery of Ancient Jerusalem. Translated from the Hebrew by Ina Friedman. Harper & Row, 1985, $24.95.

Written by the field director of the excavations, this book reports on the archeological activities of Jersualem's Temple Mount, a site whose history dates back more than three thousand years and a religious center since the time of King David. Ben-Dov discusses the artifacts found there and what they reveal to us about the past. He also writes about the practical difficulties of the job, including opposition from religious leaders and the political maneuvering he used to circumvent it.

Bright, John
A History of Israel: Third Edition. Westminster Press, 1981, $18.95.

Beginning with prehistory and extending through the fourth century C.E., this history of ancient Israel is readable and noteworthy for its tremendous scholarship and insight. Perhaps it assumes too much knowledge on the part of its readers. If you're not familiar with the significance of the J, E, D, and P documents, you may get a little lost now and then. Nevertheless, if you only plan to read one book on the subject, this is the one. See also Grant's history, in this section.

Finkelstein, Louis
Akiba: Scholar, Saint, and Martyr. Atheneum, 1970, $6.95 pb.

Rabbi Akiba ben Joseph (c. 40–135) is an almost legendary figure in Jewish history. Illiterate and poor, he nevertheless became probably the leading Jewish scholar of his period, during which Palestine was under Roman rule. After destroying the Temple, the Romans banned the teaching of Torah. Akiba defied the ban and continued to teach publicly. Warned of the risk, he said, "If there is no safety for us in Torah, which is our home, how can we find safety elsewhere?" He was tortured and killed by the Romans. His martyrdom has become a symbol of love of God and faithfulness to Judaism.

Grant, Michael
The History of Ancient Israel. Scribner, 1984, $19.95.

Grant is an excellent and prolific writer on the ancient world, and he is a first-rate popularizer. This history traces the Israelites from their earliest settlements in Canaan to the destruction of the Second Temple. Compared to Bright's history (listed earlier), Grant's is more concerned with politics and society, less concerned with religious developments. It's a solid work and, in many ways, easier for beginners than Bright's.

Josephus

The Jewish War. Translated by Goalya Cornfeld,Zondervan, 1982, $39.95; translated by G. A. Williamson, Dorset Press, 1985, $7.95.

It's hard to like Josephus (38– 100 C.E.), but impossible not to be fascinated by him. He was at best a scoundrel and self-serving political realist. He has been called a traitor and a liar for abandoning the Jewish side and joining with the Romans. He was unquestionably a shrewd and able observer, and he is our single best source of information about the war between the Jews and the Roman Empire. His history is where the story of Masada can be found, and it provides one of the few contemporary records of events that permanently shaped Jewish history. The Zondervan edition includes extensive commentaries and information on the archeological background, plus many color and black-and-white photos. The Dorset Press edition is a hardcover reprint of the Penguin Classic text, and includes a glossary, appendixes, maps, and other helpful material.

Levine, Lee I., ed.

Ancient Synagogues Revealed. Wayne State University Press, 1982, $24.

The development of the synagogue as a replacement for the Temple as a center of Jewish worship, is one of the most important events in Jewish history. It is also an event about which not a great deal is known. This book is a survey of ancient synagogues, both in Israel and in the Diaspora, examining them both from archeological and historical perspectives. The contributors include such noted figures as Yigael Yadin, Nahman Avigad, and M. Avi-Yonah. The book is slightly dry, but interesting reading.

Neusner, Jacob

First-Century Judaism in Crisis: Yohanan ben Zakkai and the Renaissance of Torah. Ktav, 1982, $11.95 pb.

After the destruction of the Second Temple by the Romans in 70 C.E., the Jewish people were at one of their historic low points. Rabbi Yohanan ben Zakkai was one of the leaders who helped to overcome the despair and, as founder of the Academy at Yavneh, was a crucial figure in perpetuating the Judaism that is still practiced today. This book, condensed from a longer scholarly work by Neusner, provides a portrait of Yohanan and also describes the world of Pharisaic Judaism.

Pearlman, Moshe

The Zealots of Masada: Story of a Dig. Scribner, 1967, $2.45 pb.

This account of Yigael Yadin's archeological exploration of the fortress at Masada describes the methods used and the reasons the excavation was of such historical importance. Yadin's own book (listed later in this section) makes an excellent companion to this one—it's bigger and has many more photos, but it is also not currently in print. They're both worth reading.

Vermes, Geza
The Dead Sea Scrolls in English. Penguin, 1962, $4.95 pb.

The Dead Sea Scrolls are a group of ancient manuscripts, dating back to the first century C.E and earlier, that were discovered in caves near the Dead Sea starting in 1947. Most, although not all, were discovered near Qumran. The dramatic story of their recovery, filled with the kind of negotiations and shady characters that sound like they belong in an Eric Ambler spy thriller, added to the public fascination with the Scrolls. They have had a major impact on all studies of the period. They are by far the oldest manuscript versions available for large parts of the Bible. Fragments of nearly every biblical book were found, and some books were found in complete form. They showed that the transmission of the Bible text from antiquity had been far more accurate than many scholars thought possible. The Scrolls also include information about the religion and life of an extremist Jewish community, now generally identified as the Essenes, which is considered to be an important link between Judaism and early Christianity. Little was known about the Essenes before the Scrolls were found.

The Vermes translation of the Scrolls is generally accepted as authoritative.

Wilson, Edmund
Israel and the Dead Sea Scrolls. Farrar, Straus & Giroux, 1978, $9.25 pb.

The major part of this book is a splendidly written account of the discovery, acquisition, and historical background of the Dead Sea Scrolls. Wilson also writes of the people who studied the Scrolls, the teachings of the sect that produced them, and, in a supplemental section, of the response to the first publication of the book. Several essays on topics related to Israel are also included. The writing is accessible to the general reader without ever being simplistic.

Yadin, Yigael
Hazor: The Rediscovery of a Great Citadel of the Bible. Random House, 1975, out of print.

Yadin was an archetypal modern Israeli—both soldier and scholar. One of its leading archeologists, he was also the chief of operations during Israel's War of Independence and chief of staff of the Israeli Army from 1949 to 1952. His account of the excavation of Hazor makes for exciting reading, as Yadin tells of the missteps and false trails as well as the successes. Hazor is a city with a long and interesting history. Dating back to 2,500 B.C.E., it was destroyed by Joshua—an event recounted in the biblical book,

Chronicles—and was later rebuilt by Solomon. Yadin's expedition demonstrated that the biblical account is an accurate one. The book is extensively illustrated.

Masada: Herod's Fortress and the Zealots' Last Stand. Out of print. This book is one of the classics of modern archeological writing. The story of Masada is a dramatic one, and Yadin's telling of its history and his excavation of the ruins effectively conveys the drama. Masada is an isolated mountain on which Herod built a spectacular multilevel fortified palace. A Roman garrison stationed there was annihilated in 66 C.E., and it became a Zealot fortress. In 73 C.E., facing capture by Roman forces, the nearly one thousand surviving Zealots committed suicide. (See Josephus, noted earlier, who is our major source of information about these events.) Masada is the site of the oldest known synagogue, the only one preserved from the Second Temple Period. Today, recruits of the Israeli Armored Corps are brought to Masada, where they swear that "Masada shall not fall again."

MEDIEVAL AND MODERN HISTORY BOOKS

We know of no one-volume survey of Jewish life in the Middle Ages that can be recommended as a good starting point for study. To become acquainted with this period, most readers would do best to turn to the appropriate section of a survey such as Roth's or Grayzel's (see the HISTORICAL SURVEYS section of this chapter). Abrahams' *Jewish Life in the Middle Ages* is fine for readers with some background in Jewish history, but deals with selected topics only. Dawidowicz's outstanding anthology *The Golden Tradition* covers both the medieval and modern eras, but deals only with Eastern Europe.

The Middle Ages saw one of the high points in Jewish history, the Jewish civilization of the Iberian Peninsula. During the flourishing of this community, some of the greatest thinkers and literary figures in Jewish history lived and worked. Heschel's *Maimonides* is a biography of one of the most important of them. Ashtor's three-volume survey, *The Jews of Moslem Spain,* is too lengthy to be suggested for all readers, but it is an important, basic, and readable survey of the subject.

Moving into the modern era, Sachar's *The Course of Modern Jewish History* is the single best survey of modern Jewish history available. To supplement it, *The Jew in the Modern World,* edited by Mendes-Flohr and Reinharz, is a collection of documents that makes for fascinating reading and provides a more intimate sense of history than most surveys can. Zborowski and Herzog's *Life Is with People* is an unexcelled portrait of Eastern European Jewish life. Dealing with a crucial contemporary theme, Gilbert's *Jews of Hope* is a vivid and moving report on the problems of Soviet Jews.

No attempt to understand modern Jewish history is complete without looking beyond the limits of this section of the book. Many religious developments, especially the growth of Hasidism, are dealt with in the MODERN JEWISH THOUGHT section. Among the other subjects you need information on are American Jewish life, the Holocaust, and Israel and Zionism. For American Jewish history, Karp's *Haven and Home* is a readable and comprehensive survey. An understanding of Israel's past can be gained from reading Sachar's *History of Israel,* and Oz's *In the Land of Israel* provides a good sense of the current mood of the country as seen by a noted Israeli writer. *The War Against the Jews, 1933–1945,* by Lucy Dawidowicz, is a history of the Holocaust notable for its thoroughness and readability.

—R. S. F. & W. W.

Abrahams, Israel
Jewish Life in the Middle Ages. Atheneum, 1978, $7.95 pb.

A study of many aspects of medieval Jewish life, placing it in the context of the Christian world. Information is included on such topics as business, home life, the slave trade, and social morality. The discussion of the synagogue as the center of social life describes weddings, flagellations, and even excommunications—the most famous of those being that of Uriel Acosta in Amsterdam in 1633.

Ashtor, Eliyahu
The Jews of Moslem Spain. Translated from the Hebrew by Aaron Klein and Jenny Machlowitz Klein. Jewish Publication Society, 1974–1984, Vol. 1, $12; Vol. 2, $12; Vol. 3, $19.95.

Jewish civilization reached one of its high points—some would say its highest point—on the Iberian Peninsula during the Middle Ages. Ashtor's history is based on an extraordinary familiarity with both Moslem and Jewish sources, and covers social, economic, political, and cultural developments. He is especially good at showing the ways in which the

Sephardic Jewish communities were part both of the Moslem world in which they were located and the broader Jewish world. This is a basic text for anyone wishing to learn about the period.

Begin, Menachem

White Nights: The Story of a Prisoner in Russia. Translated from the Hebrew by Katie Kaplan. Harper & Row, 1977, out of print.

This is an account of Begin's imprisonment by the Soviets for "anti-Soviet" and "anti-Revolutionary" activities—that is, being a Zionist. He tells of the endless interrogations, how he preserved his humanity under extreme conditions, and his eventual release and arrival in Palestine.

Dawidowicz, Lucy S., ed.

The Golden Tradition: Jewish Life and Thought in Eastern Europe. Schocken Books, 1984, $11.95 pb.

Dawidowicz says that when the Jews of Eastern Europe were faced with the opportunities—and perils—of emancipation, they searched for ways to harmonize tradition and modernity, to preserve their Jewish identity against assimilation. This excellent anthology contains autobiographies, memoirs, letters, and other documents of Eastern European life from the sixteenth century to its destruction in the Holocaust. The topics it covers include Hasidism, education, scholars and philosophers, literature and the arts, Zionism, and politics.

Dobroszycki, Lucjan, and Barbara Kirschenblatt-Gimblett

Image Before My Eyes: A Photographic History of Jewish Life in Poland. Schocken Books, 1977, $29.95 hc, $19.95 pb.

Using photographs from the archives of the YIVO Institute, this book presents an evocative look at Polish Jewish life—a klezmer band, a newly-wed couple posing with their families, market day in the crowded streets of Krzemieniec, a wonderfully tough-looking eighty-seven-year-old blacksmith, an elegant-looking star of the Yiddish stage. As with Roman Vishniac's *Vanished World* (see the ARTS section), these photographs make real what was lost in the Holocaust.

Gilbert, Martin

Jews of Hope: The Plight of Soviet Jewry Today. Viking/Penguin, 1985, $15.95 hc, $6.95 pb.

Gilbert is a historian who has written frequently on Jewish subjects. In this book he brings up to date the story of Soviet Jewry that Elie Wiesel described so eloquently in *The Jews of Silence* (see later.) In 1983, Gilbert went to the Soviet Union where he met with "refuseniks," Soviet Jews who were attempting to emigrate but whose requests for visas had been refused. He reports on his trip and the personal stories of those he met, and writes also of the broader picture of Soviet anti-Semitism and the resurgence of

Jewish identity that followed the 1967 Arab-Israeli war.

Hanover, Nathan
Abyss of Despair (Yeven Metzulah). Translated from the Hebrew by Abraham J. Mesch. Transaction Books/Rutgers University, 1984, $14.95.

Nathan Hanover was an itinerant preacher and prolific writer who was driven from his home by the notorious Chmielnicki Massacres of 1648–1652. These pogroms, which took place during a Ukrainian rebellion against Russian rule led by Bogdan Chmielnicki, destroyed more than three hundred Jewish communities and resulted in the death of perhaps 100,000 Jews. *Abyss of Despair* is based primarily on eyewitness accounts, plus material drawn from other books. It has had enduring appeal, resulting from its strong narrative and powerful language.

Heschel, Abraham Joshua
Maimonides. Translated from the German by Joachim Neugroschel. Farrar, Straus & Giroux, 1982, $15.

Moses ben Maimon (1135–1204), known as Maimonides, was an extraordinary man. He was a major codifier of Jewish law, a rabbi and communal leader, physician, and important figure in the court of Egypt's Moslem rulers. Heschel, one of the twentieth century's leading Jewish thinkers, wrote this biography in 1935. It shows Maimonides as more than the cold rationalist he is often depicted to be, and presents him as a warm person well aware of the mysteries that no intellect can penetrate. The description of his last days is especially moving. For more information on Maimonides, see the section headed JEWISH THOUGHT BEFORE 1600.

Katz, Jacob
From Prejudice to Destruction: Anti-Semitism, 1700–1933. Harvard University Press, 1980, $25 hc, $7.95 pb.

The central issue in this study of modern anti-Semitism is how anti-Jewish attitudes eventually gained so much social power as to make the Holocaust possible. Katz also deals with the complex question of why anti-Semitism reached its most virulent and intense form áfter the European Enlightenment and the beginning of "modern rationality"— events that might have been expected to lead to a diminishing of irrational hatreds. See also Poliakov's *The History of Anti-Semitism,* listed in HISTORICAL SURVEYS.

Marcus, Jacob R.
The Jew in the Medieval World: A Source Book 315–1791. Greenwood Press, 1975, $21.50 hc; Atheneum, $10.95.

This book is a useful and comprehensive collection of documents about Jewish life in the Middle Ages. Major sections include documents about relations between Jews and the state (for instance, the Jews under Islamic law); the Catholic Church and the Jews, including documents relating to the Crusades, charges of ritual murder, and the burning of the Talmud; and Jewish self-government, sects, mystics, and notables. Originally published in 1938.

Mendes-Flohr, Paul R., and Jehuda Reinharz, eds.
The Jew in the Modern World: A Documentary History. Oxford University Press, 1980, $35 hc, $16.95 pb.

A rich collection of over two hundred and fifty documents, selected with an eye toward illustrating the processes at work in modern Jewish history. The editors have chosen material not readily available elsewhere, arranged it in eleven thematic sections, and provided brief explanatory notes putting the material into context. Among the items included are excerpts from the notorious Protocols of the Elders of Zion, the Writ of Excommunication against Baruch Spinoza, Franz Kafka on his father's "Bourgeois Judaism," George Washington's reply to a message of welcome from the Hebrew Congregation of Newport, the Balfour Declaration, and a report on the destruction of the Warsaw Ghetto by the German general who carried it out.

Metzger, Therese, and Mendel Metzger
Jewish Life in the Middle Ages: Illuminated Hebrew Manuscripts of the Thirteenth to the Sixteenth Centuries. Translated from the French. Alpine Fine Arts, 1982, out of print.

A lot of books are described as profusely illustrated; this one is. It is an account of European Jewish life in the Middle Ages based on miniature illustrations from medieval Hebrew manuscripts, including prayer books, ritual and legal documents, and philosophic treatises. Of the nearly four hundred illustrations, more than half are in color. Major sections of the book deal with the Jewish Quarter, the house and family life, costume, the professions, and religious life. It is beautiful to look at and filled with information.

Roskies, Diane K., and David G. Roskies
The Shtetl Book. Ktav, 1979, $9.95 pb.

The word **shtetl** is the Yiddish term for the small Jewish towns scattered throughout Eastern Europe and in which so many Jews used to live before the Bolshevik Revolution and the Nazi Holocaust destroyed them and their way of life. *The Shtetl Book* is a collection in English translation of both primary and literary sources about the shtetl. The emphasis is on the everyday life of ordinary Jews. While the book is intended for use as a school text, it is interesting reading for anyone. It makes a good companion volume to Zborowski and Herzog's *Life Is with People*, described later.

Ross, Dan

Acts of Faith: A Journey to the Fringes of Jewish Identity. St. Martin's, 1982, $15.95 hc, Schocken Books, $8.95 pb.

This book is an excursion into Jewish communities such as the Ethiopian Jews and the Bene Israel of India, and some other groups whose Jewishness is marginal or problematic—the Chuetas of Majorca, the Samaritans, and the Karaites. Ross describes them and their lives, in part to explore the issue of just who is a Jew. *Acts of Faith* is well written, and although intended for the general reader, it does a good job of explaining the scholarly controversies that surround some of its subjects. It's interesting reading.

Roth, Cecil

A History of the Marranos. Ayer, reprint of 1932 edition, $35.50 hc; Schocken Books, $11.95 pb.

If the Jews experienced a "Golden Age" in medieval Spain, they also experienced some of the most systematic and prolonged persecution in their history—a hundred years of forced conversions, leading to their expulsion from Spain in 1492. Many of those forced to convert remained secretly loyal to Judaism despite the risk of death from the Inquisition. The word *Marrano,* probably derived from a word meaning swine, was the term used to refer to these "New Christians." In some cases, families still preserved a secret Jewish life after generations of outward Christian observance. As recently as 1917, a community of these "crypto-Jews" was found in Portugal. Roth's history is readable and comprehensive. See also *Dona Gracia of the House of Nasi,* Roth's biography of an extraordinary Marrano woman in the section headed WOMEN.

Rothchild, Sylvia

A Special Legacy: An Oral History of Soviet Jewish Emigres. Simon & Schuster, 1985, $17.95.

More than 65,000 Soviet Jews came to America in the 1970s. Rothchild studied interviews with 178 of them from the archives of the William E. Wiener Oral History Library of the American Jewish Committee, and from their personal stories has created a portrait of Soviet Jewish life. Rothchild previously edited *Voices from the Holocaust,* an anthology of first-person accounts that is now regrettably out of print.

Sachar, Howard M.

The Course of Modern Jewish History. Dell, 1977, $12.95 pb.

This authoritative survey of modern Jewish history begins with the period of the French Revolution and the rise of Western European Jewry and continues through World War II and the birth of the State of Israel. It examines political, social, economic, and cultural developments, and the interrelation between events in the Jewish world and the larger world around it. Jewish life in the United States is given extended treatment. Sachar's book offers the best one-volume coverage of the subject.

Diaspora: An Inquiry into the Contemporary Jewish World. Harper & Row, 1985, $27.50.

Sachar offers a very readable report on the current condition of the Jewish communities of the world outside of Israel and North America. Based on academic research and on his own travels and interviews, Sachar tells us about Jews living in the Soviet Union and Eastern Europe, in South and North Africa, in Western Europe and Latin America. In each area, Sachar focuses on one person, weaving a history of the community around that person. Sachar sees these diverse communities as being strongly tied together by an awareness of their common destiny as Jews, by loyalty to Israel, by philanthropic and other communal activities.

Scholem, Gershom

Sabbatai Sevi: The Mystical Messiah. Translated from the Hebrew by R. J. Zwi Werblowsky, Princeton University Press, 1973, $65 hc, $19.50 pb.

In discussing Scholem, the *Encyclopaedia Judaica* refers to his "combination of painstaking analysis, penetrating philosophical insight, and profound historical understanding." And of all his brilliant works, *Sabbatai Sevi* is generally regarded as the most brilliant, a monumental contribution to Jewish scholarship.

Shabbetai Zevi (the more common transliteration of his name) was a false messiah who in the 1600s produced a wave of religious fervor throughout world Jewry. It was the largest messianic movement since the destruction of the Second Temple and the Bar Kokhba revolt in the second century. So intense were the feelings stirred by Shabbetai Zevi that not even his conversion to Islam could dissuade his more ardent followers. Following his death, his adherents maintained that he would reappear, but schisms appeared and they split into a number of sects that eventually disappeared. This book is both a biography and a study of messianic movements and their theology. It is indispensable to any study of the false messiah and the movement he inspired. Werblowsky's translation is masterly. For other books by Scholem, see the MODERN JEWISH THOUGHT section.

Shereshevsky, Esra

Rashi: The Man and His World. Sepher-Hermon Press, 1983, $17.50.

Rabbi Shlomo Yitzaki (1040–1105), known as Rashi, was the author of commentaries on the Bible and the Babylonian Talmud. His Bible commentaries became immediately popular and have remained so to this date. (See Rosenbaum and Silbermann's *Pentateuch with Rashi* in the BIBLE section.) Rashi's Talmud commentary is now a standard part of modern editions of the Talmud. His style is remarkably simple, concise, and lucid. This biography deals extensively with his scholarly methods and interpretative techniques.

Singer, Isaac Bashevis

In My Father's Court. Translated from the Yiddish by Channah Kleinerman-Goldstein, Elaine Gottlieb, and Joseph Singer. Farrar, Straus & Giroux, 1966, $5.95 pb; Fawcett, $2.50 pb.

The rabbinical court—the **Beth Din**—is an ancient Jewish institution that has continued down to our day. It is more than a mere court of law, incorporating also aspects of a house of worship and a social service agency. As Singer says, it is based on the concept that "there can be no justice without godliness." This work is based on Singer's childhood in Warsaw and his memories of the court over which his father presided. It is, admittedly, not a purely "historical" work, but it is such an informative picture of a now-lost world that it cannot be omitted.

Stillman, Norman A.

The Jews of Arab Lands: A History and Source Book. Jewish Publication Society, 1979, $10.95 pb.

There is a tendency to write the history of Jewish life in Islamic countries in extremes— either the Jewish communities suffered terrible and unrelenting persecution, or they were astonishingly free of the persecution European Jews faced. This survey is balanced in its presentation, and a good choice because of that balance.

Werblowsky, R. J. Zwi

Joseph Karo: Lawyer and Mystic. Jewish Publication Society, 1977, $5.95 pb.

Joseph Karo (1488–1575) is known today principally as the author of the *Shulkhan Arukh,* which more than four hundred years after its composition remains the guide to Jewish law most accepted by the Orthodox, the *de facto* standard of reference. (See Appel's *Concise Guide of Jewish Law* and Ganzfried's *Code of Jewish Law,* both in JEWISH THOUGHT BEFORE 1600.) He was also the author of a major mystical work, the *Maggid Mesharim,* a diary in which he recorded what he believed were visits from a heavenly mentor *(maggid)* that occurred regularly for many years. This biography of Karo focuses on the *Maggid Mesharim* and its importance as a source of information on the mysticism of its time. In the process, Werblowsky also provides an insightful discussion of the spiritual world in which Karo lived. A knowledge of Hebrew is useful in reading this book.

Wiesel, Elie

Jews of Silence. Holt, Rinehart & Winston, 1966, out of print.

Wiesel visited the Soviet Union

in the 1960s and wrote this report on Jewish life there and the difficulties faced by those attempting to preserve their faith despite the opposition of authorities. Wiesel writes with passion and eloquence. It's a shame this book is out of print.

Zborowski, Mark, and Elizabeth Herzog
Life Is with People: The Culture of the Shtetl. Schocken Books, 1962, $7.95 pb.

A rare combination of scholarship with popular appeal, this book, based on a study by a team of Columbia University sociologists and anthropologists, draws on interviews with Eastern European Jews and analysis of history, literature, drama, and pictorial records. It attempts to present as a whole the culture of the *shtetl* and show the ways in which many of its values have survived in modern Jewish life even though the *shtetl* itself is no more. It's a book of deep humanity.

American Jewish Historiography

Jeffrey Gurock

Peace is now within reach in the world of American Jewish historiography. Respectful coexistence may soon characterize the relationship between those who study this history as a search for their roots and those who labor to make this discipline a recognized part of the Jewish and American historical academy. A thirty-year struggle for definition of this field's goals is moving toward conclusion. At least this armistice proposal can be made: those who dig and write for the adventure of research and the need to tell the stories of their families can be effectively used by those who are intent on placing this people's experience in the broadest possible contexts. In return, the university historians can accord a grudging respect to the undaunted amateurs for what these well-meaning history "buffs" have unearthed over the decades.

The struggle began in the mid-1950s when the first generation of professionally trained American Jewish historians, inspired by their senior practitioners in the wider fields of Jewish history and American immigrant and social history, challenged their amateur elders—both in age and orientation—for control of the field. Of course, until that time, American Jewish history had been, with few exceptions, the province of "the antiquarian, necrologist and undaunted sentimentalist," to quote but one early observer of the battlefield.

Those who sought out Columbus's "Jewish" roots or who chronicled the activities of the first Jews in the Thirteen Colonies or who preserved records of those Jews who gave their

Dr. Jeffrey Gurock is associate professor of American Jewish History, Yeshiva University, New York City.

lives in American wars were moved to their writings by the need to uphold the good name of their people in this country. Those, for example, who founded the American Jewish Historical Society in the early 1890s, fervently believed that if the gentile world was only made aware of the greatness of the Jewish contribution to the birth and growth of America, these facts would "be an answer, to all time to come, to anti-Semitic tendencies in this country."* In an era that saw groups such as the Daughters of the American Revolution argue that *Mayflower* descendants built America and later arrivals only broke it down, Jews rushed to prove that their coreligionists awaited the Pilgrims at Plymouth Rock and that all other Jews who followed in their wake played major roles in the upbuilding and upgrading of America. Practically, that meant that if general historians lionized the Founding Fathers, then Jewish colonial elders also had to be dug up. And if these writers could not come up with a Jewish counterpart to Nathan Hale, at least they could wax patriotic over Haym Solomon, a Jew who supposedly gave his fortune to save his country.

By the 1950s, most of the fears and concerns that had first motivated this dedication to history were gone, but the tendentiousness of American Jewish history remained. Now the agenda of the amateurs was filiopietism pure and simple. Most works looked only at community notables, and those best known to the outside world. The basic social, cultural, and intellectual history of American Jewry was left unexplored.

At that time, two new powerful phalanxes of scholars entered and transformed the field. Americanists formed by the new academic interest in immigrant and social history began to submit the Jewish historical experience to the same critical scrutiny then being applied to the examination of all other new American groups. High on their list of concerns was understanding the processes of foreigner adaptation to American culture and of immigrant economic and social mobility over the past century. For these young professional historians, no aspect of Jewish culture was off limits, and every possible

---

*Naomi W. Cohen, *A Dual Heritage: The Public Career of Oscar Straus* (Jewish Publication Society, 1969), p. 171.

modern methodology was appropriate. Such terms as *census tract* and *land use map* entered the American Jewish historian's vocabulary. And these sources took their honored place alongside ethnic and foreign language newspapers—the primary source most used in uncovering Jewish social history. That history came to include not only the success stories of the patriots, but also the poor, the slow to acculturate, and ultimately the criminal element.

In the meantime, Jewish historians also began, during the past generation, to cast their attention upon this unique Diaspora community's history. Central to their concerns were the questions surrounding the survival of the Jewish community and Jewish identity under the conditions of freedom. Of related relevance was the understanding of how Jewish movements born and bred within Europe either found a home, were transfigured, or were destroyed under the pressure of American assimilation. These interests translated themselves into important works on the progress of Zionism in America, the checkered career of Jewish radicalism in America, and most recently, interest in the denominational history of American Jewry.

Still, even as American and Jewish historians began to speak about this country's Jews and started to confer with colleagues in related fields about the academic relevance of the discipline, pockets of the old-style history remained. Local and communal history was the residual stronghold of the old-timers. Indeed, the efflorescence of the search for roots in the past two decades gave some incremental strength to the old agenda for American Jewish history. Numerous local Jewish historical societies were formed across the country. And if these groups did not have much communication with the world of academe, at least they spoke to each other.

But even as these societies proliferated, they did not keep professional historians from looking at their communities with a dispassionate eye. Indeed, some of the best works that have emerged in the past decade have focused on local and neighborhood history as American Jewish history reached toward a new maturity. However, in so doing, a certain serenity came to those who have made the rapid one-generational change in the discipline. They came to realize that even if the amateurs did not write the type of history they appreciated and recognized, the buffs more often than not came up with information and documents that could be put in the service of serious Jewish scholarship. The following list of books represents much of the best of both traditions. These books may be judged fairly both for their scholarship and communal intentions.

AMERICAN HISTORY BOOKS

For a survey of American history in one volume, Abraham Karp's *Haven and Home* is the best choice. It contains numerous primary source materials and sensible, straightforward historical analysis. A more detailed look at specific aspects of American Jewish life can be gained from Irving Howe's *World of Our Fathers*, which is about the vibrant Jewish community that existed on New York's Lower East Side at the turn of the century, and from Kenneth Libo and Irving Howe's *We Lived There Too*, which is about the role of Jews in settling the American West.

Dealing with the current state of affairs in America, Marc Lee Raphael's *Profiles in American Judaism* is a solid report on the four major branches of Judaism—Conservative, Orthodox, Reconstructionist, and Reform. *An Orphan in History* by Paul Cowan is the absorbing personal account of one man's attempt to discover what it means to recover and preserve a Jewish identity in a country where assimilation into the "melting pot" is considered desirable.

To gain a full sense of the texture of American Jewish life, you also need to read some fictional treatments. Two good novels about the immigrant experience are Meredith Tax's *Rivington Street*, a popular novel, and *Jews Without Money*, a searing account of the difficulties of immigrant life. The novels of Chaim Potok deal extensively with the tensions between modern, secular society and life as an observant Orthodox Jew. Robert Greenfield's *Temple*, winner of a National Jewish Book Award for fiction, is a fine story dealing with some of the same themes as Cowan's *Orphan in History*.   —R. S. F. & W. W.

Angel, Marc D.

La America: The Sephardic Experience in the United States. Jewish Publication Society, 1982, $15.95.

Rabbi Angel has specialized in the study of Sephardic Jewry. In this book he writes of the Sephardic Jews who migrated to America between 1899 and 1925 from Bulgaria, Turkey, Syria, and other places. He also writes of Moise Gadol, editor of the newspaper *La America*, who attempted unsuccessfully to consolidate the Levantine Sephardim into a central organization. The life of these immigrants is little known, and Rabbi Angel has done a good job of revealing it to us.

Belth, Nathan C.

A Promise to Keep: A Narrative of the American Encounter with Antisemitism. Schocken Books, 1981, $7.95 pb.

This popular history of anti-Semitism in America includes substantial coverage of the creation and efforts of the Anti-Defamation League of B'nai B'rith.

Birmingham, Stephen

Our Crowd. Berkley Books, 1985, $4.50 pb.

A history describing German-Jewish immigrants of the late nineteenth century. Birmingham is not a historian, he's a popularizer. He is, however, a very good one, and an engaging writer. The book is not profound, but is nonetheless informative and always entertaining. *The Rest of Us* (Little, Brown, 1984, $19.45 hc; Berkley Books, $4.50 pb) is Birmingham's look at Eastern European Jewish immigrants, especially those who rose to great wealth, such as Samuel Goldwyn, David Sarnoff, and Helena Rubenstein.

Cohen, Naomi W.

Encounter with Emancipation: The German Jews in the United States 1830–1914. Jewish Publication Society, 1985, $25.95.

Winner of the 1985 National Jewish Book Award for history, this book is a study of what the author sees as the first genuine encounter of Jews with emancipation—the one with American society. It traces the struggle of German-Jewish immigrants to build businesses, communal institutions, and political influence, and to adjust to the problems brought on by Americanization. Cohen writes well, and the book includes many first-person accounts that add immediacy to the scholarly account.

Cowan, Paul

An Orphan in History: Retrieving a Jewish Legacy. Doubleday, 1983, $15.95; Bantam Books, $3.50 pb.

Paul Cowan speaks for a generation of young American Jews who have returned to Judaism and refused to dissolve in the melting pot. A "Jewish WASP," with Christmas celebrations and a prep school education, Cowan was raised with no knowledge of his

Jewish heritage. Feeling "an orphan in history," he set out to rediscover his patrimony. His book combines autobiography, family history, and an exploration of the meaning of Jewish identity in modern America. It is very much a personal story, and sometimes painfully honest.

Eisen, Arnold M.
The Chosen People in America: A Study in Jewish Religious Ideology. Indiana University Press, 1983, $17.50.

The chosenness of the Jewish people is one of the central concepts of Judaism. Eisen's book is a study of how this idea of particularity has come into conflict with the desire to assimilate into American society, which is egalitarian and pluralistic in nature. He feels that both the Reform and Conservative branches of Judaism have failed to come to grips with this issue.

Feingold, Henry L.
Zion in America: The Jewish Experience from Colonial Times to the Present. Hippocrene Books, 1981, $10.95 pb.

This survey of American Jewish history is concise and clear, emphasizing the broad sweep of events rather than concentrating on details. Feingold sees the American Jewish community as being unique among American ethnic groups in the extent to which it has preserved its sense of group identity. He also sees it as unique among world Jewry in

the pressures it faces—and opportunities it is offered—to assimilate into the general culture around it.

Harris, Lis
Holy Days: The World of a Hasidic Family. Summit Books, 1985, $18.95.

A portrait of Hasidic life in general and one Lubavitcher family in particular. Harris visited the family over a period of years, and she describes its private life, the role of women in the Hasidic community, and the history of the Hasidic movement. Although she remains an outsider, Harris is a sympathetic observer who reports accurately on what she sees. She writes well and does a good job of conveying the religious fervor of Hasidic life. For readers who have never been able to understand Orthodox life or why someone would choose to live it, this book may answer some questions.

Helmreich, William
World of the Yeshiva: An Intimate Portrait of Orthodox Judaism. Free Press/Macmillan, 1982, $19.95.

Helmreich, a sociologist who was himself a **yeshiva** student when younger, spent seven years investigating the world of the yeshiva, attempting to understand how it functioned and the reasons for its success in America. As part of his research, he enrolled as a student at a major yeshiva for more than a year. This book is a report, based on interviews, questionnaires, and personal observation. It is engrossing reading—free of sociological jargon, objective yet sympathetic, and filled with interesting information. Anyone wishing to understand the yeshiva world would profit from reading this book.

Hertzberg, Arthur
Being Jewish in America: The Modern Experience. Schocken Books, 1979, $16.95 hc, $7.95 pb.

These essays examine modern American Jewish life. Hertzberg looks at problem areas such as the challenges of modern times, the politics of church and state, and black-Jewish relations. He also writes in celebration of Jewish New York, on why Jewish education *must* be religious education, on the role of the American rabbinate, and on the importance of Zionism and Israel in American Jewish life.

Howe, Irving, ed.
World of Our Fathers. Simon & Schuster, 1978, $12.95 pb.

Using newspaper reports, memoirs, and photographs, Howe recreates the life of Jews on New York's Lower East Side at the turn of the century. He covers politics, culture, religion, economic hardship, labor conflicts, and daily life. His text is dry, but the original documents provide a vivid sense of the people and their lives. For fiction about this period, see Max Rosenfeld's *Pushcarts and Dreamers* in the YIDDISH LITERATURE

section, and the works of Anzia Yezierska in FICTION.

Joselit, Jenna Weissman
Our Gang: Jewish Crime and the New York Jewish Community, 1900–1940. Indiana University Press, 1983, $19.95 hc, $9.95 pb.

Criminality is often seen as "un-Jewish," but the enormous dislocations produced by the massive migration to America in the late nineteenth and early twentieth centuries, combined with the grinding poverty faced by many of the immigrants, produced a generation of Jewish criminals: crime became a form of upward mobility. This book is an extensively researched and well-reasoned analysis of crime in the Jewish community and a fascinating history of how the community attempted to combat it. (*Prostitution and Prejudice: The Jewish Fight Against White Slavery* by Edward J. Bristow, a more narrowly focused study, deals specifically with Jewish prostitution, its causes, and the response to it by the Jewish community. It is described in the WOMEN section and is also worth reading.)

Karp, Abraham J.
Haven and Home: A History of the Jews in America. Schocken Books, 1985, $24.95, hc, $9.95 pb.

This lively history of Jews in America, from their first arrival in Nieuw Amsterdam in 1654 to the 1970s, makes extensive use of original documents such as letters and diaries to convey the flavor of life in past times. Karp concerns himself with social, religious, and cultural aspects of the American Jewish experience and argues that the diversity of the American Jewish community is a principal source of its strength. Also by Karp is *To Give Life: The UJA in the Shaping of the American Jewish Community* (Schocken, 1980, $12.95), a history of the United Jewish Appeal.

Libo, Kenneth, and Irving Howe

We Lived There Too. Marek/St. Martin's Press, 1984, $24.95 hc, $13.95 pb.

Using an approach similar to that of *World of Our Fathers,* this book is a collection of documents, photos, and ephemera portraying the important role Jews played in the opening and development of the West from 1630 to the twentieth century. Despite the selection being more limited and less interesting than that in *World of Our Fathers,* it makes clear that American Jewish history extends beyond the borders of the Lower East Side and other big-city ghettos. The documents are well chosen, and many are published here for the first time.

Madison, Charles

Jewish Publishing in America. Hebrew Publishing, 1976, $15.

Although not especially penetrating in its analysis and now somewhat dated, this work is valuable as one of the very few on the subject.

Marinbach, Bernard

Galveston: Ellis Island of the West. State University of New York Press, 1983, $49.50 hc, $14.95 pb.

A reminder that not all the Jewish immigrants to America entered through the port of New York, this book is a study of the Texas port of Galveston, which was a major entry point to America between 1907 and 1914. Much of the book is an analysis of organizational and ideological issues. For the many Jews who now live in the South and "Sun Belt," this book will be of special interest.

Metzker, Isaac, ed.

A Bintel Brief: Sixty Years of Letters from the Lower East Side to the "Jewish Daily Forward." Behrman House, 1982, $5.95 pb.

Both a delight to read and a profoundly revealing look at Jewish immigrant life. Abraham Cahan, editor of the *Jewish Daily Forward,* started a "letters to the editor" column in 1906. This book is a selection of those letters, ranging from the trivial and comic to the poignant and even tragic. They deal with the problems of love and jealousy, of poverty and unemployment, of deserted wives and abandoned children, of adjusting to the ways of a new world. Cahan's editorial replies are shrewd, warmhearted but not foolishly sentimental, practical, and often hortatory. Unless you read these letters the first time they appeared, read them now.

Quinley, Harold E., and Charles Y. Glock

Anti-Semitism in America. Transaction Books/Rutgers University, 1983, $12.95 pb.

This book by two social scientists is a study of current American attitudes toward Jews. Its findings are based on a specially commissioned survey on anti-Semitism and on other public opinion polls. Chapters cover such subjects as the role of education in decreasing anti-Jewish sentiment, anti-Semitism among blacks, and the interaction between politics and prejudice. The authors conclude that, especially among working-class people, anti-Semitic attitudes continue to affect America. They also say that American anti-Semitism is less virulent and open than it once was, but remains a factor in such social areas as club membership or marriage.

Raphael, Marc Lee

Profiles in American Judaism: The Reform, Conservative, Orthodox, and Reconstructionist Traditions in Historical Perspective. Harper & Row, 1985, $19.95.

A thorough and reliable survey of the history, beliefs, and organizational forms of the four major branches of Judaism. Raphael

also speculates on future directions and looks at such current developments as the growth of Hasidism, and the **havurah** movement, which has attempted to make Jewish life more personal and less "institutional" by forming small prayer and study groups.

Rischin, Moses

The Promised City: New York's Jews, 1870–1914. Harvard University Press, 1962, $18.50 hc $8.95 pb.

This major and illuminating history of immigrant Jewish life on New York's Lower East Side is in many ways superior to Howe's *World of Our Fathers*, although it lacks the many photographs and first-person accounts that lend Howe's work so much impact. Rischin describes the changes in nearly every aspect of their lives that the Eastern European Jews underwent on their arrival in America as transforming them physically, economically, and spiritually and argues that it was the most rapid and revolutionary transformation in the entire history of the Jewish people. His aim of making us understand what life was like even leads him to include the floor plan of a typical tenement building.

Rochlin, Harriet, and Fred Rochlin

Pioneer Jews: A New Life in the American West. Houghton Mifflin, $17.95.

The authors have produced a

richly illustrated record of Jewish life in the Far West. It covers new ground and retells the stories of Jewish peddlers and entrepreneurs in nineteenth-century frontier society. And the picture of Wyatt Earp's wife must be seen to be believed.

Rudin, A. James, and Marcia Rudin

Prison or Paradise: The New Religious Cults. Fortress Press, 1980, $9.95.

These authors warn of the dangers posed by religious cults and offer suggestions as to how they can be countered. They examine why there has been a boom in cult membership, what their characteristics are, who joins them, and how their challenge can be met. Nine major cults are profiled, including the Unification Church, the International Society for Krishna Consciousness, and the Church of Scientology. Of the anticult books available, this is one of the more temperate. Although not specifically a Jewish book, the subject is of enough concern to Jewish people to merit including it.

Schoener, Allon

The American Jewish Album: From 1654 to the Present. Rizzoli International, $45 hc, $19.95 pb.

As wonderful as the personal narratives, letters, essays, and documents collected in this book are, what gives it its real excitement are the pictures—hundreds of them. It's unfortunate the proofreading is so sloppy.

Silberman, Charles

A Certain People: American Jews and Their Lives Today. Summit Books, 1985, $19.95.

A study of the current state of American Jewry that is glowingly optimistic in its findings. Silberman reports that Jews are secure in America, that anti-Semitism is not a significant factor in their lives, and that all aspects of American society are open to them. He also says that intermarriage is not the major problem many people feel it is. He claims the rate of intermarriage is lower than usually reported and, in any case, it actually strengthens the Jewish community by bringing in new converts. Silberman has been criticized for such specifics as paying insufficient attention to the Orthodox community and the role of Israel, and for his overall upbeat tone. Some have felt that his optimism is superficial, that he makes the mistake of seeing good external conditions and ignoring the inner content of American Jewish life.

IV

Holocaust

*Wherever they burn books
they will also, in the end,
burn human beings.*

—Heinrich Heine, 1823

Holocaust

Judith Herschlag Muffs

In 1960, fifteen years after World War II, there were few books on the Holocaust, and publishers were reluctant to print more. "Enough," they said—"there is no market for them." In 1960, almost no high school history text devoted more than a few lines—if that—to the Holocaust. University and secondary school teachers didn't teach it, few scholars investigated it, and not too many people spoke about it. As a matter of fact, the term *holocaust* had not yet come to mean the Nazi murder of six million Jews; *holocaust* still meant "consumed by fire" and referred to the burnt sacrifices of ancient times. In the years following World War II, Jews called what had happened "the Catastrophe," "the Destruction" (*Hurban*). In the 1950s there was a great (though not total) silence about the Holocaust. It was the silence of numbness, the silence of guilt, the silence of fear. It was the silence of purposeful forgetting—by victims, perpetrators, and bystanders.

Among the most influential writers to break this silence, to bring the Holocaust to our consciousness, were Elie Wiesel, with his searing, autobiographical novel, *Night*, published (in English) in 1960, and Raul Hilberg, whose magisterial pioneering study, *The Destruction of the European Jews*, published in 1961, documents the Nazi machinery of death. In 1966, Richard L. Rubenstein provoked us with his radical theological essays, *After Auschwitz*. In 1968, Nora Levin became one of the first to use the term, calling her book on the history of that event, *The Holocaust*.

In the last ten to fifteen years, there has been an outpouring

Judith Herschlag Muffs is the author of *The Holocaust in Books and Film* and associate director of interfaith affairs for the Anti-Defamation League in New York.

of all kinds of publications on the Holocaust. Its theological and religious dimensions, the role of the Christian churches and the implications for Judaism and Christianity, continue to be examined and anguished over by Jewish and Christian thinkers such as Emil Fackenheim, Frank Littell, Roy and Alice Eckhardt, Arthur Cohen, and Eliezer Berkovitz. Psychological and psychoanalytic analyses have been made of camp inmates and perpetrators. In recent years, the children of survivors have been both the subjects of investigation and the investigators.

In this past decade, increasing attention has been paid to the bystanders—individuals, institutions, and nations. The roles of the United States, Great Britain, the Vatican, Christian churches, and the Red Cross have undergone very sharp and damning criticism (see the works of Arthur Morse, Henry Feingold, David Wyman, John Morley, Gunther Lewy, Walter Laqueur, and Bernard Wasserstein). A number of writers in the last few years also have condemned the American Jewish community of the 1930s and 1940s for its lack of effectiveness, its lack of power in stopping the Holocaust.

Every survivor has a story to tell. Many of them, so long silent, are now eager to tell of their experiences. And so the number of memoirs grows. Among the earliest, and still one of the best, is Alexander Donat's *The Holocaust Kingdom*. Some of the titles reflect a mind set that was perhaps only seen in retrospect—"I Chose to Live," "I Dared to Live." The memoirs themselves are uneven. Some convey a great deal of information, a few are well written. More often they are books (or manuscripts looking for publishers) that, painful as the experience may have been, had to be written: "I suffered, I survived, I am."

Novelists—Jews and non-Jews, survivors and those who did not personally "come out of Egypt"—have played important roles in bringing the story and the emotional experiences of that time into our consciousness. One of the very first was John Hersey, a non-Jew, who in 1950 gave us *The Wall*, his powerful story of the Warsaw Ghetto.

Since then the Holocaust has been the setting of hundreds of novels, plays, and short stories, and part of the plot of thousands more. They have made the Holocaust real to hundreds of thousands (if not millions) of readers. As is to be expected, these works of fiction have been of very uneven quality and value.

In the late 1950s, Andre Schwarz-Bart, a French Jew, wrote *The Last of the Just*, a literary masterpiece. Some German novelists, grappling with their own and their nation's experiences and guilt, have created important literary works (i.e., Günter Grass and Nobel Prize winner Heinrich Böll). Others have exploited the event. Mostly, they tell stories about people caught in the all-too-real nightmare and try to convey the suffering, the bravery, the hope and despair, and the humanity.

In the last few years, there seem to be fewer novels about the Holocaust. But the number of fictional works and memoirs has been such that there has developed a field of literary analysis of the subject, to which Lawrence Langer, Alvin Rosenfeld, and Sidra Dekoven-Ezrahi have made major contributions.

While we may never fully understand the "why" of the Holocaust, it is crucial that we learn as fully as possible its dynamics—the "whats" and the "hows." We now have several good synthetic histories for readers of all ages and backgrounds. Scholars, therefore, to stand the metaphor on its head, are now beginning to see the trees of the forest. Some of the current crop of books deal with very specific topics; that is, psychotherapy and psychoanalysis in the Third Reich, the role of big business, and the rise of Hitler. Still to be studied on a country-by-country basis are the role of the police, the role of lawyers and judges, of the medical profession, of union leaders, and so on in aiding or abetting, or acquiescing, or thwarting the Nazi rulers. What latitude did they have? What independence did they—could they—show? Were they rubber stamps for Nazi policy? What were the differences in Rumania, the Netherlands, Belgium, Poland, and France, and how are we to explain these differences? (Some of this in-depth study of the role of individual nations occupied by the Germans has been done by Helen Fein in *Accounting for Genocide*.)

The Holocaust looms large on our screen. We are both drawn to and repelled by it. But there is a caveat—a warning. Jewish life and Jewish history are not to be equated with the

Holocaust. Too often in teaching about the Holocaust, the subject is introduced within the context of the history of anti-Semitism. The average student-reader, with little else to go on, then equates the history of anti-Semitism with the history of the Jewish people. Such an equation is both inaccurate and dangerous. The Holocaust was a watershed in both Jewish and world history, and thus it is something that must be studied, explored, and dealt with. But it is important that it not be the only aspect and experience of Jewish life with which the Jewish or non-Jewish reader becomes acquainted.

HOLOCAUST BOOKS

The section on the Holocaust is one of the longest in this book. The enormity of the Holocaust, its appalling uniqueness in history, is such that it must be dealt with in extra detail. For that reason, this is also the only section to include both fiction and nonfiction. In addition to fiction, the books selected include histories, memoirs, diaries, theoretical analyses of genocide, and studies of specific aspects of the Holocaust. Many books in print deal with the Holocaust in specific countries. We have not attempted to include even one book for each major Jewish community, only to list books about some of the most important.

Although not specifically a Holocaust book, Shirer's *The Rise and Fall of the Third Reich* provides much essential background material. *The War Against the Jews*, by Dawidowicz, is a learned and readable one-volume history of the Holocaust, and as good an introduction to the subject as is available. For readers seeking a more detailed study, Hilberg's three-volume *The Destruction of the European Jews* is the work to get.

Focusing on the small-scale human experience of the Holocaust, readers can turn to *Night*, Wiesel's fictionalized account of his childhood experiences in Auschwitz, or Eisenberg's two excellent collections of first-person accounts, *The Lost Generation* and *Witness to the Holocaust*. Also on a smaller scale are two books about the destruction of the Warsaw Ghetto—Hersey's moving fictional version, *The Wall*, and Kurzman's journalistic history, *The Bravest Battle*. An excellent introduction to the religious implications of the Holocaust can be gained from Kirschner's *Rabbinic Responsa of the Holocaust Era*, a collection of documents dealing with the efforts of religious Jews to preserve their way of life despite persecution. For accounts of those exceptional non-Jews who came to the aid of Jews, Keneally's *Schindler's List*, a fictionalized account of Oskar Schindler; Lester's *Wallenberg*; and Yahil's *The Rescue of Danish Jewry* are all rewarding.

There are also books in other sections of this guide that readers might wish to consult. Among them are Szonyi's *The Holocaust*, an extensive annotated bibliography described in the REFERENCE BOOKS section. In ARTS, Blatter and Milton's *Art of the Holocaust* and Kalisch's *Yes We Sang! Songs of the Ghettos and Concentration Camps* should be seen. Two classic diaries, those of Anne Frank and Moshe Flinker, are listed in CHILDREN'S BOOKS, AGES TWELVE AND UP, but are also highly recommended for adult readers. Uris's *Exodus*, in FICTION, is also of value. —R. S. F. & W. W.

FICTION

Appelfeld, Aharon

At the age of eight, Appelfeld was sent to a Nazi labor camp. He escaped and spent the next three years on the run. Eventually, he made his way to Italy and, in 1946, from there to Palestine. Today he is an Israeli citizen and a teacher of Hebrew literature. He is one of Israel's greatest writers, writing prose that is spare, subtle, understated, and elegant—making his stories all the more powerful. See the HEBREW LITERATURE section for more of Appelfeld's work.

Badenheim 1939, translated from the Hebrew by Dalya Bilu. Godine, 1980, $12.95 hc; Bantam Books, $3.50 pb.

The first of Appelfeld's books to be translated into English, *Badenheim 1939* does not talk directly of the horrors of the Holocaust. Nonetheless, it depicts the ominous, foreboding atmosphere of pre-Holocaust Austria with chilling intensity. It describes a resort town brimming with Jewish vacationers looking forward to the annual music festival. Instead, they must deal with a faceless, demonic bureaucracy that slowly but inevitably drives them all toward deportation and an unknown end.

Tzili: Story of a Life. Translated by Dalya Bilu. Dutton, 1983, $12.95 hc; Penguin, $4.95 pb.

As does *Badenheim 1939*, this novel indicts European Jewry for its blindness to the signs of the approaching Holocaust. It is the story of Tzili, a dull-witted young Jewish girl who survives the war by wandering the forests although she suffers terrible hardships. While the story ends with Tzili alive and on a boat headed toward Palestine, it is hardly an upbeat ending.

Hersey, John
The Wall. Knopf, 1950, $12.50.

This fictionalized narrative describes the events leading to the destruction of the Warsaw Ghetto. Told in the form of a diary, it is written in clear and understated prose and focuses as much on the relationships among the imprisoned people as it does on the great events going on around them.

Hochhuth, Rolf
The Deputy: A Christian Tragedy. Translated from the German by Richard and Clara Winston. Grove Press, 1964, $4.95 pb.

This play tells about a young Catholic priest who tries to convince the Church to respond to the plight of European Jews during the Holocaust. Hochhuth, a German Protestant, wrote it to condemn the failure of Pope Pius XII and the Roman Catholic Church to fight more actively against the Holocaust. It generated great controversy when it was first performed in Germany in 1963 and has remained controversial ever since. See Morley's

Vatican Diplomacy and the Jews During the Holocaust (listed later) for a more balanced account.

Keneally, Thomas
Schindler's List. Penguin, 1983, $5.95 pb.

A fictionalized account of the surprising real-life heroism of Oskar Schindler. Schindler was a German industrialist more publicly noted for his hard drinking and many mistresses than for his hidden compassion. As the head of a factory in occupied Cracow, Schindler wheeled and dealed and practiced any number of devious strategies to protect his Jewish workers against the Nazis. His activities and successes verge on the astounding. More than a thousand lives were saved, and today a tree planted in his honor stands at **Yad Vashem**, the Holocaust memorial in Israel.

Schwarz-Bart, Andre
The Last of the Just. Translated from the French by Stephen Becker. Atheneum, 1977, $9.95 pb.

The Talmud says that "the world must contain not less than thirty-six righteous men who are vouchsafed the sight of the Divine Presence." This statement became the basis of a legend that there were thirty-six just men on whose virtue the very existence of the world depended. The identity of these men was a secret, unknown even to themselves, although in a time of crisis they would be revealed and help to save their people. This legend underlies *The Last of the Just*, a frequently difficult but ultimately rewarding novel of the Holocaust and one young boy who may, in fact, be the last of the thirty-six. As a teenager, Schwarz-Bart joined the anti-German French forces. At the end of the war, he returned home to learn that his entire family had been killed during the Holocaust.

Uris, Leon
Mila 18. Doubleday, 1961, $15.95 hc; Bantam Books, $4.50 pb.

Although the characters in this novel about the Warsaw Ghetto uprising are fictitious, the events it describes are real, and Uris tells the story effectively.

Weiss, Peter
The Investigation. Translated from the German by Alexander Gross. Atheneum, 1966, $6.95 pb.

The dialogue in this play is based on actual excerpts from war crimes trials. It deals with the people responsible for Auschwitz, and although not easy to stage, it is an effective indictment.

Wiesel, Elie
Night/Dawn/Day. Aronson, 1985, $17.95.

Night was Elie Wiesel's first book. It is, in somewhat fictionalized form, the story of his childhood experiences as a prisoner in Auschwitz, where his mother and sister died. It is considered by many to be his finest work. *Dawn* is a novel telling of an Auschwitz survivor who is now

a member of the anti-British underground in Palestine. As a member of that underground, he now faces the ironic need to commit an act of murder himself, executing an English prisoner. *Day*, originally published in English as *The Accident*, deals with another survivor, one who, instead of facing a possible murder, must deal with his attraction to suicide. (*Night* and *Dawn* are also available in paperback editions from Bantam Books.)

NONFICTION

Abella, Irving, and Harold Troper
None Is Too Many: Canada and the Jews of Europe 1933–1948. Random House, 1982, $17.95.

This disturbing and important book, a 1983 winner of the National Jewish Book Award, explores the reasons Canada virtually sealed its borders to European Jewish immigrants in the 1930s and 1940s—allowing in only 5,000 refugees between 1933 and 1948. The emphasis is on political history, rather than cultural or social factors. Its title is a quotation from a Canadian official, his answer to the question of how many Jews should be allowed into the country following the war.

Arendt, Hannah
Eichmann in Jerusalem: A Report on the Banality of Evil. Peter Smith, 1983, $14.25 hc; Penguin, $6.95 pb.

Hannah Arendt was commissioned by *The New Yorker* to cover the trial of Adolf Eichmann and her report is the basis of this book. Arendt's sometimes critical comments on the prosecution and her belief that European Jewry was less energetic in its defense than it should have been caused an enormous furor and the book remains controversial. Her theories on the bureaucratic, "banal" nature of the evil personified by Eichmann are, to say the least, provocative. Controversy aside, this is a work of stunning intelligence. *Justice in Jerusalem*, by Gideon Hausner (Holocaust Publications, 1978, $10.95 pb) is by the man who was Israel's attorney general from 1960 to 1963 and was chief prosecutor during the Eichmann trial. His book is an account of the trial and his preparations for it. Hausner emphasizes his efforts to convict Eichmann without overstepping the limits of justice.

Baker, Leonard
Days of Sorrow and Pain: Leo Baeck and the Berlin Jews. Oxford University Press, 1980, $8.95 pb.

A philosopher and theologian, Rabbi Leo Baeck was one of the leaders of German Jews during World War II. Although he could have escaped, he chose to stay in Germany to do whatever he could for the Jewish people. He was imprisoned in Theresienstadt concentration camp, but survived the war and emigrated to the United States. This biography of an exceptional man won a Pulitzer Prize. (See *The Essence of Judaism* by Baeck in the section headed MODERN JEWISH THOUGHT.)

Braham, Randolph L.
The Politics of Genocide: The Holocaust in Hungary. Columbia University Press, 1981, 2 vols., $90.

In his masterly and exhaustively detailed history of the destruction of Hungarian Jewry, Braham analyzes the historical, political, and socioeconomic factors that contributed to the tragedy, and the context of world events in which it took place. Although stating clearly that the primary responsibility lies with the Germans and their Hungarian accomplices, Braham concludes that "considerable blame" also falls on such "onlookers" as the Allies, the neutral powers, the International Red Cross, the Vatican, and the local Christian churches for their apathy, insensitivity, and lack of urgency. He also believes that Hungarian and world Jewish leaders share some of the blame for their shortsightedness and disunity. This work of restrained and meticulous scholarship was a winner of the 1981 National Jewish Book Award—Holocaust.

Cargas, Harry James
A Christian Response to the Holocaust. Holocaust Publications,

1986 (tentative), $17.95 hc, $12.95 pb.

Cargas describes himself as a "post-Auschwitz Catholic" and the Holocaust as "the greatest tragedy for Christians since the crucifixion." In this impassioned book, he traces the history of Christian anti-Semitism, and he details the atrocities of some— and the silence of many—during the Nazi era. He also offers suggestions for steps Christians must take to become reconciled with Jews. Along with Rosemary Reuther, Cargas is one of the leading Christian thinkers who insists that Christianity must reform itself of the anti-Semitism that pervaded its past and led to the Holocaust.

Dawidowicz, Lucy S.
The Holocaust and the Historians. Harvard University Press, 1983, $16.50 hc, $5.95 pb.

The author here examines the treatment of Jews and of the Holocaust in historical writings. Dawidowicz argues—with considerable force—that the Holocaust has been overlooked or trivialized by many historians. She is frequently hard, even harsh, in her judgments and is especially critical of Hannah Arendt. Her book is marred by her habit of seeing only the flaws in the work of other historians and not the merits.

The War Against the Jews, 1933–1945. Bantam Books, 1976, $4.95 pb.

This is the best single-volume history of the Holocaust. Dawidowicz deals with three main questions: How was it possible for a modern state to carry out the systematic murder of a people for no reason other than that they were Jewish? How did that people allow itself to be destroyed? and How could the world stand by without halting this destruction? The book has been criticized for focusing too exclusively on the Jews of Poland and for downplaying the fate of German Jews. Nonetheless, it is an outstanding work. No one can read the appendix, with its country-by-country account of the fate of Europe's Jews, and not feel despair. (A revised and updated edition was announced by the Free Press shortly before this book went to press, too late for us to review it. Its price is $22.95.)

Des Pres, Terrence
The Survivor: An Anatomy of Life in the Death Camps. Oxford University Press, 1976, $18.95 hc, $6.95 pb.

Based on his study of Holocaust literature, Des Pres set out to understand what contributed to survival—why some people survived Nazi and Stalinist concentration camps and others didn't. He makes clear that survival was more than mere chance, but often a reflection of specific psychological factors and a determination to preserve human dignity under the most desperate of circumstances. A brilliant and important book.

Dobroszycki, Lucjan, ed.
Chronicle of the Lodz Ghetto. Yale University Press, 1984, $35.

The Department of Archives in the Lodz Ghetto was founded by Mordecai Chaim Rumkowski, a figure of great controversy who carried out the orders of the Gestapo and controlled the Ghetto as if he were royalty. The chronicle that was kept on his instructions recorded the events of daily life in the Ghetto: the weather, the births, deaths, marriages, concerts—and the shootings, suicides, and deportations to Auschwitz. This English edition is an abridgement of that chronicle and its editor was himself a resident of the ghetto before being sent to Auschwitz. It is a record of decline and demoralization that is all the more powerful because of its matter-of-fact tone and lack of dramatics. (See also Grossman's *With a Camera in the Ghetto,* later in this section.)

Donat, Alexander
The Holocaust Kingdom: A Memoir. Holocaust Publications, 1983, $9.95 pb.

Donat's is one of the major memoirs of life during the Holocaust. After the war, Donat became the founder of the Holocaust Library, later renamed Holocaust Publications. This nonprofit organization has been dedicated to publishing historical and first-person accounts of the Holocaust

and to the establishment of an archival resource center. It has produced a series of mostly excellent works and is an essential resource for anyone wishing to study the Holocaust. Its address is 216 West 18th Street, New York, NY 10011.

Donat, Alexander, ed.
The Death Camp Treblinka: A Documentary. Holocaust Publications, 1979, $11.95 hc, $4.95 pb.

Treblinka was one of the largest Nazi extermination camps, the place where most of Warsaw's Jews died. This book includes background essays and analysis and devastating accounts by Treblinka survivors. Of special interest is the material on the prisoners' revolt of 1943, a futile but heroic effort to break out of the camp.

Ehrenburg, Ilya, and Vasily Grossman
The Black Book. Translated from the Russian by John Glad and James S. Levine. Holocaust Publications, 1980, $12.95 pb.

An important collection of eyewitness accounts of Nazi crimes and the Jewish experience in those parts of the Soviet Union occupied by the Germans during World War II. Although originally compiled with the cooperation of the Soviet government, the Soviets later suppressed the book because it brought too much attention to Jews and to Soviet anti-Semitism. In 1946 an abridged edition of the manuscript, combined with some additional material, was published in the United States. In the 1960s, a more complete version of the book was smuggled out of the Soviet Union, and that is what is published in this edition. Nexus Press has recently published a reissue of the 1946 version.

Eisenberg, Azriel, ed.
The Lost Generation: Children in the Holocaust. Pilgrim Press, 1982, $17.95.

Eisenberg has compiled an enormously depressing work containing more than a hundred eyewitness accounts of children in the Holocaust. Gathered from books, memoirs, diaries, and other sources, they combine to produce a harrowing picture of one of history's saddest episodes. The excerpts cover the period from the 1920s through the postwar period, and in addition to the accounts of torment and suffering, there are also accounts of resistance, including by non-Jews.

Witness to the Holocaust. Pilgrim Press, 1981, $22.50 hc, $12.95 pb.

The eyewitness accounts of the Holocaust gathered in this book are excerpted from diaries, letters, and books. They are grouped under such subject headings as "Adolf Hitler," "Exodus and Flight," "The Destruction and Rescue of Jewish Books and Religious Treasure," "The Death

Camps," "Extermination of Russian and Polish Jewry," and "Jewish Partisan Fighters." This collection is excellent—both in its scope and in its selections.

Eliach, Yaffa
Hasidic Tales of the Holocaust. Oxford University Press, 1982, $17.95 hc; Bantam Books, $4.95 pb.

The Hasidic tale is a tradition dating back to the very beginnings of Hasidism. These true tales combine real events with elements of folklore and a deep religious faith. This book contains a varied collection of them, most recorded for the first time. Focusing on spiritual rather than material resistance to the Nazis, the tales tell of faith and how it sustained Hasidic Jews through the devastation of the Holocaust. Eliach devotes a considerable portion of the book to stories involving women.

Epstein, Helen
Children of the Holocaust: Conversations with Sons and Daughters of Survivors. Bantam Books, 1960, $3.95 pb.

The suffering of Holocaust survivors often carries over to the next generation, to children who cannot come to grips with their parents' experiences. Epstein, herself the daughter of Auschwitz survivors, writes in this book of her own struggle to live with her parents' nightmare. She also interviewed many other children of survivors and presents their stories and her conclusions about how the younger generation has tried—not always successfully—to deal with the horrors of the past. This book was one of the first to study the children of survivors, and it helped focus attention on a previously ignored issue.

Ezrahi, Sidra
By Words Alone: The Holocaust in Literature. University of Chicago Press, 1980, $15.

A survey of novels, drama, and poetry dealing with the Holocaust. Ezrahi has done a thorough job and discusses many different authors, including some not well known. Her remarks are cogent, her erudition obvious, and her critical judgments sound. The wide range of her survey inevitably means that some authors receive only the briefest treatment, but that defect is minor. Ezrahi never offers an answer to the question of whether art can deal with the realities of the Holocaust—perhaps because there isn't one.

Fackenheim, Emil
The Jewish Return into History: Reflections on the Age of Auschwitz and a New Jerusalem. Schocken Books, 1978, $14.95 hc, $6.95 pb.

Fackenheim has written extensively on the religious implications of the Holocaust. The essays in this book deal with the necessity of coming to grips with the Holocaust, and Fackenheim argues that in a post-Auschwitz world all Jews are obliged to be concerned with Jewish continuity and survival, since to do otherwise would be to give Hitler a posthumous victory.

Fein, Helen
Accounting for Genocide: National Responses and Jewish Victimization During the Holocaust. Free Press, 1979, $17.95 hc; University of Chicago Press, $13.95 pb.

Fein concentrates on the sociology of genocide and how "civilized" nations could permit it to happen. Noting that 95 percent of the Jews in Poland and Lithuania were killed while 95 percent of the Jews in Denmark survived, Fein provides a country-by-country analysis of attitudes and how they affected the ways in which those countries acted during the Holocaust. Her goal is an understanding of why national responses to the persecution of Jews varied in the ways they did.

Feingold, Henry L.
The Politics of Rescue: The Roosevelt Administration and the Holocaust, 1938–1945. Rutgers University Press, 1970, $35; Holocaust Publications, $10.95 pb.

Feingold set out to discover reasons that the Roosevelt administration failed to take effective action to save European Jews from the Holocaust. While he credits the War Relief Board with some imaginative programs, he says that they came too late to be of much value. He has produced a well-researched and fair-minded book.

Ferencz, Benjamin
Less Than Slaves. Harvard University Press, 1979, $16.50 hc, $5.95 pb.

This history focuses on Jewish workers forced into the service of German industry during World War II, and "less than slaves" because slaves were treated with a greater concern for their welfare and survival. Ferencz's account focuses on the postwar attempt of some of the workers to be compensated for their labors and to make German industry acknowledge its legal and moral responsibility. The indifference of the postwar German government and legal system to the justice of their claims is most depressing. The book won a National Jewish Book Award in 1980.

Fleming, Gerald
Hitler and the Final Solution. University of California Press, 1984, $15.95.

In recent years, David Irving and other historians have questioned whether Hitler directly ordered the extermination of the Jews, claiming that there is no documentary evidence that he did so. Using information from British, American, Russian, and German archives plus interviews with German eyewitnesses, Fleming convincingly refutes those arguments, showing that there is no doubt that the "Final Solution" was deliberately designed, personally willed, and ordered by Hitler.

Friedlander, Albert, ed.
Out of the Whirlwind: A Reader of Holocaust Literature. Schocken Books, 1976, $10.95 pb.

An excellent anthology of Holocaust literature, somewhat more given to reflection and analysis than is Eisenberg's *Witness to the Holocaust*, listed earlier. Among the works excerpted are Anne Frank's diary, *The Last of the Just*, *Holocaust Kingdom*, and *The Deputy*. Each selection is briefly introduced.

Friedman, Philip
Roads to Extinction: Essays on the Holocaust. Jewish Publication Society, 1980, $27.50.

The late Philip Friedman, himself a survivor of the Holocaust, was one of the major Holocaust historians and is considered by some to be the "father" of Jewish Holocaust literature. The essays in this book are valuable for readers who wish to explore the subject in depth. Among the topics covered are the Karaites under Nazi rule, crimes in the name of science, "righteous gentiles," and whether there was an "other Germany" during the Nazi period. An extensive section deals with the methodological problems associated with studying the Holocaust. Friedman is also the author of *Their Brothers' Keepers* (Holocaust Publications, 1978, $8.95 pb), which profiles several non-Jews who helped Jews escape the Nazis.

Gilbert, Martin
Auschwitz and the Allies. Holt, Rinehart & Winston, 1982, $8.50 pb.

Martin Gilbert is a respected scholar specializing in modern history, especially the World War II period. He is the author of several volumes of the official biography of Winston Churchill, continuing the work begun by Randolph Churchill. He has also written extensively on Jewish history. Unfortunately, his *Atlas of the Holocaust* is currently out of print. Some publisher ought to reissue it. In *Auschwitz and the Allies*, Gilbert explores the reasons why the Allies did so little to interfere with the operations of the Auschwitz death camp, refusing even to bomb the rail lines over which so many Jews were being carried to their deaths. It is not a comfortable book to read.

Grossman, Mendel
With a Camera in the Ghetto. Edited by Zvi Szner and Alexander Sened. Schocken Books, 1977, $12.95.

Grossman was a resident of the Lodz Ghetto who documented with his camera what was happening under Nazi control. His photographs are combined in this book with excerpts from the *Chronicle of the Lodz Ghetto* and the result is a portrait of despair. The pictures show bread lines, deportees, scavengers, and death.

The reproduction quality is poor—most of the photographs are copies of prints, as the negatives were lost, and the layout is undistinguished. The overall effect remains powerful.

Gutman, Yisrael
The Jews of Warsaw 1939–1943: Ghetto, Underground, Revolt. Translated from the Hebrew by Ina Friedman. Indiana University Press, 1982, $24.95.

Gutman is director of the research center of Yad Vashem, the Holocaust memorial in Israel. Although himself a survivor of the Warsaw Ghetto uprising, this is not a first-person account but an impressive scholarly work examining how isolated, starved, and persecuted Jews were able to resist German might for so long. He does not avoid such controversial questions as the role of the **Judenrat** (Jewish ruling council). Gutman describes the growth of the resistance movement in the context of the overall situation within the Ghetto and also studies the German view of events. He is very critical of the Polish indifference to the Ghetto residents and the lack of assistance provided them.

Hilberg, Raul
The Destruction of the European Jews. Holmes & Meier, 3 vols., 1985, $105.

First published in the 1960s, this work has been recently revised and updated. It is considered by many to be the definitive history of the Holocaust, although it has been criticized for its conclusion that European Jewry was drawn into cooperating with the Nazis in its own destruction. The author's focus is on the German bureaucratic machinery of destruction, and his mastery of the historical documentation is unequaled.

Keller, Urich, ed.
The Warsaw Ghetto in Photographs: 206 Views Made in 1941. Dover, 1984, $8.95 pb.
A collection of pictures made by German Army photographers. The pictures are grouped in such categories as street scenes, children, internal Ghetto administration, and amusements of the Ghetto elite.

Kirschner, Robert, ed. and trans.
Rabbinic Responsa of the Holocaust Era. Schocken Books, 1985, $17.95.
This collection of responsa (rabbinic answers to questions about Jewish law) was written during the Holocaust and reflects the struggle of Orthodox Jews to preserve their lives and integrity under the most extreme conditions. Also included are responsa on postwar issues arising out of the Holocaust. For each responsum, there is an introduction, a digest, the complete text, and notes. This collection of responsa is more accessible for most readers than Ephraim Oshry's *Responsa from the Holocaust* (Judaica

Press, 1976, $14.95), which can also be recommended.

Korczak, Janus
Ghetto Diary. Translated from the Polish by Jerzy Bachrach and Barbara Krzywicka (Vedder). Schocken Books, 1978, $11.95 hc, $8.95 pb.
One of the most moving of all Holocaust documents. Korczak was the head of a children's home for orphans in the Warsaw Ghetto. Although he was given the opportunity of saving his own life, he refused to do so if he could not also save the lives of the children in his care. He went to his death with them.

Two other valuable records of life in the Ghetto are *The Warsaw Diary of Emanuel Ringlebaum* (Schocken Books, 1974, $8.95 pb) and *Scroll of Agony: The Warsaw Diary of Chaim A. Kaplan* (Macmillan, 1981, $6.95 pb). Ringlebaum was a resistance leader who died fighting the Nazis. His diary, which is not so much a diary as the notes for a history that was never written, was a major source for Leon Uris's *Mila 18* (see FICTION). Kaplan, an author and the principal of a Hebrew school in Warsaw, kept a diary that is one of the finest and most detailed records of Jewish life under Nazi rule. He is believed to have died in Treblinka in 1942.

Kowalski, Isaac, ed.
Anthology on Armed Jewish Resistance, 1939–1945, Vol. 1.

Jewish Combatants Publishing, 1984, $30.

An anthology of more than forty accounts of Jewish resistance to the Nazis by partisans, underground activists, and Jewish soldiers in the Allied armies. The book includes many photographs and its contributors include Abba Kovner, Judah Nadich, Yehuda Bauer, and Alexander Donat.

Kugelmass, Jack, and Jonathan Boyarin, eds. and trans.
From a Ruined Garden: The Memorial Books of Polish Jewry. Schocken Books, 1981, $18.95 hc, $8.95 pb.

After World War II, Jewish emigrants and survivors produced an outpouring of *yizker bikher*, books memorializing the now-destroyed towns from which they came. *From a Ruined Garden* contains more than sixty selections from these memorial volumes, some dealing directly with the Holocaust, others portraying the towns and townspeople, and some depicting returns to towns now without Jews. The portrait of small-town life presented in this book is valuable as social history. But knowing that the world being portrayed was soon to be destroyed is an always-haunting fact for the reader.

Kurzman, Dan
The Bravest Battle: The 28 Days of the Warsaw Ghetto Uprising. Pinnacle Books, 1978, $2.75 pb.

This popular history provides a day-by-day account of the Warsaw Ghetto battle. It focuses on the experiences of its participants, especially Mordechai Anielewicz, leader of the Jewish Fighting Organization, and SS Major-General Jürgen Stroop, leader of the German forces.

Laqueur, Walter
The Terrible Secret: Suppression of the Truth About Hitler's Final Solution. Little, Brown, 1980, $12.95; Penguin, $5.95 pb.

A persuasive analysis of the disbelief that greeted accurate information about the Holocaust during its course, and the reasons why reports of the intensifying horror failed to register on both sides of the Atlantic.

Lester, Elenore
Wallenberg: The Man in the Iron Web. Prentice-Hall, 1982, $6.95 pb.

During World War II, Raoul Wallenberg, a young Swede, went to Budapest to help save Jews otherwise sure to die in the Holocaust. His efforts saved tens of thousands of lives. In 1945 he was taken prisoner by the Soviets, who accused him of being a spy, and he disappeared. Recently his story has received considerable attention as speculation that he was still alive surfaced. Lester's book is short and thoroughly researched. It is the best of the books about Wallenberg. *With Raoul Wallenberg in Budapest* by Per Anger (Holocaust Publications, 1981, $8.95 pb) is also worthy. Anger was an attaché at the Swedish embassy in Budapest and was Wallenberg's collaborator and friend. He tells the story of this remarkable, heroic man simply and straightforwardly, although he offers little insight into Wallenberg's character. John Bierman's *Righteous Gentile: The Story of Raoul Wallenberg, Missing Hero of the Holocaust* (Viking, 1981, $12.95) is another account that can be consulted.

Levi, Primo
Survival in Auschwitz: The Nazi Assault on Humanity. Translated from the Italian by Stuart Woolf. Collier Books/Macmillan, 1961, $3.95 pb.

This description of life in Auschwitz was first published in Italy in 1947. Levi reports on the daily routine and the exceptional events, analyzing both what happened and his reactions to it. He makes clear how intentionally dehumanizing life in the camps was.

Marrus, Michael, and Robert O. Paxton
Vichy France and the Jews. Basic Books, $20.95 hc; Schocken Books, 1981, $12.95 pb.

A historical examination that uses a broad range of documentation to reveal the difficulties faced by French Jews during the Vichy era. The authors make painfully clear that Vichy France did not need any prodding from the Germans to begin its anti-Semitic policies; it was more than willing to do so on its own initiative. They conclude that of all the countries occupied by the Germans, France cooperated most fully in the program to annihilate the Jews. The book won the National Jewish Book Award in 1982.

Mendelsohn, John, ed.
The Holocaust: Selected Documents. Garland, 1982, $837.

Mendelsohn is the supervisory archivist of the U.S. National Archives and Records service. The documents in this eighteen-volume set, drawn from the U.S. National Archives, are arranged into four groups: Volumes 1 through 7 cover "Preparation and Planning"; Volumes 8 through 13, "The Killing of the Jews"; Volumes 14 through 16, "Rescue Attempts"; and Volumes 17 and 18, "Punishment." Individual volumes are available for $61 each.

Morley, John F.
Vatican Diplomacy and the Jews During the Holocaust, 1939–1943. Ktav, 1980, $25.

Calling the Vatican role during the Holocaust a sensitive subject is an understatement. Given its extreme touchiness, this massively documented discussion (based on access to Vatican archives) is remarkably reasoned, measured, and cautious in its judgments. It is also appalling. The author, a Catholic priest, says that although the Vatican was aware of what was happening to the Jews there is little evidence of consistent humanitarian concern. Further, in most cases where the Catholic church did protest racial laws or persecution of the Jews, other factors were involved such as the concern for converts from Judaism or the church's abhorrence of prostitution. He concludes (1) that little could have been done to save the Jews, but much could have been done to assert the Vatican's moral position, and (2) that the church's failure to do more represents a betrayal of its ideals. This is an important book.

Penkower, Monty Noam
The Jews Were Expendable: Free World Diplomacy and the Holocaust. University of Illinois Press, 1983, $21.95.

In this collection of historical studies, Penkower demonstrates again and again how the greatest horror of modern Jewish history was either ignored or became a kind of irritating side issue for the British and American governments, the Vatican, and the Red Cross. Penkower traces this inaction to disbelief that such horrors could occur, to anti-Semitism, and to Jewish disunity.

Sachar, Abram
The Redemption of the Unwanted: The Post-Holocaust Years. St. Martin's Press, 1985, $9.95 pb.

The end of the war was not the end of the suffering for the survivors of Nazi concentration and death camps. They faced the often excruciating problems of readjustment to "normal" life after being physically and emotionally ravaged by the Holocaust. This history traces how the survivors found new homes and built new lives for themselves—and dealt with the realization that they were unwanted by the world.

Shirer, William
The Rise and Fall of the Third Reich: A History of Nazi Germany. Simon & Schuster, 1970, $13.95 hc; Fawcett, $3.95 pb.

Shirer was a journalist living in Germany at the time that Hitler came to power. He combined his first-person knowledge with extensive research in the captured German archives to produce this solid and readable history. It does not concentrate specifically on the Holocaust, but it is one of the best ways to understand its background and context.

Suhl, Yuri, ed.
They Fought Back: The Story of the Jewish Resistance in Nazi Europe. Schocken Books, 1975, $9.95 pb.

Disputing claims that Jews did not fight back against Nazi persecution, this anthology offers a collection of accounts, most of them by participants, of active Jewish resistance. Suhl says that Jewish resistance groups existed in virtually every ghetto and concentration camp, resistance that in some cases included armed revolts. Suhl also disputes Hilberg's view that there was little resistance, saying that Hilberg relies too much on German sources.

Trunk, Isaiah
Judenrat: The Jewish Councils in Eastern Europe Under Nazi Occupation. Stein & Day, 1977, $12.95 pb.

In many cities, Jewish councils (*Judenräte*) were set up by Nazis through which they controlled the lives of the Jewish citizens. These councils are among the most controversial elements of the Jewish response to the Holocaust, with some of the Judenrat leaders, most notably Mordechai Chaim Rumkowski of the Lodz Ghetto, becoming figures of opprobrium. Trunk's study of these councils won a National Book Award.

Wyman, David S.
The Abandonment of the Jews: America and the Holocaust, 1941–1945. Pantheon, 1984, $19.95.

The son of a Protestant minister, Wyman writes with great feeling—and considerable research to back his conclusions—of the failure of American churches, government, and the Jewish community to fight against the Holocaust energetically, promptly, and effectively. He blames anti-Semitism for this late and inadequate response. A winner of a 1985 National Jewish Book Award.

On the same subject, *While Six Million Died: A Chronicle of American Apathy*, by Arthur D. Morse (Overlook Press, 1983, $18.95), is a revealing and thoroughly depressing account of American inaction and inertia first published in 1966. Morse is especially critical of the U.S. State Department, contending that it was more than merely uninterested in the plight of European Jews—it often worked to block efforts to save them.

Yahil, Leni
The Rescue of Danish Jewry: Test of a Democracy. Translated from the Hebrew by Morris Gradel. Jewish Publication Society, 1983, $9.95 pb.

The heroism of Denmark in refusing to cooperate with the Germans in the Final Solution is one of the brightest moments in all of World War II. This book is an account of the saving of Danish Jewry and the role played in that rescue by Sweden. A genuinely inspiring story. *Rescue in Denmark* by Harold Flender (Holocaust Publications, 1963, $8.95 pb) also reports effectively on the Danish resistance.

ν

Israel and Zionism

Israel and the People of the Book

David C. Gross

The Bible tells it all, succinctly and pointedly. In Genesis, the first of the five books of the Torah, God makes a covenant with Abram (later renamed Abraham, the forefather of the Jewish people and generally considered the first Jew). The covenant between God and this one historic individual states clearly, referring to the land of Canaan, which is modern Israel: "Unto thy seed have I given this land" (Genesis 12:7).

Since time immemorial, the land of Israel has been part and parcel of the Jewish people and the Jewish heritage, even during those long historic periods when the Jews were forcibly exiled from their ancient homeland. The prayerbook of the observant Jew constantly refers to a return to Zion. The concluding prayer of Yom Kippur—Judaism's most sanctified day—as well as the final words of the Passover Haggadah all enunciate the same hope and prayer—*L'shana habaah b'yerushalayim*, "Next year in Jerusalem."

Throughout all the centuries of Jewish history, the link between the people and the land has been unique, even mystical. It has never wavered. When impoverished Jews living in a tiny hamlet in tsarist Russia had an extra kopek or two, they would deposit the money into a small blue and white coin box—a *pushka*—which in the course of time would be collected, combined with donations of other Jews in all parts of the world and used for one purpose—to redeem the land of Israel, to prepare it for the return of the Jewish people. (Most of these

---

David C. Gross is the author of eight published books, including the forthcoming *Justice for All Our People: The Story of Louis D. Brandeis*. He was the editor of the *Jewish Week* in New York.

coins were given to the Jewish National Fund, one of whose principal programs was reforesting the land that had been neglected for nearly two millennia. During the last eight decades, this organization has planted no fewer than 100 million trees in Israel, transforming the landscape and helping to usher in its former glory as a "land flowing with milk and honey.")

Yehudah Halevi, the great Hebrew poet and scholar of Spain during the period that historians now refer to as the Golden Age of Spain (prior to the Inquisition and the expulsion of the Jews from the Iberian Peninsula), wrote that his "heart was in the east" but he was still living in the west. The famous biblical commentator, Nahmanides, wrote that "the Torah cannot assume perfection except in Israel." The late and widely revered chief rabbi of pre-Israel Palestine, Abraham Kook, said that "only in the Holy Land can the spirit of our people develop and become a light for the world." One talmudic commentator went so far as to say that "residence in Israel is equivalent to the observance of all the biblical precepts" (Eleazar ben Shammua) while another talmudic scholar claimed that "to consummate the purchase of a house in Israel, the deed may be written even on the Sabbath."

Each visitor to Israel has expressed the Jew's tie to Israel differently. Alan King, the comedian and producer, said to him America was his wife, and Israel his mother. Other tourists have claimed that the moment they set foot on Israel's soil, the heavy psychological burden that many never knew they were bearing suddenly seemed to lift from their shoulders. "We felt immediately, totally at home," visitors exclaim time and again.

There is a magnetic pull about the land for Jews, stretching back to biblical days and continuing to this century. Louis D. Brandeis, the first Jew ever named to the U.S. Supreme Court, who was not Bar Mitzvah, who until the age of fifty hardly acknowledged his Jewish origins, made a complete about-face later in his lifetime and became for many years America's leading Zionist personality. Although he spent no more than sixteen days on a visit to Palestine, this brief visit seemed to revive in him all his dormant ties to the Jewish people. Despite the malaria that prevailed in the 1920s in Palestine, Brandeis wrote that there is majesty in the country. "It is a miniature California," he wrote to his wife, and is producing a new kind of Jew, one inexorably linked naturally and eternally to the land.

The first Lubavitcher rabbi, in 1796, wrote that "love for Israel must be a fire burning in the Jew's heart." Another great Hasidic master, Rabbi Nachman of Bratslav, said a few years later, "No matter where I go, it is always to Israel."

There is a talmudic dictum that *avira d'ara machkim*—"the air of Israel makes one wise." One ancient scholar wrote that "a sage who leaves Israel diminishes in worth" while the great Rabbi Shimon ben Yohai taught that "as long as food is available, even though prices are exorbitant, it is forbidden to move from Israel to a foreign land." A rabbi, in response to a query from a congregant, wrote that the latter should "reside in Israel, even among a majority of idolators, rather than outside of Israel, even among a majority of Jews."

In centuries past, it was a custom among elderly Jews to wend their way to Israel, to die there and be buried in its soil. To this day there are some Jews whose remains are sent to Israel for burial, and there are interments outside of Israel into which are sprinkled a few handfuls of soil from the Holy Land.

A glance at the Jewish calendar tells the story of the Jew's attachment to the land of Israel. In addition to the High Holy Days (the ten days of awe and atonement, between **Rosh Hashanah** and Yom Kippur), the holidays and celebrations are Israel-oriented. Jews celebrate Passover not only as the time of the ancient Exodus from Egypt but also as the "early harvest" while **Shavuoth** is commemorated not only as the day of rejoicing for God's giving of the Torah to the Jewish people but also as the "festival of first fruits." Similarly, Sukkot, the happy eight-day holiday that culminates with the completion of the annual cycle of the reading of the Torah in the synagogue every week, is also marked as the final harvest festival of Israel's calendar. (Some historians claim that the Pilgrims who began the holiday of Thanksgiving Day were merely emulating the ancient harvest festival of Sukkot, which is also a reminder of the Israelites' wandering in the desert for forty years before entering the Promised Land.)

The Jewish calendar also includes **Tu bi-Shevat**, Jewish arbor day, in celebration of planting new trees in the Holy Land; Hanukkah, when the Holy Temple in Jerusalem was recaptured by the Maccabees and cleansed of its desecrations; Israel Independence Day, which commemorates the reestablishment of the Jewish state in 1948, and for which special prayers are now recited in virtually all synagogues at Sabbath services; and Purim, which marks the deliverance of the Jews from planned genocide by their hated enemy, Haman.

Thus, with the exception of the High Holy Days and Purim, all of the other Jewish holy days are linked to the land of Israel.

The growth and development of the Zionist movement in the latter part of the nineteenth century and the creation of Israel in 1948 have helped many Jews to clarify their own sometimes ambivalent feelings about their Jewish origins. The many years of oppression, pogroms, discrimination, and massacre were endured by Jews since the beginning of the exile in the year 70 by the everlasting hope that they would one day be able to return home—to the land of Israel.

In the 1930s, when Nazism surfaced in Germany and anti-Semitism was on the rise in the United States and in many Western countries, partly because of Nazi influence and partly because of the worldwide depression that engulfed the peoples of almost all countries, Jews suffered the anguish of fear, uncertainty and a future that looked bleak indeed. Despite the expanding anti-Semitic attacks that Hitler launched against the Jews of Germany, and then of Austria and Czechoslovakia prior to World War II, no country opened its doors to the Jews, no one offered them asylum—except the small Jewish community of Palestine. This embryonic Jewish community, severely restricted by the British mandatory authorities and suffering the attacks of Arabs, became the sole haven for tens of thousands of Jews in the prewar era.

When World War II was ended, and the Nazi regime had been defeated, a horrible reality encompassed all Jews everywhere. Six million Jews, one-third of the entire Jewish people, had been murdered, while by and large the civilized world had stood idly by. When the British mandate over Palestine insisted on continuing the restrictions of Jewish immigration to Palestine, the Jews of the world united in a historic undertaking, and succeeded in transporting "illegally" tens of thousands of Nazi death camp survivors to the Promised Land.

And when Israel formally announced its independence, it seemed to almost every Jew that a new dawn had finally come for the Jewish people. Since 1948, the 650,000 Jews of Israel have grown to a community of three and a half million Jews, many of them Holocaust survivors or escapees from oppression in Moslem lands. In less than four decades, the State of Israel has—with the all-out support of the world's Jews and with massive help from the United States—built a modern, democratic nation on the ancient land promised to Abraham by God.

Israel today is not only a country that treasures learning and study (its per capita book reading and publishing record are the highest in the world), it has evolved into a state that remains true to its ancient biblical precepts (the ideas of releasing slaves, canceling debts, and providing aid to the needy are biblical in origin), but it has also emerged as a highly technologically advanced nation that can and does compete with many Western industrialized countries.

Jewish tradition and Jewish prayers have always talked of the fact that from "Zion shall go forth the Law," and indeed the Jewish people gave the Bible to the world, with its high moral precepts and its belief in monotheism. In the twentieth century, Jews have seen their great communities in eastern Europe obliterated under Hitler (Poland, once the center of Jewish study and religious observance, is today practically *Judenrein*— rid of Jews.) The two or three million Jews in the Soviet Union have been cruelly cut off from contact with the rest of Jewry, and unless Moscow allows open and free emigration, there can be little doubt that the ravages of time and assimilation will totally erode that once-great Jewish community.

While the United States contains the world's greatest Jewish community, both in terms of size and affluence and influence, valid fears for the future exists, in light of the continuing increase in intermarriage, apathy toward Jewish religious life, and the impact of the majority culture.

For a vast majority of the world's Jewish population, Israel remains a great hope for the future. Despite its economic, social, and political problems, Israel continues to hold true to its tenets of justice and morality. The universities are packed with eager students, studying Judaic and secular subjects. The birthrate, unlike that of Jews in the Diaspora, is high. The dream of its first president, Chaim Weizmann, that Israel may become the "Switzerland of the Middle East" looks more and more attainable.

Perhaps the strong links that tie Jews to Israel can be summed up in the phrase of Yiddish poet and dramatist Itzak Manger, after the Holocaust, after the establishment of Israel, and after the infant state succeeded in defeating six invading Arab armies, "It seems to me that the Jews of the world are now standing taller and straighter than ever."

The Bible has taught Jews to remember. "Remember Amalek," the Jews are cautioned. (The Amalekites were a people who attacked the Jews during the Exodus.) The late American longshoreman-philosopher, Eric Hoffer, said that the Jewish people and Israel were a barometer for him as to where the world is heading. Jews remember that, and sense that as time goes on their ties to Israel, spiritual and physical, will become ever stronger.

BOOKS ON ISRAEL AND ZIONISM

The books in this chapter all deal with the modern state of Israel. If you want to learn about its ancient past, several books in the ANCIENT HISTORY AND ARCHEOLOGY section can be recommended. They include Aharoni's *The Archaeology of the Land of Israel* and Bright's *History of Israel*. Moving to the modern era, the best one-volume history of Israel is Howard Sachar's. It is thorough, readable, and interesting. If you want to supplement it with some personal accounts of the building of the country, *Momentous Century*, edited by Soshuk and Eisenberg, is the perfect choice.

To study Zionist ideology and thought, the first place to turn is Laqueur's *History of Zionism*, a combination of history and acute analysis. A good second step would be Hertzberg's *Zionist Idea*, which includes substantial excerpts from the major Zionist works, along with Hertzberg's perceptive comments. The two books by Vital provide a detailed study of the early years of Zionism, and are important to any advanced study of the subject. Herzl's *Jewish State* is, of course, *the* basic Zionist work, and it is still stimulating to read.

Two works dealing with specific aspects of Israeli history should be mentioned here. *O Jerusalem!* by Collins and Lapierre, is a work of popular history that does a skillful job reporting on the 1948 War for Independence. And *The Claim of Dispossession*, by Avneri, is a convincing refutation of arguments that the creation of the Jewish state unjustly displaced Palestinian Arabs.

A sense of the tensions of present-day Israel can be gained by reading *In the Land of Israel*, a report by one of Israel's leading novelists. Finally, if you plan to take a trip to Israel, we have described several travel books. The Vilnay *Guide* has, by far, the most historical background.

Going beyond the limits of this chapter, you should also look at the HEBREW LITERATURE section, where are listed several books by Israeli writers that can give you a good feeling of the mood of the country. In PERIODICALS, you will find publications that are the best way to keep current on Israeli affairs.

—R. S. F. & W. W.

Ahad Ha-am

Selected Essays of Ahad Ha-am. Atheneum, 1970, $8.95 pb.

Ahad Ha-am was the pen name of Asher Zvi Ginsberg (1856–1927). It means "one of the people" in Hebrew. In his writings, he called for the cultural revival of the Jewish people. Although he was not in the mainstream of early Zionist thought—he criticized Herzl for being estranged from traditional Jewish values and believed that it was premature to begin settling in Palestine before the necessary spiritual and cultural foundation was built—he became an influential and respected thinker. He was also an important shaper of modern Hebrew prose style, the possessor of a style noteworthy for its clarity and precision.

Avineri, Shlomo

The Making of Modern Zionism: The Intellectual Origins of the

Jewish State. Basic Books, 1981, $15.50 hc, $7.95 pb.

A history of Zionist thought presented in the form of profiles of eighteen of its major figures, including Moses Hess, Theodor Herzl, Vladimir Jabotinsky, David Ben-Gurion, and Abraham Isaac Kook. Avineri, formerly the director-general of the Israeli Foreign Ministry, is a member of the Labor Party and he tends to concentrate on those figures with whom he is most in agreement. The result is that the role of Orthodox Jewry in the Zionist movement is substantially downplayed.

Bazak Travel Guide to Israel: 1984–85. Harper & Row, $11.95.

This good travel guide offers extensive tourist information. See also Lewensohn's *Masada Guide* and Vilnay's *Israel Guide*, described later.

Avishai, Bernard
The Tragedy of Zionism: Revolution and Democracy in the Land of Israel. Farrar, Straus & Giroux, 1985, $19.95.

Avishai argues that Zionism is a "good revolution that long ago ran its course," and that while Zionism was an adequate ideology for building a nation, it is not capable of sustaining one. He also says that there is an inherent conflict between Zionism and democracy. He is especially critical of Israel's lack of a written constitution or bill of rights. Even readers who disagree with Avishai will find that he raises some serious issues with important implications for Israel's future.

Avneri, Arieh L.
The Claim of Dispossession: Jewish Land Settlement and the Arabs, 1878–1948. Transaction Books/Rutgers University, 1984, $9.95 pb.

A dispassionate and scholarly analysis of claims that the Jewish settlement of Palestine and the creation of the State of Israel resulted in the unjust displacement of Palestinian Arabs. Using documentary evidence rather than rhetoric, Avneri shows these claims to be ungrounded and false. The book is similar in its argument to Joan Peters's *From Time Immemorial*, but sharper and more concise.

Begin, Menachem
The Revolt. Dell, 1978, out of print.

A memoir of Begin's years as a leader of the underground group Irgun Zvai Leumi and the role he played in fighting against British rule of Palestine. The book is opinionated and unapologetic and provides considerable insight into Begin's politics and personality.

Bell, J. Bowyer
Terror Out of Zion: The Shock Troops of Israeli Independence. University Press, 1984, $17.95.

A detailed history of the roles of the Irgun Zvai Leumi and LEHI (the "Stern Gang") in the

Zionist underground in Palestine. Bell argues that the "official" view that Ben-Gurion and the Haganah were the principal liberators of Palestine and that the Irgun and Stern Gang were terrorists is misleading and false, that, in fact, the Irgun and LEHI were major contributors to the winning of Israeli independence.

Bellow, Saul
To Jerusalem and Back: A Personal Account. Viking/Penguin, 1976, $11.95 hc; Penguin, $3.95 pb; Avon Books, $1.95 pb.

Bellow has a novelist's eye for the telling detail, and he uses it in this beautifully written and perceptive report on his visit to Israel in 1975. He provides portraits of the people he meets, discusses the troubled relationship between America and Israel, and reflects on the tensions, stresses, and problems of Israeli life. Not uncritical, but written with great and obvious love for Israel and Judaism. For information on Bellow's novels, see the FICTION section.

Chafets, Ze'ev
Double Vision. Morrow, 1984, $16.95.

Chafets has written a knowledgeable and informed critique of American press coverage of the Middle East and why it is so often inaccurate and unbalanced. The author, formerly director of Israel's Government Press Office, blends personal observations with well-researched examples of how news is covered in the Middle East and writes with an awareness of the practical difficulties facing reporters covering a part of the world where a story with only three sides is a simple one.

Collins, Larry, and Dominique Lapierre
O Jerusalem! Pocket Books, 1973, $3.95 pb.

This history of the Israeli War for Independence is told largely through the stories of individuals—Jewish, Arab, and British—who were involved in it. While they emphasize the human drama, the authors also do a creditable job of presenting the military and political events.

Devir, Ori
Off the Beaten Track in Israel: A Guide to Beautiful Places. Translated from the Hebrew by Hazel Arieli. Adama Books, 1985, $14.95.

Based on an Israeli television series that each week describes a different "beauty spot," this book has information on nearly a hundred outdoor parks, landmarks, monuments, and other places of interest. For each, there is a full-page color photo, and a page of information, including how to get there. The book is too bulky to carry with you as a travel guide, but it is a good source for anyone planning a trip to Israel, especially if they love the outdoors.

Elon, Amos
Herzl. Schocken Books, 1986, $12.95 pb.

Theodor Herzl is considered to be the "father of Zionism," the man who through force of personality, intelligence, and unceasing labors, created the modern Zionist movement and laid the basis for the founding of the State of Israel. (See Herzl's *The Jewish State*, listed later.) Elon's biography gives a vivid sense of Herzl's personality and does a fine job of explaining his political ideas and life. The story is told with a sense of drama and excitement. *Theodor Herzl: A Biography of the Founder of Modern Zionism* by Alex Bein (Atheneum, 1962, $4.75 pb) focuses on Herzl's intellectual development and public life, not his psychology and private life. Within those limits, it is thorough and provides a solid portrait of both Herzl and the Zionist movement he did so much to further. Elon is also the author of *The Israelis: Founders and Sons* (Penguin, 1983, $5.95 pb), a well-crafted history of Israel's early years.

Frankel, William
Israel Observed: An Anatomy of the State. Thames & Hudson, 1980, $18.95 hc, $9.95 pb.

This is a somewhat dry but useful analysis of "how Israel works"—the institutional structures of power in Israel—the Knesset (parliament) and officers of state, electoral system, political parties, religious organizations, labor unions, business, education, legal system, communications, and defense forces. William

Frankel was editor of England's *Jewish Chronicle* for several years.

Gavron, Daniel
Walking Through Israel. Houghton Mifflin, 1980, $12.95.

Gavron, an Israeli journalist, traveled the length of Israel talking to the people he met, and he reports in this book on what they said. The voices he includes come from all parts of the Israeli political spectrum and while Gavron's sympathies are clearly with the left, he does a good job of letting people speak for themselves. His writing is entertaining, and his love for his country is evident. The picture he presents is one of an Israel badly split and facing troubled times.

Gilbert, Martin
Jerusalem: Rebirth of a City. Viking/Penguin, 1985, $25.

Gilbert is a major author on Jewish subjects—intelligent, informative, knowledgeable, and original. In this book he writes about a sixty-year period in the history of Jerusalem—from 1838 to 1898—a period during which the city's population nearly tripled and it was transformed from a crumbling and dismal rural backwater into a modern city. Gilbert has included quite a few period photographs and does an effective job of conveying the atmosphere of the times. Another recently published book on the same subject, Yehoshua Ben-Arieh's *Jerusalem in the 19th Century: The Old City* (St. Martin's Press,

1985, $29.95) is more scholarly in its approach than Gilbert's book and drier to read, but is also filled with fascinating period photographs and illustrations. Both books will delight lovers of Jerusalem.

Grose, Peter
Israel in the Mind of America. Knopf, 1983, $17.95 hc; Schocken Books, $9.95 pb.

The idea of a "return to Zion" had a strong emotional and religious reverberation in Christian America throughout the nineteenth century and laid the groundwork for the American government's later support for the creation of the modern State of Israel. Grose does not romanticize this attachment though, and makes clear these emotions only come into play when not in contradiction with America's interests in the Middle East. He also discusses the anti-Semitic attitudes within the U.S. government, which contributed to inaction during the Holocaust and to an arms embargo on Palestine after the war. Grose has worked as a foreign reporter for the *New York Times* and in the U.S. State Department. His inside knowledge, combined with his painstaking research, makes this a notable book; it won a National Jewish Book Award in 1984.

Hertzberg, Arthur
The Zionist Idea: A Historical Analysis and Reader. Greenwood Press, reprint of 1959 edition, $23.50 hc; Atheneum, $7.95 pb.

A combination of source book and analysis, this 600-page (plus) volume presents the development of Zionist thought from its origins in the eighteenth century up to the works of Ben-Gurion, and reflects all shades of Zionist opinion. It includes work by Moses Hess, Theodor Herzl, Ahad Ha-am, Hayyim Nachman Bialik, Nahman Syrkin, Berl Katznelson, Martin Buber, Solomon Schechter, Mordecai Kaplan, Vladimir Jabotinsky, and Abba Hillel Silver. Hertzberg's lengthy introduction provides an excellent survey of the material.

Herzl, Theodor
The Jewish State. Translated from the German by Harry Zohn. Herzl Press, 1970, $5.

This book quite literally changed the world. It is the seminal work of the man considered to be the founder of modern Zionism. Herzl (1860–1904) was a writer of light and topical newspaper pieces who was shocked by the anti-Semitism triggered by the Dreyfus trial. In *The Jewish State*, he expressed with great eloquence his conviction that Jews would never be able to assimilate, that they would always remain outsiders in the countries where they lived. He argued that the only solution to their economic and social ills was the founding of a Jewish state—"a publicly recognized, legally secured, home in Palestine."

Herzog, Chaim
The Arab-Israel Wars: War and Peace in the Middle East. Random House, 1983, $20 hc, $8.95 pb.

In this succinct and readable history of the six Arab-Israeli wars, Herzog offers explanations for Israel's military success—flexibility, improvisation, and the leadership of Israeli officers—and is also candid about Israeli failures and Arab successes. If the book has a weakness, it is its concentration on purely military matters, with little attention paid to larger political issues.

Katz, Samuel
Battleground: Fact and Fantasy in Palestine. Steimatzky, 1985, $4.95 pb.

Katz offers a good and forceful statement of the Israeli right wing's position on the origins and history of the Arab-Israeli dispute. He was a member of the underground Irgun Zvai Leumi during the Israeli War for Independence, and a member of the first Knesset. He argues that any Arab flight from Israel in 1948 was voluntary, that there really is no such thing as a Palestinian Arab, and that Jerusalem is not really a sacred city to Moslems. Further, he opposes the Camp David treaties as being no more than part of an Arab plan to destroy Israel, saying that the guiding idea behind all Arab actions

continues to be the elimination of the Jewish state.

Kurzman, Dan
Ben-Gurion: Prophet of Fire. Simon & Schuster, 1983, $19.95 hc, $10.95 pb.

This biography of David Ben-Gurion, Israel's first prime minister, deals both with his public life and with his private life, and it conveys a sense of his intense and driven nature. It is admiring of its subject but willing to present his flaws—his often ruthless nature, his lack of leadership during the Holocaust, his troubled marriage, his failed political comeback attempt. Kurzman hasn't written the definitive biography of Ben-Gurion, but he has written a very, very good one. The book is a National Jewish Book Award winner, 1985. Kurzman is also the author of *Genesis 1948*, a history of the first Arab-Israeli war that is now, unfortunately, out of print.

Laqueur, Walter
A History of Zionism. Schocken Books, 1976, $12.95 pb.

A history of the Zionist movement, its background, intellectual origins and development, its many political factions, its leaders, and its eventual success in founding the State of Israel—a success that Laqueur believes has not achieved all that the Zionists had hoped it would. Laqueur is a brilliant writer and thinker, and while demanding effort, this book rewards it. Readers who want even more detail will be interested in the two volumes by David Vital described later.

Lewensohn, Avraham
Masada Guide to Israel. Masada, distributed by Golden Lee, 1985, $10.95 pb.

In its more than five hundred pages, this guidebook lists over 1,800 towns, villages, and places to visit in Israel. For each site, there is a short description, information on things to see, biblical references, and names of approved hotels and tourist offices. Also included is information on Israel's geography, history, culture, and people; suggested tours, and assorted tourist information. The guide is intermediate between Bazak's emphasis on tourist information and Vilnay's on history.

Lilker, Shalom
Kibbutz Judaism: A New Tradition in the Making. Herzl Press/ Cornwall Books, 1982, $14.95.

Lilker, a Reform rabbi and longtime kibbutznik, sees the Israeli kibbutz movement as the most successful alternative to traditional industrial society. Unlike most other religious communities, the kibbutz is open and pluralistic and not isolated from the modern technological world. Lilker believes the kibbutz movement is a distinct outgrowth and expression of something within Judaism and is making an important contribution to the spiritual

and sociopolitical renaissance of modern Jewish culture.

Meir, Golda
My Life. Dell, 1975, out of print.

Golda Meir was a Zionist pioneer, and the prime minister of Israel from 1969 to 1974. While not totally forthcoming about her private life, Meir's autobiography is gripping reading and we can only hope that it will not remain out of print for long.

Moskin, Robert J.
Among Lions: The Battle for Jerusalem, June 5–7, 1967. Ballantine Books, 1984, $4.95 pb.

A winner of a National Jewish Book Award in 1983, this is a powerful and moving account of the battle that reunited Jerusalem. It is based on interviews with people who fought on both sides of the battle and is told with energy and excitement.

Netanyahu, Yonatan
Self-Portrait of a Hero. Random House, 1981, $12.95 hc, $3.50 pb.

An American-born Jew who emigrated to Israel, Netanyahu was the sole Israeli casualty during the raid on Entebbe that rescued a planeload of passengers taken hostage by terrorists. This book is a collection of his letters, and it gives considerable insight into the ideas that made him an ardent Zionist.

Oz, Amos
In the Land of Israel. Harcourt Brace Jovanovich, 1983, $12.95 hc; Random House, $5.95 pb.

This book by the noted Israeli novelist tells of his encounters with Israelis from across the spectrum of political and social opinion. A kibbutznik and leader of the Peace Now movement, Oz listened to— and argued with—ultra-Orthodox Jews, Arabs, right-wing nationalists, a Catholic priest, West Bank settlers, and others. In the one chapter where Oz directly presents his views, he argues strongly against right-wing ideas. It is a thought-provoking and well-written book. For information on Oz's fiction, see the HEBREW LITERATURE section.

Peters, Joan

From Time Immemorial: The Origins of the Arab-Jewish Conflict Over Palestine. Harper & Row, 1984, $26.95 hc, $12.95 pb.

Peters contends that demographic and population statistics contradict the statements of Israel's enemies who blame it for producing a wave of displaced Palestine Arabs. Rather than displacing a native Arab population, a major Arab migration took place into those areas being settled by Jews. She presents figures indicating that the number of Jews displaced from Arab countries far exceeds the number of Arabs driven from Palestine. Peters has been criticized for being somewhat naive in her understanding of Middle East history and accused of distorting the statistics, but her book remains a powerful

one. Winner of a 1985 National Jewish Book Award.

Raz, Simcha

A Tzaddik in Our Times. Translated from the Hebrew by Charles Wengrov. Feldheim, 1978, $13.95 hc, $8.95 pb.

A biography of Aryeh Levin, an Orthodox rabbi and Torah scholar who became a popular hero during the period of the British Mandate in Palestine for his support of imprisoned underground fighters. He visited them, gave encouragement, and smuggled messages in and out of jail. "Tzaddik" is a Hebrew word meaning "righteous person," and is used to refer to pious religious leaders.

Rubenstein, Amnon

The Zionist Dream Revisited: From Herzl to Gush Emunim and Back. Schocken Books, 1984, $14.95.

The author offers an analysis of the current political climate in Israel. Rubenstein, a leader of the Shinui party and a member of the Israeli parliament, deplores the recent ascendancy of right-wing religious militancy in Israel as a development that repudiates classical Zionism. He believes that religious extremism is blind to pragmatic politics, producing an "us-against-them" mentality that is both unhealthy and unproductive. Israel, he says, is a "home and not a temple, a secular nation and not a recluse willing to live alone."

Sachar, Howard M.
A History of Israel: From the Rise of Zionism to Our Time. Knopf, 1979, $14.95.

This history of Israel is notable for its erudition and its constant awareness of the larger context in which events took place. It covers politics, cultural history, the interplay between Israel and world Jewry, and the role of Israel in world affairs. Sachar, a widely respected scholar and author, also provides vivid portraits of the major personalities of Israel's history.

Schiff, Ze'ev, and Ehud Yaari
Israel's Lebanon War. Simon & Schuster, 1984, $17.95.

The authors, both prominent Israeli journalists, trace the history of the war in Lebanon—its causes, military conduct, and legacy. They believe that Israel's involvement in Lebanon was an unmitigated mistake, both militarily and ethically, and are especially critical of Ariel Sharon for his role in beginning and broadening the war.

Shazar, Rachel Katznelson, ed.
The Plough Woman: Memoirs of the Pioneer Women of Palestine. Translated from the Hebrew by Maurice Samuel. Herzl Press and Pioneer Women, 1975, $3.95 pb.

In 1928 the Council of the Women Workers of Palestine commissioned the original edition of this book, inviting fifty women to recount their personal experiences as pioneers in early twentieth-century Palestine. The women were as much committed to redefining the role of women politically and socially as they were to the dream of establishing a Jewish state. They write about the hardships they encountered in founding a kibbutz or in reclaiming wasteland—and about their frustrations and disillusionments when as women they were denied what they felt was their rightful place. The problems of family and child rearing in a communal setting are given special attention. As might be expected from an anthology of this nature, the quality of the contributions varies, but the overall effect is to provide a powerful sense of the life these women lived. An excellent supplement to Soshuk and Eisenberg's *Momentous Century.*

Silberman, Neil Asher
Digging for God and Country: Exploration, Archeology, and the Secret Struggle for the Holy Land, 1799–1917. Knopf, 1982, $16.95.

Silberman has written a history of the archeological exploration of the Holy Land from the beginning of the nineteenth century to the early twentieth century. Rather than focusing on the findings of archeology, he concentrates on biblical archeology as a manifestation of the times and the scientific impulse toward knowledge. He also writes about the ways in which archeological discovery became an arena for political and diplomatic rivalries. If all that sounds dry, it isn't. The cast of characters is more than a little eccentric, and includes people of occasionally inspiring heroism—and occasionally splendid roguishness. The subject is something of a side road in the history of Israel, and a very entertaining one.

Silver, Eric
Begin: The Haunted Prophet. Random House, 1984, $17.95.

Given how controversial a figure Menachem Begin is, this biography is especially noteworthy for its objective and dispassionate tone. It sees Begin as a complex, even paradoxical man, but does a solid job of explaining him and his views.

Soshuk, Levi, and Azriel Eisenberg, eds.
Momentous Century. Herzl Press/Cornwall Books, 1983, $25.

This book is an excellent complement to Sachar's history of Israel, described earlier. It contains more than a hundred eyewitness accounts of the rise and development of Israel as the Jewish homeland. The accounts are those both of Zionist leaders and of ordinary people, and they have been selected with an eye to their emotional impact and ability to convey the experiences of the men and women who built the country. The selections range in time

from the middle of the nineteenth century to the Egyptian-Israeli Peace Treaty.

Uris, Jill, and Leon Uris
Jerusalem: Song of Songs. Doubleday, 1984, $19.95.

The Urises have here made a loving tribute to the city of Jerusalem. The text, by Leon Uris, traces Jewish history from Abraham in biblical times to Mayor Teddy Kollek in the present, with Jerusalem as the focal point. The volume is of special interest for the beautiful color photographs by Jill Uris. They show Jerusalem's grand vistas and its little-known obscure corners, and include portraits of the many different types of personalities who live there.

Vilnay, Zev
The Guide to Israel, 1985.

Although this is the best guide to Israel, it has no American distributor. It probably can be found in Jewish bookstores. The layout is unattractive, and the *Bazak Guide* is stronger on tourist information, but Vilnay's *Guide* is jammed full of historical information (some of it possibly legendary), biblical references, and charming old illustrations. A full-color map is tucked into a pocket in the back of the book.

Legends of Galilee, Jordan, and Sinai. Jewish Publication Society, 1978, $10.95.
Legends of Jerusalem. Jewish Publication Society, 1973, $8.95.

These two volumes of legends about sites in Israel are drawn from biblical, talmudic, and other sources. The volume about Jerusalem includes more than three hundred sites, ranging from caves and valleys to walls and gates. *Legends of Galilee* also is based on traditional sources and also uses Arab tales and the writings of pilgrims during the Middle Ages. Both books are enjoyable, and include black-and-white photographs and illustrations.

Vital, David

The Origins of Zionism. Oxford University Press, 1975, $14.95 pb.

An account of the early years of the Zionist movement, tracing it up to the First Zionist Congress in 1897, which Vital sees as one of the pivotal events in the modern history of the Jews: "Zionism re-created the Jews as a political nation; and by so doing it revolutionized their collective and private lives." Vital attempts to describe the events as the men and women involved in them saw them. His work is detailed and scholarly.

Zionism: The Formative Years. Oxford University Press, 1982, $29.95.

This sequel to *The Origins of Zionism* concentrates on the decade following the First Zionist Congress. Vital considers this period the decisive one, during which the movement acquired its definitive institutional and political shape and its main ideas and programs of action were developed.

Zidon, Asher

Knesset. Herzl Press, 1967, $5.95.

Although now dated, this is a still-useful study of the Israeli parliament, the Knesset: how it compares to the parliaments of other countries, how it is organized, what its legislative processes are, and the role it plays in Israeli political life. The author was for many years the Knesset's deputy secretary.

VI

Jewish Living

Happy is the one
who finds wisdom,
and the one who
derives understanding.
Its ways are ways
of pleasantness
and all its paths are peace.
It is a tree of life
to those who hold fast to it,
And those who uphold it
are happy. PROVERBS 3

אשרי אדם
מצא חכמה
ואדם יפיק תבונה:
דרכיה דרכי־נעם
וכל־נתיבתיה
שלום:
עץ־חיים היא
למחזיקים בה
ותמכיה מאשר:
משלי ג

"Tree of Life." Drawing by Betsy Plotkin Teutsch, artist and calligrapher, Philadelphia, © 1985.

Hands On

Mae Shafter Rockland

The story is told that a very long time ago, two brothers, both of whom were farmers, lived on either side of a medium-sized hill in the Promised Land. Both brothers worked very hard, and their land rewarded them with substantial crops. One brother was married and had many children; the other lived alone. One clear bright night at the end of the harvest, the brothers stood on their respective sides of the hill thinking about their good fortune. The unmarried brother looked over his abundant crop and thought how lucky he was. He decided that his brother, who had so many more people to be concerned about, deserved to have more than he. So he gathered up many sheaves of grain and began to climb the hill to deliver them to his brother. At the very same time the married brother thought of how fortunate he was to have a wonderful family around him as well as his rich crops. He felt *rachmones* (compassion) for his brother's solitary state, and so he too piled bundles of grain on his shoulders to carry to his brother. At midnight, at the top of the hill, the brothers met and, seeing one another's intentions, embraced. When God saw the concern and love of the brothers for one another, he chose that hill to be the location of Jerusalem—the City of Peace.

This legend, illustrating as it does the Jewish longing and love for Jerusalem that has always been the focus of their national dreams as they wander through history, romantically illustrates that even for God, "actions speak louder than words."

Mae Shafter Rockland is an artist-author based in the Boston area. Her works include *The Hanukkah Book, The Work of Our Hands, Jewish Needlework for Today, The Jewish Party Book, The Jewish Yellow Pages,* and *The New Jewish Yellow Pages.*

Judaism is an ortho*praxy* much more than simply an ortho-*doxy*. That is, Jews are known more by what they *do* than by what they profess to believe.

The contemporary Jewish world is much more complex than the simple rural lifestyle described in the preceding story. American Jews are pushed and pulled by the demands and lures of the secular, materialistic, high-tech, high-speed world in which they live. It is hard to know what to do or what to believe. But, as the Hasidic saying goes, "God sends the cure before the disease." Along with the confusion of media over-stimulation comes the blessing of "how-to" books. It is possible at your local bookstore, by plunking down a few dollars or a plastic card, to learn how-to-do,-be,-build,-buy,-grow,-invest in, -motivate,-renovate, and/or -change in some way, large or small, anything your heart desires. And when one turns to the Ju-daica shelves, there are books detailing every aspect of being or becoming Jewish. We need not feel embarrassed at joining the "how-to" parade; after all, the first book of the genre is the Torah itself. All the rest are commentary. The contempo-rary guides to Jewish life are extremely useful and valid in a number of ways. On the simplest level, they provide a basic introduction to the age-old question of what it means to be a Jew, both for the Jew and to gentile observers. They then offer guidance through the many interpretations of the Jewish life and holiday cycles as well as through philosophy. At their best, the how-to books offer creative solutions that may subtly or dramatically enhance and change the rich Jewish traditions. Nothing happens without affecting the future, and so some of the books described here not only teach about the past but may be instrumental in shaping the world of our Jewish grand-children and beyond. Another aspect of these books that should not be overlooked is their usefulness to future historians and anthropologists. The how-to books of today, whether cook-books or marriage guides, document the way people live and encapsulate our immediate preoccupations and lifestyle.

The books listed here are useful for readers who want an introduction to Jewish life, those who seek a novel or alterna-tive way of enhancing their tradition, and those who want to explore deeply a particular aspect of Jewish life.

HOW-TO BOOKS

The term "how-to" is something of a catchall for books with an emphasis on the practical details of Jewish living. Some of the books are very concrete, and some of them have larger spiritual dimensions. Especially for people who are seeking to increase the level of Jewish observance in their lives, these books can be extremely helpful. For a general discussion of Jewish living, Donin's *To Be a Jew* is unexcelled. It is comprehensive and clear. For a more informal approach, the three *Jewish Catalogs* are a good choice. They cover every aspect of Jewish life and are packed with information.

Much of Jewish life is centered around the home. The subject is dealt with in Greenberg's *How to Run a Traditional Jewish Household*, which is notable for its down-to-earth and warm approach. The second part of this chapter includes some cookbooks, obviously important for any Jewish home—or for anyone who enjoys good food.

Several books listed elsewhere in this guide also deal with practical details of daily life. In particular, you should refer to the section on HOLIDAYS. —R. S. F. & W. W.

Asheri, Michael
Living Jewish: The Lore and Law of the Practicing Jew. Dodd, Mead, 1983, $9.95 pb.

Written from the viewpoint of an Orthodox Jew, this is a solid explanation of Jewish observance. Asheri writes on a basic level, assuming little Jewish knowledge on the part of his readers. He covers daily life, prayer, the holidays, Jewish ethics, and the basics of Jewish religious belief. The book is not as consistently good as Rabbi Donin's books (described later), but nonetheless a good introduction.

Diamant, Anita
The New Jewish Wedding. Summit Books, 1985, $16.95.

Diamant offers information on planning a Jewish wedding and the party that follows it. In addition to giving advice on practical matters such as wording the invitations, finding a rabbi, and renting a hall, Diamant writes about the spiritual dimension of the event and how it can be enhanced. She also offers ideas on how couples can design their own celebrations and rituals, including suggested wordings for the **ketubah** (wedding contract). Also see Helen Latner's *Your Jewish Wedding*, described later.

Donin, Hayim Halevy

Rabbi Donin was one of the finest popularizers of Orthodox Jewish belief and practice. His books (see also *To Pray as a Jew*, in the section on PRAYER BOOKS) are thorough and easily understandable without being superficial. All are of value, even to non-Orthodox Jews.

To Be a Jew: A Guide to Jewish Observance in Contemporary Life. Basic Books, 1972, $15.95.

Written from an Orthodox viewpoint, *To Be a Jew* is one of the best introductions to Jewish living available. The writing is clear and to the point. There is information on how to observe and discussion of the ideas and traditions lying behind the observance. The topics include the Sabbath, the dietary laws, family life, synagogue services, the Holy Days, and the major life cycle events—birth, Bar or Bat Mitzvah, marriage, divorce, and death.

To Raise a Jewish Child: A Guide for Parents. Basic Books, 1977, $15.95.

This book offers advice on child rearing in general and on transmitting Jewish values to your children. Donin also includes advice on selecting the right school and lists a variety of resources for the Jewish education of children—books, records, games, camps, and so on. A chapter of "cases from a rabbi's study" discusses coping with contemporary "situations."

Epstein, David and Suzanne Singer Stutman

Torah With Love: A Guide for Strengthening Jewish Values Within the Family. Prentice-Hall, 1986, $14.95.

The authors, an attorney and a psychologist, are enthusiasts of weekly Torah study in the family as a good way to pass on Jewish values, help children develop as Jews, and create stronger family ties. They aim to bring the Scriptures to life by raising contemporary moral and religious issues and getting the whole family involved through games and role playing. There is much encouragement for people who do not have a good Jewish education.

Greenberg, Blu

How to Run a Traditional Jewish Household. Simon & Schuster, 1984, $19.95.

Written with warmth, humor, and a commonsense awareness of the difficulties of living in a world not geared to the needs of Orthodox Jews, this is a valuable guide for people who wish to run their home in accordance with Orthodox practice. Greenberg explains every detail of Jewish living in a direct and anecdotal style, drawing on her own life and the experiences of her family.

The Jewish Catalog Series. All published by the Jewish Publication Society.

This series of oversized paperbacks made a great impact when they first appeared, with their lively, informal tone and graphics. All are filled with photos and drawings. It's now ten years since the first of the *Catalogs* was published, and they're still an excellent source of information on a wide variety of Jewish topics. An updated edition would be welcome. The three titles are

Siegel, Richard, Michael Strassfeld, and Sharon Strassfeld
The (First) Jewish Catalog: A Do-It-Yourself Kit. 1973, $7.95 pb.

This volume covers information on the Jewish calendar, keeping kosher, getting married, creating a Jewish library, bringing the Messiah, Jewish travel, and more.

Strassfeld, Sharon, and Michael Strassfeld
The Second Jewish Catalog: Sources and Resources. 1976, $8.95 pb.

The Jewish life cycle, sex and sexuality, Jewish education, synagogue and prayer, the arts, and a Jewish "Yellow Pages" are given in this volume.

The Third Jewish Catalog: Creating Community. 1980, $9.95 pb.

Focusing on Jewish communal responsibility, the last of the *Catalogs* discusses charity, social action, ecology, Israel and Zionism, and so on. Also included are chapters on Yiddish, Jewish genealogy, and an index to all three volumes.

Kertzer, Morris N.
What Is a Jew? Bloch, 1953, $7.95; Macmillan, $4.95 pb.

With a minimum of theorizing and an emphasis on direct, factual information, Kertzer offers brief answers to questions about Jews, Israel, Jewish-Christian relations, Jewish customs and traditions, the tenets and practices of Judaism, and Jewish attitudes toward marriage and family, religion, and law and ritual. Kertzer's approach is liberal and probably not acceptable to the Orthodox. His book is one of the simplest and easiest to understand of all the one-volume introductions to Judaism, and its question-and-answer format is easy to read.

Kitov, Eliyahu
The Jew and His Home. Translated from the Hebrew by Nathan Bulman. Shengold, 1963, $10.50.

Written from a very Orthodox viewpoint, this is a concise statement of the Jewish tradition as it applies to family life. Kitov covers such topics as the value of Jewish marriage, the character of the wedding ceremony, harmony in the home, the laws of family purity, the meaning and purpose of modesty, child rearing, kosher laws, and such events as circumcision and Bar Mitzvah. Kitov's traditionalist attitudes toward the role of women will not appeal to feminists.

Klein, Isaac

A Guide to Jewish Religious Practice. Jewish Theological Seminary; distributed by Ktav, 1979, $20.

A detailed, comprehensive, and authoritative guide to Jewish practice, written from the perspective of Conservative Judaism. Like Orthodoxy, Conservative Judaism accepts the supremacy of *halakhah* (Jewish law) in guiding our lives, but it argues that as historical circumstances change so must our interpretations of the law. The material covers all aspects of life, is well organized, and clearly presented. Sources are quoted, making further research easier.

Krohn, Paysach J.

Bris Milah. Mesorah, 1985, $11.95 hc; $8.95 pb.

A fifth-generation **mohel**, Rabbi Krohn has compiled here everything you might want to know about the customs and laws, the ritual, and the meaning of **bris**, the rite of circumcision. He has also included an essay on the choice and significance of names and information on Sephardic customs and rituals.

Kukoff, Lydia

Choosing Judaism. Union of American Hebrew Congregations, 1981, $10 hc; Hippocrene Books, $5.95 pb.

Written by a convert to Judaism, this is a guide for other converts on what to expect, both from their non-Jewish families and from their new fellow Jews. The emphasis is on the practical, rather than on the religious issues involved. She writes with wisdom and emotional insight. This book is excellent for anyone who has converted or who knows someone who has.

Kurzweil, Arthur

From Generation to Generation: How to Trace Your Jewish Genealogy and Personal History. Schocken Books, 1982, $8.95 pb.

This detailed guide shows how to trace your family history, telling you where to find the documents and records you need and how to use them. Kurzweil discusses the basic techniques of genealogical research, lists Jewish historical associations, offers advice on interviewing elderly relatives, and much more. The guide is indispensable for anyone interested in tracing their family background. *Finding Our Fathers: A Guidebook to Jewish Genealogy* (Genealogical Publishing, 1986, $12.95 pb) is a good source of information about Jewish surnames.

Lamm, Maurice

The Jewish Way in Death and Mourning. David, 1972, $6.95 pb.

This book gives a clear explanation of the traditional Jewish understanding of death and customs surrounding it. Lamm's personal warmth is evident throughout the book, which can be used both as a guide to observance and a general reference on the subject.

The Jewish Way in Love and Marriage. Harper & Row, 1982, $9.57 pb.

Writing from a strictly Orthodox viewpoint, Lamm discusses Jewish sexual ethics and marriage customs. Includes both philosophical discussion and practical information, although the emphasis is scholarly, and the Latner or Diamant books are more useful for planning a wedding. Among the topics covered are matchmaking, marriage contracts, the wedding ceremony, and appropriate prayers.

Latner, Helen
The Book of Modern Jewish Etiquette. Schocken Books, 1981, $19.95.

This useful guide for Jews and non-Jews covers all aspects of Jewish etiquette in both home and synagogue, including dress, food, and ritual. Daily life, holidays, and special ceremonial occasions are all included, drawing on traditional sources and with information on the practices of Orthodox, Conservative, and Reform.

Your Jewish Wedding. Doubleday, 1985, $4.95 pb.

A handbook for planning a Jewish wedding, concentrating on the practical aspects such as selecting a caterer, sending invitations, who pays for what, and what

to wear. Information on Jewish traditions and law is included. There are several helpful checklists to assist in your planning. See also Anita Diamant, *The New Jewish Wedding.*

Maslin, Simeon J., ed.
Gates of Mitzvah: A Guide to the Jewish Life Cycle. Central Conference of American Rabbis, 1979, $9.95 hc, $7.95 pb.

This book was written to encourage Reform Jews to be more religiously observant. It is very much a part of Reform's mainstream, with its emphasis on individual choice, but it is also quite traditional in its belief that the performance of *mitzvot* (good deeds and religious obligations) is an essential part of a meaningful Jewish life. (For example, while it doesn't say you *must* keep a kosher home, it suggests that doing so is a good thing.) It covers the major events of life, from birth to marriage to death, and includes essays on such topics as charity, divorce, and conversion. The approach is abstract and somewhat dry, but this is the best introduction to Reform Jewish practice available.

Silver, Abba Hillel
Where Judaism Differed: An Inquiry into the Distinctiveness of Judaism. Macmillan, 1972, $5.95 pb.

This book can be read as an introduction to Judaism, but its special strength is its constant focus on the traits that distinguish

Judaism and Christianity. While he seeks to find areas of agreement between them, Silver makes no bones about the major issues dividing them and does not try to paper them over. Silver's book is likely to be particularly useful to Christians or converts from Christianity, although there is plenty in it for all readers.

Steinberg, Milton
Basic Judaism. Harcourt Brace Jovanovich, 1975, $2.95 pb.

Considered by many to be the best one-volume presentation of basics of Jewish belief and practice, *Basic Judaism* is brief without being superficial. Although Steinberg was a Conservative rabbi, his book presents the approaches of all the major branches of Judaism impartially. The writing is clear and crisp, interpretative as well as descriptive, and doesn't avoid the difficult issues such as the presence of evil in the world. Steinberg is frank in expressing his hope that "a lucid and ordered formulation" of the faith will encourage his readers to "live that faith more consistently and forthrightly." His novel *As a Driven Leaf,* described in the FICTION section, is well worth reading.

Trepp, Leo
The Complete Book of Jewish Observance: A Practical Manual for the Modern Jew. Summit Books/Behrman House, 1980, $16.95.

Trepp's book is especially helpful for beginners and for readers seeking information on the practices of the major branches of Judaism, as he clearly spells out their differences of belief and practice. Trepp assumes no knowledge on the part of his readers and presents his information in a simple, step-by-step manner.

COOKBOOKS

David, Suzy
The Sephardic Kosher Kitchen. Illustrated by Jean David. Jonathan David, 1984, $14.95.

When Spanish Jews, or Sephardim, were expelled from Spain in 1492, they brought their culinary traditions with them to their new homelands, where they blended with local specialties. One of the countries where they settled was Bulgaria, and the recipes in this book come from there. They include many dishes made with eggplant, tomatoes, peppers, onions, homemade white cheese, and phyllo (or filo) dough. The recipes are, for the most part, clearly presented and represent an authentic and important part of the Jewish heritage.

Goldberg, Betty S.
Chinese Kosher Cooking. Jonathan David, 1984, $14.95.

These recipes adapt classic Chinese dishes to the Jewish kitchen. The book is filled with bits of folklore, shopping hints, suggested menus, and explanations of Chinese cooking techniques and is a treat to read.

London, Anne, and Bertha K. Bishov
The Complete American-Jewish Cookbook. Crowell, 1971, out of print.

This is probably the best all-around Jewish cookbook. The recipes are varied, presented in an easy-to-understand fashion, and taste good. The publisher, Crowell, has informed us that it plans to reissue this book soon.

Machlin, Edda Servi
The Classic Cuisine of the Italian Jews. Dodd, Mead, 1981, $12.95 pb.

Machlin's family came from the village of Pitigliano in Tuscany, and she draws on her family background in this delightful book. In addition to a selection of delicious traditional kosher Italian-Jewish recipes, she presents a memoir of her life in Italy and information on how the various Jewish holidays were celebrated there. The book is a pleasure to read even if you don't try any of the recipes. The illustrations add to the charm.

Nathan, Joan
The Jewish Holiday Kitchen. Schocken Books, 1979, $14.95 hc, $10.95 pb.

Traditional recipes are given for all the major holidays, the Sabbath, many minor holidays, and such life cycle events as Bar Mitzvahs and weddings. The recipes are mostly quite easy to follow. Nathan also includes background information on the holidays and many of the recipes, suggested menus, and a discussion of kosher laws. A very good book with lots of information on folklore.

Nash, Helen
Kosher Cuisine. Illustrated by Pat Stewart. Random House, 1984, $17.95.

Nash was determined to show that food could be both "gourmet" *and* kosher. She has succeeded. She didn't simply take gourmet recipes and then substitute kosher ingredients. Instead, she has modified and altered them as needed to produce first-rate food without compromise.

Rose, Evelyn
The Complete International Jewish Cookbook. Salem House/Merrimack, 1984, $16.95.

More than 650 Jewish recipes from around the world are given here, including special foods for the holidays.

Holidays As Memory Makers

Lydia Kukoff

You have lovingly given us, O God, festivals of joy, holidays, and times of gladness.

from the festival *Kiddush*

The Jewish holiday cycle as it exists today is perhaps the clearest evidence of the evolutionary dynamism that has enabled creative Jewish survival for close to four thousand years.

From Tishri and the High Holy Days to Av with its solemn commemoration of moments of profound historical tragedy, the Jewish calendar has built layer upon layer of responses to biblical commandments, reinterpretations of one-time agricultural festivals, adaptations of customs borrowed from neighboring peoples, rituals developed by scholars and by the people themselves, and liturgies evolved over centuries of brilliant and sensitive response to the many worlds in which Jews lived. The Jewish calendar is a marvelous kaleidoscope of colorful and diverse celebrations, capturing the gamut of human emotions and enabling Jews to have the opportunity to live in "Jewish time."

For all the diversity, however, there are a number of characteristics that hold for every Jewish holiday and thus reflect a basic Jewish value system that bears examination.

Lydia Kukoff is director of the Commission on Reform Jewish Outreach of the Union of American Hebrew Congregations and the Central Conference of American Rabbis. She is the author of *Choosing Judaism*.

1. The Uniqueness of the Jewish People

Any people, any religion, must have a basis for its shared communal and individual identity. Judaism provides for that bonding in part through the holiday structure. Jews separate themselves from the outside world and gather with other Jews to strengthen and reinforce a Jewish self. There is no question that this affirmation of Jewish uniqueness helps them to live more comfortably and confidently in a world that seems to discourage uniqueness.

Shabbat, the most frequent holiday, is perhaps the most striking example of the emphasis on Jewish uniqueness. At sundown on Friday afternoon or evening, Jews throughout the world join as families to sanctify time. As Jewish women bless the *Shabbat* candles, they are aware that millions of other women, at that same moment, are welcoming the light of *Shabbat* and holiness. As Jewish men rise to chant the *kiddush*, they know that their act of sanctification is not a solitary one and that Jewish men in Israel, France, Hungary, the Soviet Union, join them in expressing this joyous reminder that Jews were specially blessed by God.

And on some primal level Jews are aware that in marking *Shabbat* they join a continuum of Jews throughout the centuries who have proudly affirmed their Jewish identity whatever the cost.

2. The Imperative of Hope

Every Jewish holiday begins at sunset. It is when the world grows dark and most frightening that Jews impose their celebration—optimism about the future—on the darkness. As the light of day disappears, they light candles as a symbol of their faith in tomorrow, confident in the coming of a new dawn and a new opportunity to live and to love.

3. The Reenactment of Jewish History

Jewish holidays emphasize the individual Jew as a link in the chain of Jewish history and, consequently, the responsibility of each Jew to preserve, protect, and convey that tradition to future generations.

Through holidays Jews remember peak moments in the history of their people and thus bind themselves inextricably to their ancestors.

The Torah service each *Shabbat*, for example, constitutes a symbolic reenactment of the giving of the Torah at Mount Sinai.

When gathering for dinner in a *sukkah* each autumn, Jews symbolically relive the wilderness experience of the Israelites. As they sit in this fragile structure exposed to the elements, they are reminded of the tenuous nature of human existence. As they remember their ancestors and their forty years in the desert, they are reminded of the many and marvelous ways in which God provided for those wandering, vulnerable Israelites. Jews invite their most ancient ancestors, a different one each night, to be with them in the *sukkah*. Wherever they celebrate *Sukkot*, they sit in the presence of Abraham and Sarah, Isaac and Rebecca, Jacob, Rachel and Leah, who are the honored guests. And, in a *sukkah* decorated with the yield of the land, they remember that they are part of a people who celebrate their closeness to the land in every generation and in every age.

Or perhaps most powerfully, when Jews assemble for the Passover *seder* to celebrate freedom and redemption, the Haggadah reminds them that in each generation all Jews must imagine themselves personally coming out from Egypt. Throughout the *seder*, they relive a vivid story that begins with the degradation of slavery and concludes with the blessing of liberation. Each holiday helps Jews remember, helps them keep what might otherwise be an ancient and distant past close to them, fresh and vital, suffusing their contemporary lives. Through their holidays, they renew themselves in a community of today and as part of a historical community. Celebrating holidays enables Jews to be a part of the chain of renewal.

4. *The Home as a Center of Celebration*

One of the notable aspects of Judaism is the centrality of the home as a locus of holiday celebrations.

It may be that this emphasis on the home emerged in part as a result of the uncertainty of Jewish existence. Jewish ancestors, who were often driven from their homes and homelands without warning, could not depend on the synagogue alone to sustain the substance and continuity of Jewish observance.

Yet it must also be stated that the preeminent Jewish value placed upon the family and family life was a primary factor in creating the awareness that the home is a *Mikdash Me'at*, a small sanctuary.

The family serves as the vehicle through which Jewish values are transmitted. *Shabbat* dinner, the *seder*, the *sukkah*, the Chanukah candles, apples and honey on Rosh Hashanah, Shabbat **Havdalah**—all these celebrations and many more are the means to a common sharing and conveying of ideas, history, and commitment.

It has been said that Jewish identity is in large measure a product of childhood memories. If so, Jews have the potential and the responsibility to be memory makers in every Jewish home.

5. The Importance of Community

Though the home is of primary importance to Jewish holiday celebration, the companionship of the larger community is crucial as well. The home is seen as a key building block of a larger whole comprising the synagogue, a house of prayer, learning, and meeting. Accordingly, there are special synagogue services for all major holidays and most minor ones.

Rosh Hashanah and Yom Kippur, in fact, are marked almost exclusively in the synagogue. The communal orientation of the liturgy, the compelling need to be with others at a time of personal self-examination, make these logical exceptions to the norm.

6. Sharing Joy with Others

Finally, no overview of the Jewish holidays would be complete without mentioning the constant emphasis on *tzedakah* and hospitality.

Tzedakah is of paramount importance in Judaism. Before *Shabbat* or festival candles are lit, it is customary to drop a few coins in the family *tzedakah* box. Before Passover, *tzedakah* was given to the poor to enable them to celebrate the holiday with dignity. On Purim, in addition to giving *mishloach manot* (baskets of "goodies") to friends, Jews give *tzedakah* to at least two people in need. During the High Holy Day period, as Jews assess their behavior of the last year, they turn their hearts toward *teshuvah* and *tzedakah*.

Hospitality is another *mitzvah* which is central to Judaism. Abraham is praised because he opened his home and his heart to the stranger. One of the most vivid accounts in the Torah is of Abraham's eagerness to welcome the three "men," really angels, and invite them into his home as honored guests. In Jewish communities throughout the ages, strangers were welcomed and brought home from synagogue for a *Shabbat* meal. Today Jews still share Sabbaths with friends and those who may be new to the community. And the *seder*, when family and friends are gathered to celebrate what is probably the most beloved holiday, begins with the words, "May all who are in need come celebrate Pesach with us."

The discovery of the joy and meaning of Jewish holiday celebration is a lifelong adventure. As Jews read about and experience rituals, foods, prayers, songs, and symbols, they slowly come to own them, and to make them a part of themselves.

To observe and cherish the Jewish holidays, to make them a part of their homes and of themselves, is an act of commitment to the future of an age-old people whose past is glorious and whose future is the Jews' common, sacred responsibility.

BOOKS ON JEWISH HOLIDAYS

Readers looking for a one-volume survey of the Jewish holidays and how they are observed will find Strassfeld's *The Jewish Holidays* to be an excellent introduction. Bloch's *The Biblical and Historical Background of the Jewish Holy Days* provides a good survey of the religious and historical development of the holidays. Additional information about observance can be gained from Kitov's *The Book of Our Heritage*, a three-volume set describing Orthodox practice. *Gates of the Seasons*, edited by Knobel, is a one-volume discussion written from the perspective of Reform Judaism. To learn about specific holidays in depth, the anthologies edited by Goodman for the Jewish Publication Society are useful. They contain material selected from a wide variety of sources and are inexpensive. Agnon's *Days of Awe*, an anthology for the High Holy Days (Rosh Hashanah and Yom Kippur), is exceptionally good.

If Yom Kippur is the most solemn Jewish holy day, the Sabbath may be the most important. Heschel's *The Sabbath* is a good introduction to the meaning of the day. Millgram's *Sabbath* is in the same format as the series of holidays books edited by Goodman, and it is equally useful. For Reform Jews, Plaut's *Shabbat Manual* is a good introduction to Sabbath observance. Additional information on the holidays can be found in the sections on CHILDREN'S BOOKS and PRAYER BOOKS. The *Jewish Catalogs*, described in HOW-TO, also contain a wealth of holiday material. —R. S. F. & W. W.

Agnon, S. Y.
Days of Awe. Schocken Books, 1965, $8.95 pb.

Many an anthology calls itself a "treasury." This one really is. Agnon compiled material on Rosh Hashanah and Yom Kippur from the Torah, the Prophets, the Writings, from the Talmud and from *midrash*, from works of mysticism and works of Jewish law— from the whole of Hebrew literature of the ages. The result is a religious meditation that is both understandable and deep although perhaps best suited to knowledgeable readers.

Birnbaum, Philip
The Birnbaum Haggadah. Hebrew Publishing, 1953, $4.95 hc, $2.95 pb.

Why choose one edition of the Passover **Haggadah** rather than another? In this case the special merits are Birnbaum's clear translation, the extensive running commentaries drawn from a wide variety of sources, and an introduction with information on the holiday and its origins, the *seder*, and the history of the Haggadah. Hebrew and English texts are on facing pages, and the illustrations are in black and white. A selection of songs is included.

Bloch, Abraham P.
The Biblical and Historical Background of the Jewish Holy Days. Ktav, 1978, $20.

This survey describes how the major Jewish holidays originated and have developed over the centuries. Bloch, an Orthodox rabbi, draws heavily on the Talmud and other rabbinic sources, but also pays attention to such historical factors as the decentralization of religious authority that followed the destruction of the Temple and the impact of life in the Diaspora.

Bronstein, Herbert, ed.
A Passover Haggadah. Illustrated by Leonard Baskin. CCAR Press/Central Conference

of American Rabbis, 1982, $27.50 hc, $7.50 pb.

Published by the organization of Reform rabbis, this Haggadah is noteworthy for its use of non-sexist language (the four *sons* become four *persons*) and for its dramatic watercolor illustrations by Leonard Baskin. The Hebrew and English are given in parallel columns, and interspersed with the text of the Haggadah are many additional readings—traditional and contemporary, secular and religious—from which the participants can choose during the course of the *seder*. A selection of songs is included.

Cardozo, Arlene Rossen

Jewish Family Celebrations: The Sabbath, Festivals, and Ceremonies. St. Martin's Press, 1982, $17.50 hc, $6.95 pb.

Written specifically for families just beginning to incorporate traditional Jewish practices into their lives, this book covers the major holidays plus such events as Bar or Bat Mitzvahs, funerals, weddings, and births. Each chapter offers information on the origin and development of the observance plus suggestions on how to celebrate it at home, including recipes, blessings, and songs. It's a good introductory text.

Gaster, Theodor H.

Festivals of the Jewish Year: A Modern Interpretation and Guide. Smith, 1952, $17 hc; Morrow, 1978, $7.95 pb.

Gaster describes the origins, rituals, customs, and meaning for contemporary life of the Jewish festivals, fasts, and holy days. He traces the holidays back to pre-biblical times, seeking to discover the universal truths lying behind their changing forms. His anthropological orientation, speculative approach, and interest in comparative religion are not always appreciated by Orthodox Jews.

Glatzer, Nahum N., ed.

The Passover Haggadah. Schocken Books, 1979, $3.95.

This straightforward presentation of the Haggadah text gives Hebrew and English on facing pages. In addition to commentaries and explanatory notes, the editor has included a section of supplemental readings on the Holocaust. Schocken has wider distribution than either the Hebrew Publishing Company or CCAR Press, and this edition is likely to be more readily available in non-Jewish bookstores.

Goodman, Philip, ed.

For many years the executive director of the Jewish Book Council of the Jewish Welfare Board, Rabbi Goodman put his knowledge of books to work assembling a series of holiday anthologies. Although, as is frequently the case with anthologies, they can be dry reading, they are wonderfully useful source books for anyone eager to explore the Jewish holidays.

Each of the books is illustrated, and each contains selections from classic Jewish writings—Bible, Talmud, *midrash*, medieval Jewish literature, codes of law, liturgy, and modern prose and poetry. Each volume includes sections on the history and observance of the holiday and a selection of children's stories and activities. The books are each more than 360 pages long, affordably priced, and excellent values. All are published by the Jewish Publication Society. (See also *Sabbath*, edited by Abraham E. Millgram.)

The Hanukkah Anthology. 1976, $10.95.

The Passover Anthology. 1961, $10.95.

The Purim Anthology. 1945, $7.50.

The Rosh Hashanah Anthology. 1970, $7.50.

The Shavuot Anthology. 1975, $9.95.

The Sukkot and Simhat Torah Anthology. 1973, $7.50.

The Yom Kippur Anthology. 1971, $9.95.

Heschel, Abraham Joshua

The Sabbath: Its Meaning for Modern Man. Farrar, Straus & Giroux, 1951, $4.95 pb.

A celebration of the Sabbath and a meditation on its nature. Heschel sees Judaism as a religion that sanctifies moments in time, a religion that teaches us "to be attached to sacred events." To Heschel, "the Sabbaths are our great cathedrals," days of separation from space and the material things that fill it, a day on which we can become aware of peace and the meaning of eternity. The book is enhanced by a series of wood engravings by Ilya Schor.

Kitov, Eliyahu

The Book of Our Heritage. Translated from the Hebrew by Nathan Bulman. Philipp Feldheim, 1978, 3 vols., $32.50 hc, $19.95 pb.

The Strassfeld holiday guide described later is the best general introduction for beginners; Kitov's set of books is probably the best second step. Writing from a traditionally Orthodox perspective, he works his way through the entire Jewish year, offering explanations, prayers, customs, parables, allusions, insights, reasons, meanings, and a guide to observance. Kitov is correct in that "a reader not acquainted with the Jewish Classics will find some difficulty in understanding" his book, but his writing is easy to understand and his knowledge is broad. Included are *two* reasons not to eat nuts on Rosh Hashanah.

Knobel, Peter S., ed.

Gates of the Seasons: A Guide to the Jewish Year. CCAR Press/ Central Conference of American Rabbis, 1983, $9.95 pb.

In this book the Reform Jewish movement for the first time provided detailed guidance on the *mitzvot* of observing the Sabbath and the Jewish holidays. Covering all the major holidays plus such recent commemorations as **Yom Ha-shoah** (Holocaust Day) and **Yom Ha-atsmaut** (Israeli Independence Day), it provides information on the background, customs, traditions, meaning, and practical aspects of observance.

Millgram, Abraham E., ed.

Sabbath: The Day of Delight. Jewish Publication Society, 1944, $8.95.

Similar to the books described earlier in the holiday series edited by Philip Goodman, *Sabbath* contains illustrations and a broad selection of materials, including a Sabbath service for the home, poetry, information on the law of the Sabbath, stories for children, examples of the Sabbath in literature (both traditional and modern), historical background, and a selection of songs.

Plaut, W. Gunther

A Shabbat Manual. Central Conference of American Rabbis, 1972, $5.95.

This introduction to the Sabbath for Reform Jews—its meaning and how to observe it—is intended to encourage *Shabbat* observance. It includes songs, services, readings, and a glossary. It is occasionally defensive about past Reform practices and attitudes, but is a useful book for beginners. A cassette for use with the book is available for $5.50, and is a great help to beginners

in learning how to recite the blessings.

Rabinowicz, Rachel, ed.

Passover Haggadah: The Feast of Freedom. Illustrated by Dan Reisinger. Rabbinical Assembly, 1982, $5.95 pb.

One of the nicest features of this Haggadah from the Conservative movement is its colorful, evocative, and cheerful illustrations. It also includes extensive marginal commentaries, with information on history and Jewish law. The editor has attempted, successfully, to stimulate discussion by the participants in the *seder.* There is not quite enough instructional information for a complete beginner, but this is otherwise a fine Haggadah. Although it is a paperback, it has a sewn binding and is sturdy enough to survive the beating that all Haggadahs take.

Raphael, Chaim

A Feast of History: The Drama of Passover Through the Ages. Out of print.

The origins of Passover, the history of the Haggadah, and the complete text of the Haggadah, combined with a wealth of color and black-and-white illustrations. Raphael is particularly good on the development of the festival throughout history and around the world.

Renberg, Dalia Hardoff

The Complete Family Guide to Jewish Holidays. Illustrated by

Amnon Danziger and Irwin Rosenhouse. Adama Books, 1985, $15.95.

A guide to the Jewish holidays, their origins, evolution over the years, observance, and customs. Included are songs, prayers, recipes, traditional and modern arts and crafts, and suggestions on how to plan holiday parties for children. Unlike the Strassfeld book described later, this book is very much geared toward children, especially those from ages five to eight. It also includes more sophisticated supplementary material for use by parents or teachers. The photographs place a strong emphasis on Israeli celebrations of the holidays.

Rockland, Mae Shafter
The Hanukkah Book. Schocken Books, 1975, $9.95 pb.

Although Hanukkah has not been an especially important event on the Jewish calendar, it has lately begun to develop into a major expression of Jewish identity. This unpretentious book is filled with ideas to help celebrate the holiday—crafts, parties, recipes, games, and gifts. It includes historical and religious background information on Hanukkah and lots of pictures.

Strassfeld, Michael
The Jewish Holidays: A Guide and Commentary. Illustrated by Betsy Platkin Teutsch. Harper & Row, 1985, $24.95 hc, $15.95 pb.

For each holiday, Strassfeld offers an introduction, a description of its rituals and customs, an exploration of its contemporary application and meaning, and a discussion of its key themes and the questions it raises. Using something like the talmudic format of marginal commentaries, Strassfeld has added observations by five modern Jewish thinkers—Arnold Eisen, Everett Gendler, Arthur Green, Edward L. Greenstein, and Zalman Schachter-Shalomi. Their commentaries are among the best parts of the book, providing intellectual insights, historic speculation, poetry, and even occasional whimsy. The two-color illustrations add to the book's appeal.

Yerushalmi, Yosef Hayim
Haggadah and History: A Panorama in Facsimile of Five Centuries of the Printed Haggadah. Jewish Publication Society, out of print.

This oversized volume surveys Passover Haggadahs from the end of the fifteenth century to the present. Yerushalmi has written an introduction and detailed descriptions of each of the approximately two hundred illustrations. An important scholarly work and also a pleasure to look at.

VII

Jewish Thought

"Kabbalistic Meditations on the Letters." There is a Jewish tradition that the Hebrew letters have a mystical essence of their own that is separate from the text. Drawing by Mark Podwal, © 1978.

Text, Tradition, and Reason: The Dynamics of Medieval Jewish Thought

David Shatz

The subject of Jewish thought before 1600 is so vast that it is impossible to discuss it meaningfully in a short essay. Instead, we have asked David Shatz, an expert in philosophy, to discuss the most dynamic period of Jewish philosophical creativity. The subject of rabbinic literature—which includes Mishnah, the Talmud, *midrash*, and responsa—merits coverage, but we do not have the space for more than our own brief remarks at the start of the book listings.   —R. S. F. & W. W.

To the uninitiated reader, Jewish philosophical thought in the Middle Ages is likely to appear forbidding, esoteric, and remote from contemporary theological and religious concerns. Medieval texts abound with fine distinctions, obscure terminology, and demanding arguments, all frequently pressed into the service of scientific and metaphysical theories long since abandoned. A vast distance separates us from medieval thinkers, and many a reader has opened Moses Maimonides' *Guide of the Perplexed,* Saadya Gaon's *Book of Doctrines and Beliefs,* or Judah Halevi's *Kuzari,* expecting to find in these classics timely ideas and clear guidance, only to give up after a few arduous pages devoted to the Active Intellect, essence and accident, and other staples of medieval intellectual discourse.

Dr. David Shatz is associate professor of philosophy at Yeshiva University. He is coeditor of *Contemporary Philosophy of Religion,* and has published articles and reviews in both Jewish and general philosophy.

Is medieval Jewish thought hopelessly timebound or anti-quated? In certain details and in idiom, perhaps yes; in general thrust and objective, no. The contemporary reader who keeps an eye on the forest rather than on the trees will find a remarkable continuity between the medievals' concerns and our own, and will come to appreciate why medieval Jewish thought has indeed been of relevance and primary importance to Jewish thinkers of virtually every period.

Beginning with the ninth and tenth centuries, intellectually inclined Jews became exposed to Greek philosophy as seen through the prism of commentators of late antiquity and philosophers of the Islamic world. Much of medieval Jewish philosophy, like much of Moslem and Christian thought of the period, is an attempt to formulate a response to the confrontation with philosophy. How should Judaism relate to this ostensibly alien culture? Must its ideas be shunned and rejected, or can they instead be integrated and synthesized with Jewish tradition?

The most important response to such questions was a view commonly known as *rationalism*. For the rationalist, Judaism and philosophy are in perfect harmony: divine revelation and human reason lead to a single body of truth. Human reason can demonstrate, through philosophy, much of what is presented in the revelation as fact—for example, the existence and unity of God. And even if reason cannot prove the truth of every doctrine contained in the revelation, in no case can a religious teaching conflict with conclusions generated by the application of human reason.

Together with this conviction that philosophy and religion could be harmonized, rationalist thinkers developed a distinctive conception of the religious ideal. Not only does Judaism permit the study of philosophy and the sciences to individuals of appropriate talents and inclinations, it actually encourages, indeed mandates, such study as an integral component of the truly religious life, a *sine qua non* for attaining the highest levels of religious devotion. By using their knowledge so as to interpret tradition and demonstrate the truth of religious teachings, philosophers infuse their commitment with a depth, understanding, and richness that can never be produced by a religious sensibility that is rooted in the unreflective acceptance of traditional teachings and norms.

This blending of a religious ideal with a philosophic one is highly controversial, and to sustain it, rationalists engaged in an extensive program of interpretation and reinterpretation of Jewish tradition. For Moses Maimonides, a towering authority on Jewish law as well as the greatest of Jewish philosophers, the commandment to study Torah comes to include the study of science and philosophy, while the imperative "and you shall love the Lord your God" (Deut. 6:5) becomes a command to know God through the exercise of reason: "according to the knowledge will be the love."

The process of reinterpretation is even more evident in the rationalists' defense of their claim that religious and philosophical doctrines can be harmonized. What of the numerous instances in which a scriptural verse or rabbinic dictum runs counter to scientific or philosophical viewpoints? The problematic passage is then to be interpreted anew so as to accord with philosophic truth. For example, when taken literally, biblical, talmudic, and midrashic passages imply that God has a body and is affected by emotions akin to ours. From a philosophical standpoint these ascriptions of human characteristics to God are unacceptable. Consequently, the relevant texts must be interpreted as figures of speech, which are used only because few people can think without the aid of such imagery. Exquisitely sensitive to the needs and limitations of its students, the Torah, the consummate teacher, "speaks in the language of human beings."

In encouraging the pursuit of philosophy and engaging in the philosophical interpretation of traditional texts, medieval thinkers did not see themselves as mavericks or innovators. On the contrary, they viewed themselves as restorers of a lost tradition in Israel. Owing to persistent pressures and persecutions, philosophy, once cultivated by Jews, was now exclusively in the hands of the non-Jewish world. The task was but to recover it.

What, then, should the reader expect to find in the writings of Maimonides and other rationalist thinkers? He or she will encounter extended attempts to explain the phenomenon of prophecy, elucidate the attributes of God, resolve the problem of evil, clarify the doctrine of creation, probe the concept of miracle, explore the notion of free will, articulate reasons for the commandments, and enunciate an ideal of human perfection. Although the intricacies of the philosophic arguments invoked in these contexts make heavy demands on the reader, the overall aim of the enterprise is fascinating. At every step of the way, the Jewish philosopher will be submitting to a dual set of constraints. On the one hand, the position the thinker adopts must be philosophically cogent. On the other hand, the position must make sense, literal or figurative, of the classic authoritative texts, and it must do so in a disciplined manner; the text could not be made to yield just any position the interpreter endorsed, for it would then lose its integrity and independent authority. It is precisely this creative tension of text, tradition, and reason that stands at the heart of the Jewish philosophical enterprise in the Middle Ages and produces discussions that are remarkable for their subtlety, novelty, and boldness.

In their openness to the realm of culture, in their insistence on interpreting and defending Judaism in the universal categories of reason while retaining a clear link to tradition and authority, the medieval philosophers formulated an agenda of continuing relevance. Yet the rationalist approach did not go unchallenged. While numerous works of the period are an elaboration and implementation of the rationalist program, others express sharp criticisms of it.

Some of the critics based their opposition on the dangers of heresy that lurked in the philosophic enterprise: philosophers were often perceived as holding suspect positions on such issues as the eternity of matter, the character of divine providence, and the separate survival of individual souls after death. Even in the absence of concrete heresies, emphasis on intellectual pursuits, on thought rather than action, might lead to neglect of the law. A particularly searching and provocative critic was Judah Halevi of Spain, who formulated a powerful critique of the rationalists' conception of religiosity even before Maimonides gave that conception its fullest expression. While recognizing the value of philosophy in its own sphere, Halevi resists all attempts to equate the religious life with the life of the intellect. The God of Abraham is the caring, vital, dynamic God of history, not the abstract, impersonal, "first cause" of Aristotle. Abstract thought, furthermore, is cold and detached; it cannot kindle the love, the fervor and the passion for religion that "invites its votaries to give their life for His sake, and to prefer death to His absence." For Halevi, it is not rational thought but, instead, direct experience and prophetic revelation that form the basis of the Jewish faith.

Despite their reluctance to confer on philosophy a religious value, let alone declare its study obligatory, many Jews did think that rationalists were right to seek a dimension of spirituality beyond study and practice of the law. In this regard an intriguing counterpoint is provided by the teachings of Jewish mysticism (**kabbalah**), another prominent genre of Jewish thought in the Middle Ages. Like philosophy, *kabbalah* held out for an elite an intellectually rigorous discipline outside of study of the law; like rationalists, kabbalists saw themselves as continuators of an ancient esoteric tradition in Judaism (*kabbalah* means "tradition"). However, as against the philosophers, the kabbalists discredited Greek learning as alien in character and presented their own teachings as authentic, indigenous Judaism. In sharp contrast to rationalism, *kabbalah* portrays God in living, dynamic terms, even to the point of using sexual imagery to describe aspects of the godhead; it explores the intimate inner workings of the deity, "the pulsation of divine life," as the preeminent historian of the movement put it. The same references to God's limbs that rationalists insisted were mere figures of speech are interpreted by kabbalists as symbols referring to processes or aspects of the divine (though the divine in itself, kabbalists made clear, is hidden and unknowable). With regard to such issues as the nature of creation, the origin and reality of evil, the aims of the commandments, the nature of the soul, the role of prayer, the place of Jews in the cosmic order, and the significance of exile, kabbalists produced solutions that, while often charged with radical elements, in many respects fitted traditional emphases and modes of thinking better than did rationalist doctrine. Perhaps because of its greater stress on tradition, its dynamic conception of God, its powerful imagery, and its focus on the nature of Jewishness and Jewish experience, *kabbalah*, unlike rationalism, was destined to evolve from esoteric doctrine to popular religion.

The discerning reader will locate in medieval thought many of the issues around which contemporary thought is polarized. The possibility of engaging the secular world in a mutually enriching encounter is in fact the paramount issue confronting Jewish thinkers in every century; and in the course of exploring this possibility, no thinker can avoid confronting the very same questions about interpreting Jewish texts and understanding Jewish law and Jewish experience that the medievals so ardently debated. The various schools of thought in the Middle Ages have themselves attained the status of traditions—albeit competing ones—within Judaism, and, to that extent, must be accorded the reverence and seriousness that Jews have always accorded tradition. In short, the reader who becomes conversant with Jewish thought in the Middle Ages will have become awakened and enriched both philosophically and Jewishly, and will have gained access not to this particular period alone, but to the whole wealth and range of Jewish reflection through the ages.

BOOKS ON JEWISH THOUGHT BEFORE 1600

Many readers will need a few terms defined before they can understand what books are included in this section. They are Mishnah, Talmud, and *midrash.*

According to tradition when the Torah, the Written Law, was given to the Jews at Sinai it was accompanied by additional explanations of its meaning and purpose known as the *Oral Law.* During the second and third centuries C.E., a group of scholars, most notably Rabbi Akiba (see Finkelstein's biography of Akiba in the section headed ANCIENT HISTORY AND ARCHEOLOGY) began the codifying and compiling of the Oral Law, including all shades of opinion on matters under dispute. This process reached its completion under Rabbi Judah Ha-Nasi and the material became known as the Mishnah (teaching). The Mishnah consists of six major sections, known as *sedarim* (orders), each of which is divided into a number of tractates. It is written in language remarkable for its density and allusiveness, and any reader not trained in the subject will find it difficult to understand even the simplest meaning of the text.

During a seven-hundred-year period, from approximately 200 B.C.E. to 500 C.E., scholarly debate took place concerning the precise meaning of various aspects of the Jewish law as expressed in the Mishnah. The Talmud is, essentially, a record of that debate. It is a dialogue with digressions, legal decisions, and stories and legends, and it expresses a variety of often contradictory opinions. Partly as a result of the way in which the Talmud was compiled, it is rare that any one subject is treated fully in one place.

The term *midrash* means "exposition" or "investigation," and refers to homiletical interpretations of Scripture. That definition fails to convey the incredible richness and complexity of midrashic thought. It deals with ethics, with the derivation of laws, with the expansion of the biblical text.

Holtz's *Back to the Sources* is a guide to studying the Jewish classics, including Talmud and *midrash*. It is very helpful. *The Judaic Tradition*, edited by Glatzner, is a comprehensive anthology of texts and includes informative explanatory notes.

Several editions of the Mishnah are available, including those of Danby and Blackman. Lipman's abridged edition is probably the best place to begin studying the Mishnah. *Pirke Avoth*, a section of Mishnah offering ethical teachings, is also accessible to nonscholars. Several editions available are listed later, under Herford. *The Essential Talmud* by Steinsaltz provides an excellent introduction to that subject. Rather than attempting to read the Talmud without first receiving a substantial education in its contents, most readers would do best to begin with excerpts such as those in Cohen's *Everyman's Talmud*.

The major collection of *midrash* is Freedman and Simon's edition of *The Midrash Rabbah*. It is, however, far too difficult for beginners. Porton's *Understanding Rabbinic Midrash* is very dry but much easier to understand. Montefiore and Loewe's *Rabbinic Anthology* includes material from the Talmud and a variety of midrashic sources. It is not easy reading, but it is an excellent introduction. Husik's *History of Medieval Jewish Philosophy* provides comprehensive coverage of the subject. *Jewish Ethics, Philosophy and Mysticism*, by Jacobs, includes a good selection of source materials and helpful commentaries. Maimonides, one of the most important Jewish thinkers, wrote several books described here. Twersky's *Maimonides Reader*, which includes excerpts from a variety of his works, is an excellent place to begin studying them. —R. S. F. & W. W.

Abrahams, Israel, ed.
Hebrew Ethical Wills. Jewish Publication Society, 1954, $10.95 pb.

Ethical wills are an important and distinctive Jewish tradition. Rather than bequeathing property, they are a parent's moral guidance to his or her survivors. The tradition can be traced back to the Bible, where Jacob and Moses, among others, produced them. Among the wills gathered here are those of Judah ibn Tibbon (notable for his specific instructions concerning the care and love of books), Maimonides, and Elijah, the **Gaon** of Vilna. In addition to the moral instruction they convey, these ethical wills provide touching and intimate insights into the personal life of Jews across the centuries. Hebrew and English texts are included on facing pages. *Ethical Wills: A Modern Jewish Treasury* (Schocken Books, 1983, $16.95), edited by Jack Riemer and Nathaniel Stampfer, is a more recent anthology of ethical wills, and includes several written by contemporary American Jews.

ArtScroll Mishnah Series. Mesorah.

Although only a few volumes of ArtScroll's Mishnah series have been published so far, they are among the best guides to the subject available for the serious student. (Lipman's abridged edition, listed later, is probably the easiest way to approach the subject.) The books are attractively designed and laid out. More important, they give the layperson the tools needed to begin understanding the meaning and implications of the text. Both the Hebrew and English texts are included, as are extensive introductions to each tractate, as well as diagrams, cross references, and commentaries. The titles currently available are

Seder Moed
Vol. 1(a): *Shabbos*, $16.95 hc, $13.95 pb.
Vol. 1(b): *Eruvin*, $16.95 hc, $13.95 pb.
Vol. 1(c): *Beitzah*, $10.95 hc, $7.95 pb.
Vol. 2: *Pesachim/Shakalim*, $16.95 hc, $13.95 pb.
Vol. 3: *Rosh Hashanah/Yoma/Succah*, $16.95 hc, $13.95 pb.
Vol. 4: *Taanis/Megillah/Moed Katan/Chagigah*, $14.95 hc, $11.95 pb.

Seder Nashim
Vol. 1(a): *Yevamos*, $16.95 hc, $13.95 pb.

Vol. 1(b): *Kesubos*, $16.95 hc,
$13.95 pb.
Vol. 2(a): *Nedarim*, $16.95 hc,
$13.95 pb.
Vol. 3: *Gittin and Kiddishin*,
$17.95 hc, $14.95 pb.

Appel, Gersion
The Concise Code of Jewish Law.
Ktav, 1977, $9.95 pb.

In the sixteenth century, Rabbi
Joseph Karo compiled a guide to
Jewish law that combined the Talmud with later rulings and put
all the material into a systematic
order. His book, called the *Shulkhan Arukh* (literally "the prepared table"), has remained the
major source for determining the
law ever since, and many Orthodox Jews turn to it for daily guidance in Jewish practice and
conduct. Appel, in his book, has
taken only those sections of the
Shulkhan Arukh pertaining to
prayer and religious observance
in daily life, combined them with
material from later commentaries, and provided brief explanatory notes. The topics covered
include daily prayer, synagogue
worship, Torah study, blessings
and grace after meals, and kosher dietary laws. This book is
valuable both for its clear exposition and for the insight it offers
the non-Orthodox into the rules
that guide Orthodox life. Also
see Solomon Ganzfried. It is
regrettable that no publisher
has undertaken the job of issuing
a complete English translation. It
would be a major undertaking—

the complete *Shulkhan Arukh* is a
massive work—but it would be a
significant contribution to American Jewish life.

Blackman, Philip
Mishnah. Judaica Press, 1977, 7
vols., $75.

This complete Mishnah in Hebrew and English is probably the
most widely available and used
edition. It is extensively annotated,
with an emphasis on the meaning
of the text. The English translation is more modern and easier
to read than some other editions.
Each tractate begins with a one-
page introduction explaining its
name, outlining its contents, and
placing it into its sequence in both
Talmuds. Beginners would be
wisest to begin their study of
Mishnah with an abridged edition. This set is most suitable for
reference purposes.

Bleich, J. David
*With Perfect Faith: The Founda-
tions of Jewish Belief.* Ktav, 1983,
$25 hc, $14.95 pb.

Maimonides' Thirteen Principles of Faith are as close to an
official creed as Judaism has ever
come. This book, meant primarily for use as a college or post-
graduate text, is an anthology
drawn from the major figures of
medieval Jewish thought and organized around those thirteen
principles. Included are excerpts
from the works of Saadia, Halevi,
Ibn Daud, Maimonides, Nahmanides, Gersonides, and others.
There is little explanatory text,

and only a few footnotes, making this book somewhat less useful than it might otherwise have been. It is a fine anthology, though.

Braude, William G., and Israel J. Kapstein, trans.
Pesikta de-Rab Kahana. Jewish Publication Society, 1975, $23.95.

The *Pesikta* is a good starting point for the study of midrashic literature, being more easily understandable than most other collections. It comprises a series of homilies on the Torah readings, known as portions, for festivals and special Sabbaths. *Pesikta* is Hebrew for "portion," and the material is attributed to Rav Kahana, hence the name. The translators won a National Jewish Book Award for this book.

Caplan, Samuel, and Harold U. Ribalow, eds.
The Great Jewish Books: And Their Influence on History. Horizon Press, $10.95 pb.

This is a genuinely useful book. The editors have taken excerpts from twelve of the "most important" books in Jewish history and combined them with useful commentaries and biographical sketches. The selections run from a few pages to more than twenty. You can argue with some of the selections—is Graetz's *History* really a "great" book?—but a book that introduces you to the Bible, Talmud, Rashi, Maimonides, *Shulkhan Arukh*, Theodor Herzl, and Hayyim Nachman Bialik has much to offer.

Cohen, Abraham, ed.
Everyman's Talmud. Schocken Books, 1975, $11.50 pb.

To make the rich material of the Talmud more accessible to the average reader, Cohen took selections from it and arranged them by subject. His emphasis is on the Talmud's ethical and religious teachings, although he also includes folklore and material dealing with jurisprudence. Although in no way a substitute for the real thing, this book does a commendable job of presenting the major ideas of the Talmud. It includes a short introduction on the history of the Talmud and related materials.

Cohen, Haim
Human Rights in Jewish Law. Ktav, 1984, $20.

This survey of human rights in Jewish legal history starts with the earliest biblical sources, continues through talmudic literature, and includes the legal codes of Maimonides (*Mishneh Torah*) and Joseph Karo (*Shulkhan Arukh*). Haim Cohen is a retired justice of the supreme court of the State of Israel.

Danby, Herbert, ed.
The Mishnah. Oxford University Press, 1933, $39.95.

This translation of the Mishnah is in clear English and spells out many of the terse and cryptic references. Compared to the Blackman edition, Danby's translation is somewhat more readable, but the Hebrew text is not

included. There are some footnotes, but they are comparatively
limited, intended only to explain
allusions and clarify confusing
points, not to be a commentary.
An introduction provides some
background on the origin and
development of the Mishnah, its
arrangement, interpretation, and
the various Hebrew editions.
Given the difficulties of understanding the implications and
meaning of the Mishnah in Jewish law without extensive commentaries, the Danby edition is
probably of greatest value as a
one-volume reference to readers
already somewhat familiar with
its contents and concepts.

Epstein, Isadore, ed.
The Soncino Talmud. Soncino
Press, 18 vols., $375.

A complete English translation
of the Talmud. Since the Talmud
consists of the **Gemara**, which is
the major interpretation of the
Mishnah, plus several other commentaries, all arranged on the
page around the Mishnah, it is
difficult to achieve a simple and
straightforward translation that
is fully satisfactory. The Soncino
edition is as good as anyone has
yet done. For most people, the best
way to get the flavor of Talmudic
discourse is to buy *The Treatise
Ta'anit of the Babylonian Talmud*,
edited and translated by Henry
Malter (Jewish Publication Society, $6.50 pb). If dipping your
toe into the waters of one tractate
appeals to you, you can always

then go for a swim in the ocean
of the Talmud.

**Freedman, H., and Maurice
Simon, trans. and eds.**
The Midrash Rabbah. Soncino
Press, 1977, 10-vol. set, $165.

This monumental collection of
midrashic literature was written
from the sixth through the twelfth
centuries. It is enormously varia-
ble in nature—sometimes cryptic
and intellectual, sometimes stun-
ningly clear and evocative. The
price of this set and its complexity make it most suitable for advanced students and libraries, but
everyone can read it with profit
if he or she is willing to work
hard enough.

Ganzfried, Solomon
*Code of Jewish Law (Kitzur
Shulhan Aruh).* Translated by
Hyman E. Goldin. Hebrew
Publishing, 1963, $8.95.

Originally published in 1864,
Ganzfried's edition of the *Shulkhan Arukh* achieved immediate
and widespread popularity among
Orthodox Jews. This popularity
may have reflected its emphasis
on the laws of everyday life and
ritual, and its attempt to be easily
understandable by laypeople. The
book is an abridgement of the full
Shulkhan Arukh and in many cases
presents only one view of an issue. As the only English-language edition covering all parts
of the *Shulkhan Arukh* (the Appel
edition listed earlier contains only
selected chapters), the Ganzfried
edition is of value. Its major

drawback is that Ganzfried represents a particularly stringent approach to Jewish law and is not the best guide to contemporary Jewish observance.

Gersh, Harry
The Sacred Books of the Jews. Stein & Day, 1972, $4.95 pb.

A basic introduction to the major religious works of Judaism: the Bible, Talmud, *midrash*, responsa, legal codes, *kabbalah*, prayer book, and important commentaries. Gersh provides extensive quotations from the sources and his explanations are easy to understand. His approach, which includes acceptance of the human authorship of the Bible, will not appeal to the Orthodox. But his book is a good survey and well suited to beginners.

Ginzberg, Louis
On Jewish Law and Lore. Atheneum, 1977, $5.95 pb.

Ginzberg was a professor of Talmud at the Jewish Theological Seminary from 1902 until his death in 1953 and was one of the greatest twentieth-century Jewish scholars. His *Legends of the Jews* (see the section headed BIBLE) is an unquestioned masterpiece. This book collects six of his essays, including the significance of *halakhah* for Jewish history, the codification of Jewish law, the *kabbalah*, Jewish folklore, allegorical interpretation of Scripture, and an introduction to the Palestinian Talmud. They are rewarding reading.

Glatzer, Nahum N., ed.
The Judaic Tradition. Behrman House, 1982, $9.95 pb.

Originally published in three separate volumes by Beacon Press in the 1960s, this book collects more than two hundred texts. The first section includes biblical Apocrypha, Dead Sea writings, Philo, Josephus, Talmud, *midrash*, and other works from antiquity. The second section draws from the Middle Ages, and includes works such as the prayer book and **Zohar**, well-known figures such as Maimonides, and those less well known, such as Nathan Hannover and Judah Loew ben Bezalel. The third section covers the modern world and includes Leopold Zunz, Moses Mendelssohn, and Abraham Isaac Kook. Each excerpt is introduced with helpful explanatory notes. Its bulk makes this book unwieldy, but its contents make it worth owning.

Ha-Levi, Judah
Kuzari. Translated from the Arabic by Hartwig Hirschfeld. Schocken Books, 1964, $4.95 pb.

Judah Ha-Levi (1075–1141) was a Spanish poet and philosopher whose religious poetry still survives, some of it incorporated into the liturgy. His love of Zion has been an inspiration to Jewish nationalists over the centuries. *Kuzari*, his major philosophic work, is a Platonic dialogue in which a rabbi, a Christian, a Moslem, and an Aristotelian philosopher engage in a disputation before the king of the Khazars, who at the end of the debate adopts Judaism as the state religion. Ha-Levi argues strongly for the superiority of revelation over philosophy and for the redeeming power of Judaism. The book is one of the classic works of Jewish thought, clearly written and readable. It is based on a real historical incident. In the eighth century, King Bulan of the Khazars—a small kingdom on the Volga, in the Crimea—did convert to Judaism, and made it the state religion—for reasons that may have been more political than religious. In *The Thirteenth Tribe*, Arthur Koestler argued (less than persuasively) that modern Jews are actually descended from the Khazars.

Herford, R. Travers
Talmud and Apocrypha. Ktav, 1971, $11.95 pb.

An English Unitarian, Herford (1860–1905) spent much of his life studying the early period of Judaism, the Pharisees in particular. *The Pharisees* and *Pharisaism, Its Aim and Its Method* are both unfortunately out of print. They are worth looking for. *Talmud and Apocrypha* starts with the Old Testament as the main source for later ethical teachings, and then traces its divergent development in rabbinic literature and in the nonrabbinic apocrypha and pseudepigrapha. Herford is unusual among Christian theologians for his understanding of the Oral Law and Talmud as a continuation of the prophetic spirit. The Apocrypha—seen by many Christians as the essence of prophecy—he viewed as preserving only its appearance, not its core.

The Ethics of the Talmud: Sayings of the Fathers. Schocken Books, 1962, $5.95 pb.

The *Pirke Avoth* is a collection of sayings and ethical teachings of Jewish sages from the third century B.C.E. to the third century C.E. Although a part of the Mishnah, it has no Talmudic commentary. It is widely looked to as a source of piety and devotion to learning and is included in the prayer book. Herford's edition includes the Hebrew text and an English translation. It is scholarly in tone, with extensive and detailed notes, information on the historical and religious background, and textual explanations. It would be perfect for all readers, even beginners, if its typography and layout were clearer and easier to follow. A reasonably priced hardcover edition of the *Avoth* is available from the World Zionist Organization as part of its Elucidated Mishnah Series (1984, $10). It includes a lucid translation, commentaries drawn from traditional sources, and new commentaries by Pinhas Kehati. It does not include as much background information, but is otherwise excellent. *The Living Talmud* by Judah

Goldin (New American Library, 1957, $3.95 pb) is another excellent translation and includes a brief introductory essay and selected traditional commentaries.

Holtz, Barry W., ed.
Back to the Sources: Reading the Classic Jewish Texts. Summit Books, 1984, $19.95.

This collection is almost indispensable for anyone pursuing a course of self-study in the Jewish classics. Included are a series of essays by experts in the field, not just telling about the texts but also explaining how to study them. The eight sections include Bible, Talmud, *midrash*, medieval Bible commentaries, medieval philosophy, *kabbalah*, the Hasidic masters, and prayer and the prayer book. Each area is described in terms of its history, perspective, and significance. Among the contributors are Arthur Green, Alan Mintz, and Edward L. Greenstein. Each chapter is followed by a "Where to Go from Here" bibliography with advice for further study. Although advanced knowledge isn't needed to read this book, it has some weaknesses as an introduction, since it sometimes leaves things unsaid. The flaws are minor, though, and this book has much to teach virtually any reader.

Husik, Isaac
A History of Mediaeval Jewish Philosophy. Atheneum, 1969, $5.95 pb.

Although originally published seventy years ago, Husik's book remains the best history of the subject. Following a general introduction, it surveys the thought of the major medieval Jewish philosophers from Isaac Israeli and Saadia Gaon through Ibn Gabirol and Maimonides to Gersonides and Crescas. This is not a work of analysis. Rather, it presents the ideas of these men as they themselves might have summarized them. It is up to the reader to understand the implications. Reflecting the biases of the time at which Husik wrote, mysticism and kabbalistic thought are dismissed as "obscurantism" and not covered at all. Despite its limitations, this is a very useful book.

Jacobs, Louis, ed.
Jewish Ethics, Philosophy and Mysticism. Behrman House, 1969, $5.95 pb.

A useful supplement to Husik's book (described above), this is a source book with material drawn primarily from the medieval Jewish thinkers. It is meant for use in education, but there's no reason to limit it to that purpose. The brief selections are interspersed with explanatory remarks by Jacobs that aid our understanding. Unlike Husik, Jacobs appreciates the intellectual quality of much Jewish mysticism. His selection includes material from the *Zohar* and from the writings of the Baal Shem Tov and Abraham Isaac Kook, among others.

Jastrow, Marcus

A Dictionary of the Targumim, the Talmud Babli and Yerushalmi, and the Midrashic Literature. Judaica Press, 1985, $15.

First published in two volumes in 1903, now combined into one "compact" edition nearly three inches thick, the Jastrow dictionary is still valuable for serious students of rabbinic literature. The words are given in vocalized Hebrew, and explained in context to elucidate shades of meaning. It is a comprehensive work, including the many words derived from Greek, Latin, and Persian that occur in the Talmud. This edition was produced using photo offset printing from an older edition, and the quality of the type is occasionally poor. Its merit as a reference and its reasonable price compensate for this.

Leviant, Curt, ed.

Masterpieces of Hebrew Literature: A Treasury of 2000 Years of Jewish Creativity. Ktav, 1969, $14.95 pb.

A very good anthology spanning the period from postbiblical Apocrypha to the eighteenth century. It includes examples of every major genre of Hebrew literature, including liturgical poetry, travelogues, ethical wills, *midrashim*, prayers, responsa, Bible commentaries, and legal codes. Leviant has provided brief introductions to each section placing the writers and their works into perspective, but there are no footnotes or other explanatory remarks, leaving readers somewhat on their own. For that reason, the book may be best suited for classroom use where there is a teacher to help explain things.

Lipman, Eugene J., ed. and trans.

The Mishnah: Oral Teachings of Judaism. Schocken Books, 1974, $7.95 pb.

For readers who want to get a taste of Mishnah, this is probably the best choice. It includes brief selections from each tractate, all with short explanatory introductions and a list of the biblical sources. The notes and commentaries are clear, straightforward, and concise, concentrating on the meaning of the text rather than on scholarly issues. While some background in Judaica is useful for full understanding, Lipman does not assume that his readers have advanced knowledge.

Maimonides

Maimonides (1135–1204)—Rabbi Moses ben Maimon—known by his initials as the Rambam, is one of the greatest figures in Jewish history. Unable to live in Palestine, then devastated by the Crusades, Maimonides settled in Egypt where he became spiritual head of the Cairo Jewish community and physician to Saladin's vizier. The high quality of his work and its enormous quantity are impressive evidence of his brilliance and productivity. In addition to his works on Jewish subjects, he was the author of many medical papers, including treatises on asthma, hemorrhoids, poisons, healthy living, and sexual intercourse. His tomb, in Tiberias, bears the inscription: "From Moses to Moses, there was none like unto Moses." Readers interested in learning about Maimonides should read Heschel's biography of him described in the section on MEDIEVAL AND MODERN HISTORY. They might also refer to *Maimonides: Torah and Philosophic Quest* by David Hartman (Jewish Publication Society, 1976, $7.95 pb), an impressive synthesis of his thought that won a National Book Award.

Maimonides' analysis of the forms of charity remains influential today. And, although there is nothing that can be considered an "official" creed of Judaism, the Thirteen Articles of Faith he propounded come as close to universal acceptance as anything has. They have been incorporated into the daily prayer book. Among them are: "I firmly believe that the Creator, blessed be his name, is the Creator and Ruler of all created things, and that he alone has made, does make, and ever will make all things. I firmly believe that all the words of the Prophets are true. I firmly believe that the Creator, blessed be his name, rewards those who keep his commands, and punishes those who transgress his commands. I firmly believe in the coming of the Messiah; and although he may tarry, I daily wait for his coming."

The Commandments. Translated by Charles B. Chavel. Soncino Press, 1967, 2 vols. $35 hc, $25 pb.

The basic concept of the Jewish religion is the observance of *mitzvot*—the divine commandments. Our task is to understand the will of God and to live according to his wishes. By the fourth century C.E., the ancient sages had decided that the Torah contained 613 commandments: 248 positive commandments and 365 negative ones. Strangely, several centuries passed before an attempt was made to enumerate all 613, and that attempt was not generally accepted as successful. In *The Commandments*, Maimonides set out to explain all the commandments given in the Torah. A foreword explains the principles he used to decide which to include and which to exclude. This is followed by a list of the commandments, with explanations of what they mean and commentaries where needed.

Ethical Writings of Maimonides. Edited and translated by Raymond L. Weiss and Charles Butterworth. New York University Press, 1975, $25 hc; Dover, 1984, $6 pb.

A collection of ethical writings by Maimonides. Not as central to an understanding of Maimonides as the *Mishneh Torah*, but fascinating and illuminating reading. This anthology includes "Laws Concerning Character Traits," "Eight Chapters," and five other works.

Guide for the Perplexed. Smith, no date, $16 hc; Dover (translated by M. Friedlander), 1904, $6.95 pb.

The perplexed of the title are those torn between the teachings of Torah and of secular philosophy. First published in 1190, the *Guide* was written to reconcile reason with faith, to demonstrate that Judaism was rational and understandable in the context of Aristotelian thought, in fact rational and understandable *only* in that context. Maimonides argues that the Torah text cannot all be taken literally, that especially those passages ascribing human qualities to God must be seen as metaphorical. Maimonides' acceptance of many aspects of Aristotelian thought caused a strong negative response among other Jewish thinkers of the time. In 1305 people under the age of twenty-five were banned from reading the *Guide*. The protests have since died down, and today Maimonides is considered acceptable by even the most Orthodox.

A Maimonides Reader. Edited by Isadore Twersky. Behrman House, 1972, $9.95 pb.

For many readers, this is probably the single best volume of Maimonides' work to buy. Twersky, who is the outstanding Maimonides scholar of our time, has written an informative and insightful introduction. He then presents a lengthy excerpt from the *Mishneh Torah*, the central work by Maimonides, a shorter excerpt from the *Guide for the Perplexed*, and miscellaneous other writings, including some of his correspondence. Each selection is prefaced with an introductory note.

Mishneh Torah: Maimonides' Code of Law and Ethics. Edited by Philip Birnbaum. Hebrew Publishing, 1974, $9.95 pb.

The Talmud, the source of Jewish law, does not offer anything like an orderly presentation of its rulings. Its vast size also complicates the task of finding the appropriate section. Maimonides apparently found this situation intolerable, and set out to produce a systematic and comprehensive codification of Jewish law. In a letter he remarked that he undertook the task "to save himself in his advanced age the trouble of consulting the Talmud on every occasion." The *Mishneh Torah* was the result, the fruit of ten years of labor. It covers every topic in the Talmud, presenting the findings in a terse and direct style, without mention of the sources or divergent views. Where the original had disagreements, Maimonides presents only his view—something that was a cause of great controversy. He also rejected customs he saw as based on superstition. While not all his conclusions were universally accepted, the brilliance of his arrangement made the *Mishneh Torah* the model for all later codes of Jewish law, including the *Turim* (fourteenth century) and the *Shulkhan Arukh* (sixteenth century). Birnbaum's edition is greatly abridged but retains the flavor and the substance of the original. His introduction is clear and very helpful.

Matt, Daniel Chanan, trans. and ed.
Zohar: The Book of Enlightenment. Paulist Press, 1983, $12.95 hc, $9.95 pb.

The Zohar, literally *The Book of Splendor*, is a cryptic and esoteric work of great power. It is a mystical commentary on the Torah, attributed to Rabbi Shimon ben Yohai, a second-century sage. Its actual authorship and origin are obscure, although it is generally believed to have been written by Moses ben Shemtov de Leon, a thirteenth-century mystic. Its subject matter is vast and profound—the origin of the universe, the redemption of humanity, the oneness of God and humanity. It is utterly impossible to summarize the Zohar, but there are two important things to know about it. First, it is a unique work on which virtually all Jewish mysticism has drawn. Second, it makes our actions quite literally the key

to the future of the universe, teaching that it is up to humanity to "mend the world" and reclaim the divine sparks. This edition, part of Paulist Press's excellent Classics of Western Spirituality Series, offers a selection of passages, beautifully translated, extensively annotated, and attractively printed. (See Maurice Simon's complete edition, described later.)

Montefiore, C. G., and H. Loewe, eds.
A Rabbinic Anthology. Schocken Books, 1974, $16.95 pb.

This wonderfully meaty and stimulating anthology of rabbinic literature focuses exclusively on religion and ethics. The sources are primarily the Talmud and *midrash*, but a broad range of other rabbinic material is included. The excerpts are mostly quite short—rarely as long as a page—and are organized around such major topics as "The Nature and Character of God and His Relations with Man," "Study, Practice and Goodness," "Hope and Faith; Miracles," and "Pity, Forgiveness and Love." Montefiore, who was a Reform Jew, and Loewe, who was Orthodox, each wrote a lengthy introduction discussing rabbinic literature and their understanding of it. There are also extensive commentaries interspersed with the excerpts. Although not easy going, there is no better introduction to this body of writings.

Nadich, Judah
Jewish Legends of the Second Commonwealth. Jewish Publication Society, 1983, $25.

The Second Commonwealth—the period from the return of Jews from the Babylonian Exile in the sixth century B.C.E. to the destruction of the Temple by the Romans in 70 C.E.—was one of the most fertile and religiously creative in all of Jewish history. It was during this time that the final books of the Bible were written and the whole of it was made canonical, that the Mishnah was written down, and the Talmud was debated and recorded. In this book, which does for the Second Commonwealth what Ginzberg's *Legends of the Jews* did for the biblical period, Nadich has woven legends drawn from a variety of sources into a narrative that presents the major people, events, and ideas of the time. The substantial scholarly apparatus is kept separate from the text, so it is available if you want it, unobtrusive if you don't.

Neusner, Jacob

One of the most prolific of Jewish scholars, Neusner has written extensively on the Talmud as well as many other issues of Jewish concern such as education and the relationship of American Jewry to Israel. He is codirector of the program in Judaic studies at Brown University.

Invitation to Talmud: A Teaching Book. Harper & Row, 1984, $18.95.

Not so much a book about the Talmud as a book about how to study the Talmud. Neusner takes one chapter of the Mishnah, shows how its meaning and implications can be learned, then moves through the various commentaries on it that are found in the Talmud, discussing their contents and method. In addition to a close reading of the texts, Neusner generalizes on the methods and modes of thought and argument they exemplify. He also provides background information on the Talmud, discussing in particular how its creators were able to conceive of practical and critical thinking as holy. Neusner can be preoccupied with methodological issues, but this is a useful book and a good starting point for readers wishing to learn how to approach the study of Talmud.

Neusner, Jacob, ed.
Our Sages, God, and Israel: An Anthology of the Talmud of the Land of Israel. Rossel Books, 1984, $19.95.

Actually there isn't any such thing as *the* Talmud—there are, in fact, *two* Talmuds. Both are commentaries on the same Mishnah, and both follow the same general format, but the two versions were compiled in different places at different times. The best-known and most widely referred-to edition is called the Babylonian

Talmud and was completed around 500 C.E. It is regarded as the most authoritative edition. The other edition is called the Palestinian Talmud, and is also known as the Jerusalem Talmud, or the Talmud of the Land of Israel. It is of selections from that Talmud that this book is composed. The Palestinian Talmud was completed about 100 years earlier than the Babylonian, is much shorter, and has fewer of the nonlegal digressions that are so filled with historical information, biblical exegesis, or ethical teaching. Neusner's anthology is composed primarily of passages that deal with "holiness and salvation" rather than commentary on Mishnah. The selections are arranged by subject.

Understanding Rabbinic Judaism: From Talmudic to Modern Times. Ktav, 1974, $11.95 pb.

An anthology of essays by various scholars on aspects of rabbinic thought and on notable authorities who, as Neusner describes them, continue to have an impact on the mind of contemporary Judaism. The topics covered include rabbinic mysticism, talmudic theology, the centrality of *halakhah*, and the career of Rashi; those anthologized include Mordecai Kaplan, Eliezer Berkovits, Louis Ginzberg, and Solomon Schechter.

Patai, Raphael, trans. and ed.
The Messiah Texts: Jewish Legends of Three Thousand Years. Wayne State University Press, 1979, $17.95.

The Jewish belief in the coming of the Messiah has been an undying thread for many centuries. Patai, who is a distinguished anthropologist, may be uniquely qualified to produce this anthology. In it, following a general introduction on Messianic ideology and its importance in Jewish history, he has assembled his own translations of texts dealing with the coming of the Messiah. His sources range from the earliest intimations in the Bible to modern authors, and include folktales, apocalyptic fantasies, and prophetic parables. Patai has also included information on the false messiahs who have cropped up in Jewish history, and on the explanations that have been advanced for the failure of the Messiah to appear so far. Some of the texts are as short as one sentence, others are several pages long. They make compelling reading.

Porton, Gary G.
Understanding Rabbinic Midrash. Ktav, 1985, $11.95 pb.

This book collects excerpts from six major midrashic works, among them *Midrash Rabbah*, each followed by comments clarifying the text, conclusions discussing its meaning, and notes on sources and references. The tone is textbookish and dry, and this is not a good choice for the general reader. It is, however, quite useful for students, since it presents not just results, but also a sense of the methods needed to understand what are often obscure, esoteric texts.

Schechter, Solomon
Aspects of Rabbinic Theology: Major Concepts of the Talmud. Schocken Books, 1961, $8.95 pb.

The author of this book was a founder of Conservative Judaism and for many years the president of the Jewish Theological Seminary of America. His scholarship was impeccable, but he managed to combine his learning with popular appeal and to write books that can be grasped by the general reader. He felt that for Jewish theology to be fully understood it must be experienced emotionally, that it must be "felt" as well as "known." In this book he presents rabbinic opinion on a number of theological issues, as much as possible letting the sources speak for themselves. The material has been arranged by topic into chapters covering such subjects as "God and the World," "Election of Israel," and "Sin as Rebellion."

Simon, Maurice, ed.
The Zohar. Soncino Press, 1934, 5 vols., $75.

The most complete English-language version of the Zohar. For most readers, the drastically abridged edition by Daniel Chanan Matt is a more sensible purchase—the translation is more readable, the commentaries more extensive. But the Matt edition constitutes only 2 percent of the entire work. For those students who cannot read the original or who can but need help to do so, the Soncino edition is very useful.

Steinsaltz, Adin
The Essential Talmud. Translated from the Hebrew by Chaya Galai. Basic Books, 1977, $15 hc, $7.95 pb.

The best introduction to the Talmud available. Steinsaltz is one of Israel's foremost scholars. He writes with unusual clarity and with enormous learning. Here, he covers the history of the Talmud, its structure and content, and its methods and modes of thought. This book is accessible even to beginners, but never condescends or oversimplifies. It is the ideal starting point for almost anyone interested in learning about the Talmud.

Diversity and Dissent: Competing Trends in Modern Jewish Thought

Charles M. Raffel

The attempt to define neatly a particular period in history is rightly mocked by the cartoon that shows a cave dweller peering out on a bright sunny day and exclaiming, "Hooray, the Dark Ages must be over!" As opposed to the cave dweller, the careful observer must realize that the movement of the Jews out of the ghetto into the mainstream of Western living— a transformation marked both by immeasurable gains and tragic losses—did not germinate suddenly one night and flourish before daybreak. The changes that mark modernity for the Jews—a striking deemphasis of the exclusive role of religious law and tradition in shaping one's life, a wider range of economic opportunities and greater political freedom—help to initiate the agenda for modern Jewish thought.

The agenda, if not the approach, is very much tied to ancient and medieval concerns: to distill somehow the essence of Judaism and determine the proper life's goal for the Jew. Nevertheless, a decisive change in method predominates. If we follow Harry Wolfson's sweeping definition, modern thought, by its nature, is that system of thought, after Spinoza, that maintains a loyalty to reason, but abandons its prior loyalty to Scripture. Considered solely by chronology, however, modern Jewish thought contains both innovative style and substance, on the

Dr. Charles M. Raffel holds the Erna S. Michael Chair in Jewish Philosophy at Yeshiva University's Stern College for Women. He has written essays and reviews in the field of both medieval and contemporary Jewish thought.

one hand, and business as usual, on the other. The Jewish response and contribution to modernity is at times flexible, pliant, and adaptive and at times resistant, cautious, and conservative. Modern thinkers include mystics and rationalists, reformers and neo-Orthodox, critical scholars and pietists, Zionists and anti-Zionists, capitalists and socialists, Yiddishists and Hebraists. Not surprisingly, between these polar extremes lies a wide area of overlap and interchange. But first and foremost, modernity means change and contrastingly different attitudes and responses to change.

There is no set table *(Shulkhan Arukh)* for modern Jewish thought. The general reader is faced with a perplexing challenge, if not collision course, of competition for the very soul of Jewish belief. The true definition of the most basic elements of any conception of Judaism—God, Israel, and Torah—is subjected to radical and intensive examination and reexamination.

God, sovereign of the universe, is transcendent. He is an idea. Or is he a process? But, then again, we are told he is being. The Hasid insists that God is immanent in daily sorrows and joys. For Martin Buber, the divine moment is the moment of true communication, of dialogue, between beings. Or is God in fact reason, and is not the divine moment that of ethical perfection? In dark and the darkest times, our modern thinkers ask, "Where is God?" and listen in chilling silence or abandon hope for a comprehensible answer.

Israel, our thinkers continue to argue, is anything but a place, it is a spiritual vision. It is an idea. Point and counterpoint. The vicious wave after wave of modern anti-Semitism demands an unflinching response. Israel is a place, it must be a place. Israel is not a notion, not just a dream, but a nation. Or is Israel ultimately the union of likeminded, fiercely committed souls that transcends time and space?

The Torah is turned over and over. Are the *mitzvot* (commandments) obligatory on all Jews forever? "Are all the *mitzvot* obligatory?" someone questions, first in a whisper and then in a shout. "The Torah is not in heaven, it is in the hands of people," we are reminded. The Torah needs to be personalized, the teaching must be modernized, emended, extended, reformed, and reconstructed. The many competing voices seem to make it unmistakably clear that while Jews have obligations, they certainly also have choices.

These differing configurations of God-Israel-Torah inhabit many different constellations in the course of modern Jewish thought. The reader may feel, at times, in need of a chart to identify them all. Jewish philosophy, by its own paradoxical nature, has always adapted its expressions to prevailing philosophical theories. The reader so inclined may identify the Jewish views based on a Kantian model, the search for the religion of reason in Jewish sources, Idealists and pragmatists and an unending assortment of existentialists. There is indeed a cataclysmic shift to the individual, to the feelings and vision of the existential "I." A concomitant search, born in both desperation and joy, to find a new sense of community is also undertaken. This new thinking, based on what the "I" sees and feels, needs a new home. The Jew is a noun in search of an adjective, be it cultural, Conservative, Reform, Orthodox, biological, Zionist, socialist, secularist, and even "self-hating."

And yet still a Jew. Listen to the individual voices, for among the thinkers you will find no real movements here. Listen to Moses Mendelssohn, Hermann Cohen, Franz Rosenzweig, and Martin Buber. Whatever their view of the blessings and curses of modernity, do they not analyze, speculate, argue, explain, define, defend, attack, and teach so that deeply felt Jewish expression and experience will take root and flourish?

Recollecting the varied configurations of God-Israel-Torah in modern Jewish thought, almost all is brought into question and, taken collectively, precious little is resolved conclusively. The general reader should approach modern Jewish thought knowing that the questions will far outweigh the answers. The reader who is particularly anxious with a multiplicity of options may be comforted by at least half of Alfred North Whitehead's dictum, "Seek simplicity and mistrust it."

Modern Jewish thought reflects a time of questioning, of redefinition, of attack and response in both realms of theory and practice. For the serious reader, the one who takes his or her reading seriously, modern Jewish thought offers a demanding freedom that is challenged by the need to define, to see between options, and to make choices on just about every question of consequence to Jews and the future of Judaism.

BOOKS ON JEWISH THOUGHT FROM 1600–PRESENT

A comprehensive collection of texts by the major Jewish thinkers of the past two centuries can be found in Glatzer's *Modern Jewish Thought,* which is an excellent starting point for students of the field. For readers who wish to learn more about the specific beliefs of the various branches of Judaism, several books are available. *Understanding Conservative Judaism* by Gordis, *Dynamic Judaism* by Kaplan, and *Reform Judaism Today* by Borowitz all provide good introductions to (respectively) Conservative, Reconstructionist, and Reform Judaism. No one book systematically details the beliefs of Orthodoxy, but Wouk's *This Is My God* is a clear and nonscholarly presentation of the basics. *To Be a Jew* by Donin, described in the HOW-TO section, focuses more on practice than theory, but is also an outstanding presentation of Orthodox belief. *Profiles in American Judaism* by Raphael (AMERICAN JEWISH HISTORY) provides an introduction to the current state of the major branches of Judaism in America. Readers who want to gain a sense of modern Jewish thought should look at the books of Buber, Heschel, and Soloveitchik.

To readers wishing to learn about mysticism, Bokser's *Jewish Mystical Tradition* is an anthology with a broad and interesting selection of documents. Scholem's *Major Trends in Jewish Mysticism* is a difficult but important study of the subject. A more accessible book is Weiner's *9-1/2 Mystics,* which includes information on mystical theories and descriptions of mystics. Hasidism, a modern Jewish movement that incorporates many mystical strands, is described well in Jacobs's *Hasidic Thought.* A more impassioned, less analytical approach is taken in Wiesel's *Souls on Fire,* which portrays some of Hasidism's founders.

—R. S. F. & W. W.

Adler, Morris, ed.
Jewish Heritage Reader. Taplinger, 1965, $5.95 pb.

A wide-ranging and stimulating collection of short essays—most under five pages in length—on Jewish topics. The contents, originally published in B'nai B'rith's quarterly, *Jewish Heritage*, cover such subjects as Jewish chosenness, sex in the Jewish tradition, Christianity and Judaism, conversion, Bible translations, Yiddish writers, American Jewish life, and the problem of evil.

Aron, Milton
Ideas and Ideals of the Hassidim. Citadel Press/Stuart, 1969, $7.95 hc, $5.95 pb.

A good introduction to Hasidic thought, which the author sees as the single most influential Jewish religious movement of the past two centuries. Aron examines the lives of the Hasidic masters, looks at the conflicts that arose within the movement and between it and other Jewish movements, and offers "gleanings" from many Hasidic masters. Although it lacks the passion and fervor of Elie Wiesel's *Souls on Fire* (described later), it is more systematically organized.

Baeck, Leo
The Essence of Judaism. Translated from the German by Victor Grubenwieser and Leonard Pearl. Schocken Books, 1948, $8.25 pb.

In this book, originally published in Germany in 1922, Baeck describes Judaism as a "classical" religion of action, one that works to improve the world, as distinct from Christianity, which is a "romantic" religion of feeling. He sees Judaism as the supreme expression of morality, a religion that is universal in content and teaching while being particularistic in its historic expression. Baeck, a Reform rabbi, was a leader of the German Jewish community during World War II. A moving account of his life is presented in Leonard Baker's *Days of Sorrow and Pain* (see the HOLOCAUST section).

Band, Arnold J., ed. and trans.
Nahman of Bratslav: The Tales. Paulist Press, 1978, $9.95 pb.

Part of Paulist Press's excellent series, the Classics of Western Spirituality, this is one of the more accessible editions of Rabbi Nahman's tales. Nahman of Bratslav (1772?–1810?) was an early Hasidic master. He emphasized faith and prayer over intellect, and his allegorical tales are fascinating but often perplexing and obscure. They blend intense kabbalistic mysticism with great narrative artistry. This edition includes
all thirteen tales, a biographical introduction, information on the text and translation, and a section of scholarly, somewhat academic commentaries. See also Adin Steinsaltz's *Beggars and Prayers*, described later. *Tormented*

Master by Arthur Green (Schocken Books, 1981, $11.95 pb) is a biography of Rabbi Nahman with an emphasis on psychological analysis.

Blau, Joseph L.
Modern Varieties of Judaism. Columbia University Press, 1966, $22 hc, $9 pb.

Blau views the changes and adjustments Judaism has made in the past two centuries as a response to the European Enlightenment and to the emancipation of Western European Jewry, which allowed Jews to enter into the secular world around them. His conviction that "every living religion is perennially changing, adapting its principles, its practices, its rituals, its beliefs, and its theology to meet the needs of the varying times and places in which its adherents live" may not be acceptable to Orthodox Jews. To those who can accept that hypothesis, Blau's discussion of the emergence of Orthodox, Conservative, and Reform Judaism is stimulating and thoughtful.

Bleich, J. David
Contemporary Halakhic Problems, Vol. 1. Ktav/Yeshiva University Press, 1977, $20 hc.

Contemporary Halakhic Problems, Vol. 2. Ktav/Yeshiva University Press, 1983, $20.

Bleich is a distinguished talmudic scholar. He is dispassionate, detached, and writes from a viewpoint that rarely allows for leniency or flexibility in the law. In these books he applies a traditional approach to the *halakhah* (the Jewish law) to a variety of contemporary social, political, technological, and religious problems—from transsexual surgery and the use of automatic cash machines to cannibalism and the use of disposable diapers. For each question, Bleich delineates the issues, discusses the positions taken by various rabbinic scholars, and examines the areas of disagreement. Among the topics covered are intermarriage, autopsies, teachers' unions, capital punishment, and the modern State of Israel. While the writing is clear, a knowledge of the sources is required to follow Bleich's reasoning.

Bokser, Ben Zion, ed. and trans.
The Jewish Mystical Tradition. Pilgrim Press, 1981, $15 hc, $9.95 pb.

A broad cross section of the most significant Jewish mystical writings, from the Bible and Talmud through *kabbalah,* Hasidic teachings, and such modern thinkers as Rabbi Abraham Isaac Kook. In between are some surprises (Maimonides, who is not generally thought of as a mystic), and items not usually anthologized (something by Nahman of Bratslav *other* than one of his tales). Included are brief biographical notes, a discussion of Jewish mysticism as compared to other mystical traditions, and an overview of the mystical dimension in human experience. This is a first-rate collection of source materials.

Borowitz, Eugene B.

Rabbi Borowitz is an articulate spokesman for the ideas of Reform Judaism. He has written several books, edited several more, and is the founder and editor of *Sh'ma* (see the PERIODICALS section). He does not hesitate to take a stand on controversial issues and his intelligent and forceful presentation makes for informative and interesting reading.

Liberal Judaism. Union of American Hebrew Congregations, 1984, $8.95 pb.

An exploration of some basic religious issues from a "liberal" Jewish perspective (mostly Reform, but encompassing more than that). The subjects covered include whether the Jews are a Chosen People, whether there is life after death, the reasons Reform Jews do not feel compelled to observe all the commandments and traditions, why religions differ, and what the State of Israel means to Jews. Major alternative points of view are discussed, and where a consensus seems to exist, it is given.

Reform Judaism Today. Behrman House, 1983, $9.95 pb.

This is three books in one, adding up to the best introduction to Reform Judaism available.

The books, originally published separately, are *Reform in the Process of Change, What We Believe,* and *How We Live.* In a direct and honest manner, Borowitz discusses the conflicts and tensions within the Reform movement, looks at how the movement has evolved over the past hundred years, explains the ways in which it is the "quintessential American form of Jewish life and worship," and offers his thoughts on where the movement is headed. It's a first-class piece of work.

Buber, Martin

Although his philosophical works are not in the mainstream of traditional Jewish thought, Martin Buber is one of modern Judaism's most interesting and appealing personalities. Born in Germany in 1878, he was an early and active Zionist. He prepared an influential translation of the Bible (see BIBLE), and wrote on a variety of Jewish subjects. His approach to Judaism was strongly influenced by Hasidism. (See Maurice Friedman's biography of Buber, described later.)

I and Thou. Translated by Walter Kaufmann, Scribner's, 1970, $20 hc, $6.95 pb; translated by Ronald Gregor Smith, Scribner's, 1984, $3.95 pb.

When asked why his company had two different editions of *I and Thou* in print, Charles Scribner III said it was much like the situation with "classic" Coca-Cola: they thought they had a better product but the public demanded that the original be brought back. Of the two translations, the more recent by Walter Kaufmann is arguably the more accurate and precise. The Smith translation is unquestionably the more poetic. Both are acceptable ways of approaching Buber's work. *I and Thou* presents the essence of Buber's philosophy in a manner that is concise, aphoristic, and allusive. Vastly simplified, we must view ourselves, he says, in terms of the types of relationships into which we enter. The I-It relationship is one that sees a world of objects that can be manipulated, an unequal relationship in which you become one more object. The I-Thou relationship is, conversely, one of mutuality, of freedom from the bounds of time or space. This concept carries forward to an understanding of God as the Eternal Thou, known not through intellectual awareness but through direct confrontation and experience. *I and Thou* is a beautiful and fascinating work that you ought to read.

The Origin and Meaning of Hasidism. Edited and translated by Maurice Friedman. Horizon Press, 1960, $5.95 pb.

Buber believed that Hasidism, more than any other religious philosophy, has the power to teach us "for what purpose we are on Earth." The essays in this book are on various aspects of Hasidism, including the life and

teachings of its founder, the Baal Shem Tov, the differences between Hasidism and other mystical movements, how Hasidism compares to Zen Buddhism, and Zionism in the Hasidic movement.

Bulka, Reuven

The Coming Cataclysm: The Orthodox-Reform Rift and the Future of the Jewish People. Mosaic Press; distributed by Flatiron Book, 1984, $16.95 hc, $8.95 pb.

Bulka argues—passionately and persuasively—that based on current practices in the areas of conversion of non-Jews, marriage, and divorce, there will soon be an unbridgeable chasm between America's Reform Jews and their Orthodox and Conservative coreligionists. He does more than simply sound the alarm—he offers a series of proposals to prevent this rift from developing further. The proposals require a shift in Reform practice and a willingness to compromise on the part of Orthodox rabbis. Whether or not you agree with Bulka's solutions, his presentation of the problem is forceful and disturbing.

Chill, Abraham

The Minhagim: The Customs and Ceremonies of Judaism, Their Origins and Rationale. Sepher-Hermon Press, 1979, $14.95 hc, $9.75 pb.

There is no exact English equivalent for the Hebrew word *minhag* (*minhagim* is the plural form). The closest would be "custom," a time-hallowed practice, generally one inspired by faith and devotion to the fulfillment of God's will. An example is the tradition of Orthodox men keeping their heads covered all the time—a practice for which there is no specific requirement in Jewish law. This book is a survey of *minhagim*, arranged by category (holidays, birth, synagogue, etc.), with the source of each examined and its rationale explained. Chill also compares variations, such as the differences between Ashkenazic and Sephardic practice. He uses an impressive range of sources, but wears his scholarship lightly. It is an interesting reflection on the Jewish attitude toward the balance between the human and the divine that the Talmud says when custom and law come into conflict, *minhag* supersedes law.

Eckman, Lester Samuel
The History of the Musar Movement 1840–1945. Shengold, 1975, $8.95.

The Musar Movement—*musar* is a Hebrew word meaning ethics, reproof, or chastisement—was founded by Rabbi Israel Salanter (1810–1883). At its heart was the belief that Jewish learning was worthless unless it contributed to a more moral life, one imbued with love of God and humanity. It taught that a person should strive to grow spiritually throughout life, and developed a system of study and meditation to be used toward those ends. This book, which discusses the history of the movement and analyzes its impact on Jewish life, is not as good as could be hoped but it is one of the only books on the subject available in English and as such is of value.

Freehof, Solomon B.
Modern Reform Responsa. Ktav, 1971, $15.

Responsa are a special type of correspondence: rabbinic answers to questions on Jewish law and observance. Freehof was chairman of the Responsa Committee of the Central Conference of American Rabbis, the organization of Reform rabbis, for more than twenty years. In that time he wrote several volumes of responsa, of which this is the fourth. Freehof had little patience for what he saw as Orthodoxy's extremism and intellectual inconsistency, and while his responsa are learned and thoughtful, there is little in them that the Orthodox will find acceptable. Freehof also edited *A Treasury of Responsa* (Jewish Publication Society, 1962), a survey of responsa spanning the last thousand years and covering such topics as polygamy in Turkey, community government, Jewish first names, and music in the synagogue. It is unfortunately not currently in print.

Friedman, Maurice
Martin Buber's Life and Work. Dutton.

Vol. 1: *The Early Years, 1878–1923*. 1982, $25.
Vol. 2: *The Middle Years, 1923–1945*. 1983, $29.95.
Vol. 3: *The Later Years, 1945–1965*. 1984, $32.50.

As a religious thinker, philosopher of education, exponent of Hasidism, existentialist, Zionist, Bible translator, spokesman for Arab-Jewish rapprochement, humanitarian, and teacher, Martin Buber is one of the most fascinating intellectual figures of our age. And, simply put, this is the definitive biography of Buber. Friedman worked to edit and translate Buber's work for more than thirty years and is intimately familiar with it. If the biography has a flaw, it is that Friedman's admiration of Buber leads him to see every aspect of his character and work in the best possible light. Volume 3 won a National Jewish Book Award in 1985.

Glatzer, Nahum N.
Modern Jewish Thought: A Source Reader. Schocken Books, 1977, $7.50 pb.

An anthology of writings by many of the most important Jewish thinkers of the past two centuries. It surveys the major intellectual concerns and adds some variety by including not just the "big" names like Zunz and Kook, but also Cynthia Ozick, Albert Einstein, Judah Magnes, and others. Glatzer has written short introductions to each selection providing basic biographical and historical background. Intended for use in the classroom—it's even divided into fifteen sections to match the typical semester of fifteen weeks—it's also a good survey for autodidacts.

Gordis, Robert
Understanding Conservative Judaism. Ktav, 1978, $15.

Although Conservative Judaism has more adherents than either Reform or Orthodoxy and although it has produced a multitude of distinguished scholars, public knowledge and awareness of its theology is not high. This may result, as Gordis says, from the conviction of many of its leaders that it is "best to avoid defining its content or demarcating its limits." Gordis, a leading figure in the Conservative Movement, was for many years a professor of Bible at the Jewish Theological Seminary in New York. Being a collection of writings, this book does not present a unified account of the beliefs and rationale of Conservatism, but it is as good as anything available on the subject.

The Hafez Hayyim (Israel Meir Kahan)
Ahavath Chesed. Translated from the Hebrew by Leonard Oschry. Feldheim, 1976, $9.95 hc, $5.95 pb.

Rabbi Israel Meir Kahan (1838–1933) is known as the Hafez

Hayyim after the name of his first book, an exposition on the laws of slander and gossip. He was noted for his piety, integrity, and humility. His best-known book is the *Mishnah Berurah,* a six-volume commentary on the section of the *Shulkhan Arukh* dealing with the laws governing everyday life for Orthodox Jews. Three volumes of this work are available in English from Feldheim Publishers. *Ahavath Chesed* is a more accessible book and a better starting point for most readers. It is an indepth discussion of the laws of **chesed**—a Hebrew word variously translated as "lovingkindness" or "benevolence." The topics covered include loans, pledges, wages, giving charity, hospitality, visiting the sick, and comforting mourners. The author's love of humanity and Jewish tradition shines throughout the book.

Heilman, Samuel
The Gate Behind The Wall: A Pilgrimage to Jerusalem. Summit Books, 1984, $14.95.

Heilman, a sociologist who had written about the world of Jewish observance, felt himself an outsider in the world of Talmud study despite being an Orthodox Jew. In this book he writes of his desire to become a participant, not an outsider. He brings us along as he travels in Jerusalem looking for a teacher who can help in his quest. Following a slow start, his account builds in power and force.

It is the story of one man's spiritual journey, a portrait of the *yeshiva* world of talmudic study and some of its fascinating people, and a thoughtful examination of the difficulties faced by Jews who wish to be part of both the secular and Jewish world.

Herring, Basil F.
Jewish Ethics and Halakhah for Our Time: Sources and Commentary. Ktav, 1984, $15 hc, $8.95 pb.

Although textbookish and dry, this is a useful introduction to the subject of ethics and Jewish religious law. Nine major ethical issues, such as civil disobedience, homosexuality, abortion, and telling the truth to a terminally ill patient, are examined. For each, a hypothetical case is offered, brief quotations from the major sources—Bible, Talmud, and rabbinic commentaries—are given and analyzed, secular views are surveyed, and the halakhic views are presented.

Heschel, Abraham J.
Rabbi Heschel (1907–1972) is one of the preeminent Jewish scholars and philosophers of the twentieth century. His concerns were amazingly wide, and his writings range over the Bible, rabbinic theology, Hasidism, ethics, and history. Heschel's work frequently combines traditional Jewish thought with modern existentialism. (See also the sections entitled BIBLE and HOLIDAYS.)

Between God and Man: An Interpretation of Judaism. Edited by Fritz A. Rothschild. Free Press/Macmillan, 1965, $8.95 pb.

The single best introduction to Heschel's philosophy of religion, this anthology includes excerpts from some of Heschel's major works—*Man Is Not Alone, Man's Quest for God, God in Search of Man,* and *The Sabbath*—plus articles, talks, essays, and other books. The selections and their arrangement are designed to present the central ideas of Heschel's thought in a systematic manner. The major sections of the book are entitled "Ways to His Presence," "The God of the Prophets," "Man and His Needs," "Religious Observance," and "The Meaning of This Hour." An introduction by the editor capably summarizes Heschel's thought.

The Earth Is the Lord's: The Inner World of the Jew in Eastern Europe. Farrar, Straus & Giroux, 1978, $4.95 pb.

Perhaps his most accessible work, this book is an appreciation of the world of Eastern European Jews between the seventeenth and nineteenth centuries, which Heschel sees as *the* Golden Age of Jewry. He tells of a world in which time, not space, was sanctified, in which Jews made the Sabbath and the Holy Days the center of their existence. Illustrated with woodcuts by Ilya Schor, this book is a pleasure to look at and read.

Hirsch, Samson Raphael
Horeb: A Philosophy of Jewish Laws and Observances. Translated from the German by I. Grunfeld. Soncino Press, 1975, 2 vols., $19.95.

Hirsch (1808–1888) was a leader of nineteenth-century German Orthodoxy and an articulate opponent of Reform. He is considered to be one of the founders of "neo-Orthodoxy," that part of Orthodox Judaism that believed a combination of Judaism and secular culture was possible while remaining loyal to rigorous observance of the traditional Jewish faith. Hirsch believed that the mechanical performance of Jewish ritual was not enough. In *Horeb* (the name comes from the Hebrew for Mount Sinai) Hirsch aimed to present the details of Jewish laws and observance while emphasizing their underlying ideas and the religious thoughts they symbolize. The result is a work that spells out the basics of Jewish observance and communicates their importance and meaning to Jewish life. It is not a book you would want to read straight through, but it is a valuable book to dip into, to refer to. It provides an interesting perspective on the time frame of Jewish thought that the publisher refers to this book as a classic in "contemporary Jewish thought." It was first published in 1837.

Jacob, Walter, ed.
American Reform Responsa: Collected Responsa of the Central Conference of American Rabbis, 1889–1983. CCAR Press/Central Conference of American Rabbis, 1983, $20 pb.

Jacob has collected the complete texts of all 172 responsa issued by the American organization of Reform rabbis, representing the official statements of Reform Judaism. Arranged by subject, the responsa cover such questions as the permissibility of euthanasia, sexual ethics, and the observance of the Holy Days. As expected in a Reform document, permissive answers dominate, but often accompanied by advice to act more in accord with tradition. Some of the viewpoints can be startling to the non-Reform. One 1955 responsum, for example, says of the wearing of skull caps during synagogue services, ". . . we should think it an act of willful and useless self-isolation when an American Jew chooses to make of the skull cap an important symbol of Jewish piety." (Other responsa in the book take a different view of the issue.) The book also includes the text of the highly controversial report of the Committee on Patrilineal Descent on the status of mixed marriages, which broke with the other branches of Judaism in declaring the children of a Jewish father and a non-Jewish mother to be Jewish if they are raised Jewish.

The responsa are reproduced from typescript.

Jacobs, Louis
The Book of Jewish Belief. Behrman House, 1984, $9.95 pb.

This book surveys the basics of Jewish faith and values. Among the topics discussed are the Torah, *mitzvot*, the Bible, rabbinic literature, mysticism, the Sabbath, dietary law, the Holocaust, Israel, ethics, marriage, and the family.

The Book of Jewish Values. Rossel Books, 1984, $6.95 pb.

A discussion of the ideas, ideals, and values of Judaism tracing their development and looking for new interpretations suitable to the spiritual needs of contemporary life.

Hasidic Thought. Behrman House, 1976, $6.95 pb.

There are many books about the Hasidic masters. This is one of the few in English that contain their own writings. The emphasis is not on the usual aphorisms but on excerpts from their books. It includes short selections by the Baal Shem Tov, Hayyim of Zanz, Menachem Mendel of Kotzk, Moses Teitelbaum, Nahman of Bratslav, Dov Baer, Shneur Zalman of Liadi, and quite a few others. Jacobs has interspersed brief explanatory notes that are more than merely informative— they are genuinely enlightening, deepening our understanding.

Kaplan, Aryeh
Jewish Meditation: A Practical Guide. Schocken Books, 1985, $17.95 hc, $9.95 pb.

Kaplan notes that while many people are surprised to hear of a Jewish tradition of meditation, Judaism has in fact produced one of the more important systems of meditation. He believes meditation is important both to enhance what can be "cold and spiritually sterile synagogue services" and as a way of keeping Jews from searching within other religions for the riches that can be found within their own. As the subtitle says, the emphasis of this book is on the practical, presenting a step-by-step introduction to such techniques as mantra meditation, contemplation, visualization, and using meditation in conjunction with the Jewish liturgy. Kaplan assumes no special background in either Judaism or meditation on the part of his readers.

Kaplan, Mordecai M.
Dynamic Judaism: The Essential Writings of Mordecai M. Kaplan. Edited and with introductions by Emanuel S. Goldsmith and Mel Scult. Shocken Books, 1985, $22 hc, $12.95 pb.

An influential and original thinker, Kaplan (1881–1983) was the founder of the Society for the Advancement of Judaism and of the Reconstructionist branch of Judaism. His ideas are too complex to be summarized briefly, although their essence is contained in his description of Judaism as an "evolving religious civilization." All three elements of that phrase are significant. He saw a need for Judaism to respond to new challenges with changes in its practices and beliefs. Religion was, Kaplan felt, the clearest expression of Jewish creativity, seeking to understand the purpose of human life. Finally, as a civilization, Judaism has the secular elements needed to provide a counterbalance to religion's tendencies toward rigidity and worship of the past. A lifelong Zionist, he remained convinced that life in the Diaspora was not only acceptable for Jews, it was vital for Jewish survival. While the Reconstructionist Movement has never become a large one, Kaplan's ideas have been felt by Orthodox, Conservative, and Reform Jews. This book includes brief excerpts from several of his works, arranged into major subject headings such as Jewish peoplehood, Torah in our day, ethics, Jewish education, worship and ritual, and Judaism and community in America. The editors have provided a biographical essay and an introduction to Kaplan's thought. *Dynamic Judaism* is the single best introduction to Kaplan and Reconstructionism available. For readers who wish to read at greater length and in greater detail, the book to consult is Kaplan's *Judaism as a Civilization:*

Toward a Reconstruction of American Jewish Life (Jewish Publication Society, 1982, $25 hc, $10.95 pb).

Kellner, Menachem Marc, ed.
Contemporary Jewish Ethics. Hebrew Publishing, 1978, $11.95 pb.

Although intended for use as a classroom text, this collection of writings on ethical issues makes for interesting reading. Essays address both general questions and such specific issues as the case of Karen Quinlan, civil disobedience, business ethics, homosexuality, and capital punishment. The contributors represent a range of Jewish views from the strictly Orthodox to the liberal Reform and include a number of leading scholars and theologians. This is a good book to dip into.

Kushner, Harold S.
When Bad Things Happen to Good People. Schocken Books, 1981, $5.95 pb.

One of, if not *the,* key questions religion must face is how a benevolent God could allow a world so filled with pain and sorrow. Kushner—a rabbi and the father of a child who died before the age of ten—attempts in this book to provide an answer that is both within the Jewish tradition and consoling to those who are facing tragedy. If his answer to a profound question is not itself always profound, it is thoughtful and it has been found helpful by many.

Luzzato, Moshe Chaim
The Path of the Just. Translated by Shraga Silverstein. Feldheim, 1982, $11.95 hc, $6.95 pb.

Luzzato (1707–1747) was a figure of controversy during his life for his belief that he was in communication with the spirits of biblical heroes and his attempts to hasten the era of redemption and the coming of the Messiah. Forced to emigrate from his native Italy, he settled in Amsterdam, where he wrote this book, also known as *The Way of the Righteous.* Long after the controversy ended, Luzzato's reputation has endured, based largely on his ethical works such as this one. In it he instructs his readers in a systematic and simple manner as to how they can improve their moral behavior and attain a higher level of religious and ethical perfection. It has become one of the most influential ethical works in Judaism. This edition contains the Hebrew text of the original (in vocalized form) and the English translation on facing pages.

Neusner, Jacob, ed.
Understanding Jewish Theology: Classical Issues and Modern Perspectives. Ktav, 1973, $11.95 pb.

This collection of essays surveys the basic issues of Jewish theology: God, Torah, and Israel. The way in which Jewish theology has responded to modern issues such as the Holocaust and the creation of the State of Israel are also explored. The contents have been selected from the works of such major Jewish thinkers as Abraham Joshua Heschel, Gershom Scholem, Solomon Schechter, Arthur Hertzberg, Emil

Fackenheim, and Moshe Chaim Luzzato.

Ostrow, Mortimer, ed.
Judaism and Psychoanalysis. Ktav, 1982, $20.

These ten essays focus on topics such as Freud's Jewishness, the psychological significance of the Bar Mitzvah experience, how Judaism's monotheism has influenced Jewish thought and character, what *midrash* tells about the meaning of anxiety to traditional Jews and how Judaism deals with anxiety, and the Jewish response to crisis. Some familiarity with psychoanalytic concepts, Jewish history, Scripture, and rabbinic literature is needed to read this book profitably.

Patai, Raphael
The Jewish Mind. Scribner, 1977, $14.95 hc, $7.95 pb.

One of the most accomplished and wide-ranging Jewish scholars of our time, Patai has written books notable for their readable style and blend of Jewish knowledge with anthropological insights. In *The Jewish Mind*, he sets out to examine the touchy issue of whether Jews really are different from gentiles. He looks at how the Jews have affected the cultures around them and how they, in turn, have reacted to those outside cultures. He looks for the roots of "the extraordinary force of the Jewish mind" throughout history and attempts to find the "essence" of Jewishness. This is a

sensible and intelligent work, well worth reading.

Reuther, Rosemary Radford
Faith and Fratricide: The Theological Roots of Anti-Semitism. Winston Press, 1979, $8.95 pb.

An important contribution to the study of anti-Semitism. Reuther, who is Christian, argues that the anti-Jewish trends in the New Testament and in Christian history are not peripheral or accidental, but deeply embedded in its theology. She condemns Christian ignorance of living Judaism, says that Christianity must find a way to affirm its message without negating Judaism, and insists that the Jewish refusal to accept the Christian message has actually had a positive effect on Christianity. For readers wishing to pursue this topic further, one particularly valuable resource is Stimulus Books, a series on Jewish-Christian dialogue published by Paulist Press.

Sandmel, Samuel
A Jewish Understanding of the New Testament. Ktav, 1974, $11.95 hc, $9.95 pb.

Sandmel was a teacher and Reform rabbi who wrote extensively on Christianity. This book is aimed at Jews who wish to gain a more thoughtful understanding of Christianity. It does not indulge in foolish attempts to "reclaim" Jesus for Judaism; it simply presents in a straightforward and judicious way an introduction to the New Testament. Among Sandmel's many other books of interest are *We Jews and Jesus, The Genius of Paul,* and *Judaism and Christian Beginnings.*

Schechter, Solomon

Studies in Judaism: Essays on Persons, Concepts, and Movements of Thought in Jewish Tradition. Ayer, reprint of 1896 edition, $19.50 hc.

Schechter is one of those rare figures who were important in the worlds of both scholarship and organizational life. He is considered to be the founder of Conservative Judaism, was instrumental in creating the United Synagogue of America, the association of Conservative congregations, and as president of the Jewish Theological Seminary in New York helped build it into a first-rate scholarly institute. As a scholar, his recovery of more than 100,000 manuscripts and manuscript fragments from a storage room in an ancient Cairo synagogue remains one of the astonishing feats of modern times. The *Encyclopaedia Judaica* refers to his *Studies in Judaism* and *Some Aspects of Rabbinic Theology* (see JEWISH THOUGHT BEFORE 1600 section) as "indispensable documents of American Jewish religious Conservatism." In *Studies in Judaism,* ten essays from the original three-volume edition of the work are collected. They cover, among other subjects, the study of Talmud, the dogmas of Judaism, Elijah Gaon of Vilna, and the history of Jewish tradition.

Scholem, Gershom

Major Trends in Jewish Mysticism. Schocken Books, 1961, $8.95 pb.

Gershom Scholem is one of the few people of whom it can be said that they revolutionized the study of Jewish history and religion. Before Scholem began his studies of Jewish mysticism, Jewish scholars treated the subject as an embarrassment—a relic of ghetto superstition, the root of dangerous movements that followed false messiahs. Scholem pioneered the modern study of Kabbalah and Jewish mysticism, placing it on a firm scholarly basis and irrefutably demonstrating its importance in Jewish religion and thought. His erudition and deep understanding remain unmatched and his work forced a major reexamination of many aspects of Jewish history. *Major Trends* surveys the subject from its beginnings in antiquity. Like all of Scholem's work, it is not easy reading, but no serious student of mysticism can be well informed without reading Scholem. (For a considerably easier introduction, see Weiner's *9-1/2 Mystics,* described later.) Other currently available books by Scholem include *Kabbalah* (New American Library, 1978, $8.95 pb) and *On the Kabbalah and Its Symbolism* (Schocken Books, 1969, $6.95 pb). See also *Sabbatai Sevi* in the MEDIEVAL AND MODERN JEWISH HISTORY section.

Soloveitchik, Joseph B.

Halakhic Man. Translated from the Hebrew by Lawrence Kaplan. Jewish Publication Society, 1983, $12.95.

One of the most revered figures of modern Orthodox Judaism, Soloveitchik has been committed to the principle that both religious and secular studies are valid for students of the Torah. His work has provided the intellectual basis for the Modern Orthodox movement, a part of Orthodox Judaism that seeks a religious life that is integrated into the secular world. In *Halakhic Man,* generally regarded as his major work, Soloveitchik says that it is only through the observance of *halakhah* (Jewish law) that humanity can obtain nearness to God. The halakhic human confronts the world bearing an ideal model as presented in Torah, and his or her goal is to make the world conform to this model. Thus the human's arena is this world, and his or her creativity expresses itself as redemption and atonement. This translation of a difficult text is unusually good. The book won a 1985 National Jewish Book Award.

Steinsaltz, Adin

Beggars and Prayers: Adin Steinsaltz Retells the Tales of Rabbi Nahman of Bratslav. Translated from the Hebrew by Yehuda Hanegbi, et al. Basic Books, 1979, $6.95 pb.

For the clarity, concision, subtlety, and depth of his commentaries, Steinsaltz is unmatched. This book includes retellings of six of Nahman's tales, each followed by a section of commentary and explanation. It is a gem.

Trachtenberg, Joshua

Jewish Magic and Superstition: A Study in Folk Religion. Atheneum, 1984, $6.95 pb.

This is *not* a how-to book, but a delightful and scholarly excursion into the world of demons and angels and the many superstitions based on them. Trachtenberg sees folk religion as the most eloquent expression of the folk psyche. His focus is on European Jewry of the eleventh through the sixteenth centuries and on practices that, while never breaking completely with the tenets of Judaism, often stretched those tenets nearly to the breaking point. Among the subjects discussed are the spirits of the dead, the Bible in magic, amulets, the potency of names, medicine, dreams, and astrology. The book is fascinating reading.

Weiner, Herbert

9-1/2 Mystics: The Kabbalah Today. Macmillan, 1985, $8.95 pb.

An exceptionally good book. The author set out to meet and learn from current practitioners and students of the *kabbalah*. He recounts his experiences in this book, along the way presenting a considerable body of information about the history and content of Jewish mysticism. The explanations are easily understandable without being simplistic and the character sketches of the people he met are vivid and sympathetic. Both as an introduction to *kabbalah* and as a piece of journalism, this is a solid job.

Wiesel, Elie
Souls on Fire: Portraits and Legends of Hasidic Masters. Translated from the French by Marion Wiesel. Summit Books, 1982, $7.95 pb.

Described objectively, this is a series of portraits of the Hasidic masters, charismatic figures presented through retelling legends and stories about them. Wiesel analyzes their characters and looks at the meaning of their message for today. That description fails totally to convey the intensity and passion of the telling. This is a book filled with ecstasy and longing for redemption, burning with religious fervor. Its explanations of Hasidic thought are fine, but the real reason to read it is to gain an understanding of the fire that burned in these men. Quite possibly Wiesel's best book.

Wouk, Herman
This Is My God. Doubleday, 1979, $14.95 hc; Touchstone/Simon & Schuster, $8.95 pb.

Wouk is best known for his fiction—for example, *The Winds of War* and *Marjorie Morningstar.* But this book is one of his best, a personal and heartfelt affirmation of the Jewish way of life and its importance to him. While less detailed than the guides by Donin or Trepp described in the HOW-TO section, it is readable and compelling. For someone looking more for a *sense* of what Judaism is than for a step-by-step guide to its practice, Wouk's book is an excellent choice.

VIII

Literature and the Arts

"The Lattice." Judaic papercuts date back to the sixteenth century. In this laser-etched papercut the Hebrew verses of the Song of Songs are interwoven with the imagery of the text. By Tsirl Waletzky, New York, © 1982.

The Literature of the Jewish Idea

Joseph Lowin

The Jewish people are known as a law-making people. But, perhaps no less than the Greeks, they are also a story-telling people. The quintessential Jewish text, the Talmud, is an amalgam of two strains, *halakhah* and *aggadah*, law and lore. While it may be said that Jewish legal authorities of the twentieth century have been reticent to innovate in legal matters, this reticence has not been evident in the realm of literature. In fact, among the most innovative of writers in this past half-century have been writers of stories not only with Jewish themes and characters, but also of narratives that display what might be classified as Jewish ideas.

But what is it that makes a story Jewish? Is it, for example, the subject matter? Can one not write a non-Jewish story on a Jewish subject the way it is possible to paint a Christian painting on an Old Testament theme? Is it the author's religion, nationality, or ethnicity that makes the story Jewish? Is it the language—Yiddish or Hebrew, or **Ladino**—in which the author writes? Perhaps it is the author's intention that his or her story be Jewish that makes it so. And what if the author—like Abraham Cahan in *The Rise of David Levinsky*—intended that his story not promote ethnicity but, rather, facilitate adjustment and acculturation. What about I. L. Peretz's story of "Bontsha the Silent" whose obvious intent it was to show the vapidity of purported Jewish passivity and small-mindedness? I choose these stories—and there are more—because, despite

Dr. Joseph Lowin is the national director of adult education at Hadassah; on leave for 1986–87 as a Jerusalem Fellow. He is writing a book on the literature of the Jewish idea.

the author's intentions, they have become part of the canon of Jewish literature and are even celebrated as classics by Jewish readers everywhere. Perhaps, then, it is Jewish readers who make a story Jewish. There is a good deal of truth in that statement. But not the complete truth.

Let us look at the issue from another angle. Jewish stories are stories that depict Jews as they really are. As we all know, Philip Roth asserts, Jews are happy, optimistic, successful, and warm. Or is it that, as he playfully continues, Jews are grieved, pessimistic, dissatisfied, and xenophobic? Both the sentimental and the coldly clinical deftly describe the Jews. Both Harry Golden and Philip Roth, both Leon Uris and Elie Wiesel are Jewish writers.

Leon Uris's depiction, in *Exodus*, of the Jews as people who fight back has literally been credited with making Jews and Zionists out of many who had previously felt only indifference, if not shame and degradation, at their "poor luck" at having been born Jews. Uris has "made" Jews because he has made Jews *look good* in the eyes of the world. But is the aim of Jewish writing the improvement of public relations? The question is neither as simple nor as complicated as it appears. Many of the people who recognize the artistic inadequacies of Uris's writing would be reluctant to dismiss him cavalierly. Saving Jews is a precious thing.

But there are other writers whose fiction has been good for the Jews. Ludwig Lewisohn's 1928 novel *The Island Within* has had an effect similar to Uris's work. Stanley Chyet, in his preface to a recently reissued edition of the novel, says, "He made a Jew of me—he, his work, and particularly this book." But there are even more contemporary writers whose writing can play a similar public relations role, and do so while remaining faithful to the idea of a Jewish idea. Who is more audible today as a voice for Jewish pride, for Jewish identity, and for Jewish moral earnestness than Elie Wiesel? Wiesel's first novel, *Dawn*, published at about the same time as Uris's *Exodus*, also depicts a Jew who fights back. Wiesel's Jew, however, seeks to place his fighting into a Jewish context. Wiesel's latest novel, *The Fifth Son*, rewrites *Dawn*, searches for an even higher moral purpose than fighting back, and does so by delving into the Jewish textual tradition.

Many contemporary literary critics have observed that the earliest stages of American Jewish writing dealt with the difficulty in acculturating encountered by a largely immigrant Jewish population. Most of the Jewish writing of this early period seemed to have a social function—the facilitation of that acculturation. Recently, Jewish writers have begun to demonstrate to their readers that Jewish culture—the Jewish textual tradition—is a subject worthy for fiction. Even more recently, as recently as today, Jewish writers are using traditionally Jewish modes to create their works.

There are few enterprises more traditional in Jewish intellectual and spiritual life than the continuing effort to interpret, reinterpret, and in some cases rewrite Judaism's classical texts. This interpretive literature of Judaism is called *midrash*. As Robert Alter, a noted scholar of both Jewish and Israeli literature, has remarked, *midrash* is "the rabbis' way of imaginatively connecting things intrinsically unconnected." To the extent that it uses the imagination, therefore, *midrash* involves fiction, story. It is the retelling by the rabbis—with the addition of commentary—of biblical and in some cases postbiblical tales. *Midrash* might better be characterized as functional embroidery, as the addition of interpretive texture to narrative text. *Midrash* is at once both fanciful invention and a way of taking story seriously.

Today, several writers are using the midrashic mode to create—or, better, to recreate—a Jewish esthetic. They are employing the Jewish textual tradition—both its subject matter and its style—as a *pre*-text for their writing. In so doing these writers are turning story into commentary. The midrashic mode can be found worldwide, in the works of very different novelists, memoirists, and short story writers. Several examples come to mind. Elie Wiesel's novel *The Fifth Son* is not only a rewriting of *Dawn*. It is also a commentary on the description in the Haggadah of the traditional four sons. (The Haggadah's assertion, by the way, is itself an ingenious interpretation of several biblical verses.) Primo Levi's novel *If Not Now, When?* is a commentary on Hillel's famous dictum, "If I am not for myself, who will be for me? And if I am for myself only, what am I? And if not now, when?" Joseph Heller's recent novel *God Knows* is a retelling of the story of King David, and, despite the superficial vulgarity, is a very Jewish book. Amos Oz's latest, *A Perfect Peace,* is not only a translation of a phrase in the *"Kel Maleh Rahamim"* prayer but also a modern rendering of the conflict among Saul, Jonathan, and David. Herman Wouk's bestselling novel *Inside, Outside* is not merely a Bronx *Bildungsroman*; it is, more importantly, a work of Jewish liturgical quality, a *kaddish* for an irretrievable past, a prayer of thanksgiving, a *sheheheyanu* for the state of Israel. And then there is Cynthia Ozick, the quintessential Jewish writer today, the one who has done the most to promote the idea of a Jewish idea, whose "Pagan Rabbi" is a *drash* (an expansion) on the talmudic affirmation that study—and this always means textual study—may not be interrupted for the appreciation of nature.

This trend toward writing in the midrashic mode is emblematic of the Jewish idea, the idea that the ordinary may be made extraordinary, that the profane may be sanctified, and that story can become liturgy.

The Jewish idea is neither Judaism (that is to say, the Jewish religion) nor Jewishness (that is, a certain ethnic identity). I do not mean to imply that it transcends these. More properly, the Jewish idea means somehow to encompass both Judaism and Jewishness. The Jewish idea relates in the first instance to traditional Jewish culture. It has to do with meaningfulness and is most clearly understood when applied to the writing— and the reading and rewriting—of stories. To be Jewish, a story may evidence one or all of the criteria listed earlier. But most of all, for a story to be Jewish, it must, like *midrash*, have meaning. A Jewish story is one that does not make a totem, an idol, out of the imagination. It is also one that insists on making distinctions. It distinguishes between what is Jewish and what is not. More often than not, it swims against the tide of Western culture and with the tide of Jewish history.

Jews are text-centered, if not to say text-obsessed, and what distinguishes the Jews is that they spend their most precious time commenting on text, judging text, and, in the process, judging the world. For the Jews, a story may be funny but it must have moral seriousness. Like the Talmud—the ocean in which the Jews have learned to swim against the tide, to float, and, when necessary, to tread water, a Jewish story must have both *halakhah* and *aggadah,* flowers and fruit. The fruit is important not only for the nourishment it provides. The flowers are important not only for their pleasant aroma. Both are crucial for the seeds and pollen they contain. Both law and lore promise that tomorrow there will be more law and lore. The Jewish idea involves an ongoing process. Story begets commentary, which in its turn begets judgment, which in its turn begets further story, and so on. Jewish history is only partly the narrative of events, however. It is only partly the story of national calamity and only fractionally the story of national triumph. What Jews occupy themselves with is not event but commentary. They comment on their history and more importantly they comment on their texts. In so doing, the Jews judge their history and the world, giving meaning to both.

BOOKS OF FICTION AND LITERATURE

More than any other type of book, the choice of fiction is very much a matter of personal taste. The titles described here have been selected to represent a cross section—novels, poems, and short stories, easy to read and hard to read. Beyond literary merit, we have also been guided by the value of a book in inspiring its readers or informing them. The twelve-volume *History of Jewish Literature* by Zinberg is an authoritative source of critical information, but needs to be brought up to date, since it ends with the nineteenth century. In addition to the books in this chapter, readers should consult the fiction section of the Holocaust chapter and the chapters on Hebrew literature and Yiddish literature, which are filled with many wonderful books.   —R. S. F. & W. W.

Ausubel, Nathan, ed.
A Treasury of Jewish Folklore.
Crown, 1948, $10.95.

Hundreds of stories, proverbs, riddles, tales, and songs from Jewish tradition telling of wise men and fools, demons and angels, scholars, **schlemiels**, rabbis, merchants, doctors, matchmakers, and misers. Truly, this book is a treasury—and a bargain also. Ausubel's *Treasury of Jewish Poetry*

(Crown, 1957) is out of print but worth looking for.

Ausubel, Nathan, ed.
A Treasury of Jewish Humor. Doubleday, 1951, $17.95.

This book collects stories, epigrams, excerpts from novels, and other examples of humor garnered from Jewish literature. Among the many writers collected here are Sholom Aleichem, Lion Feuchtwanger, Hayyim Nachman Bialik, I. L. Peretz, Heinrich Heine, S. J. Perelman, Mendele Mokher Seforim, and Ferenc Molnar.

Bellow, Saul
The winner of a Nobel Prize for Literature, Bellow is a Jewish writer who dislikes being categorized as a Jewish writer. He has said that a writer is not "something national and not associated with any race or religion." Nonetheless, his novels consistently deal with Jewish themes and Jewish characters, and his view of the world is strongly Jewish in content and style. His prose is complex and intellectual, with a tendency toward lengthy discussions of ideas. He is a writer not for people looking for "a good read," but for people wishing to be provoked, disturbed, made to think and feel.

Herzog. Viking/Penguin, 1964, $12.95 hc; Penguin, $4.95 pb.

The eponymous Moses El-khanah Herzog is a womanizer, intellectual, and writer, a man whose personal life is in disarray: his work is not progressing, his wife is unfaithful, and his mistresses and family are giving him trouble. The entire world of the novel is peopled by Jews and his identity as a Jew in a non-Jewish world is a central concern of Herzog.

Mr. Sammler's Planet. Viking/Penguin, 1970, $12.95; Viking, $5.95 pb.

This downbeat and sour novel is written with a depth of feeling and passion that make it stand out from Bellow's other work. Mr. Sammler is a Holocaust survivor, now in his seventies, who finds the present repellent and violent, and his past meaningless and misspent. He is not a comfortable man to spend any length of time with, but he forces us to examine the world in which we live and our responses to it.

Great Jewish Stories. Laurel/Dell, 1985, $4.95 pb.

Too bad there isn't a hardcover edition of this anthology—it's the best collection of Jewish stories available, and a more permanent version would be welcome. Bellow has written a short introduction, but it's his selection of stories that makes this book shine. It includes work by Nahman of Bratslav, Heinrich Heine, Stefan Zweig, Martin Buber, both I. J. and I. B. Singer, Bernard Malamud, and Grace Paley, along with several others. The stories aren't just *by* Jewish writers; they all deal with Jewish life and the Jewish view of the world. Anyone who can compare Tobit to Leopold Bloom, as Bellow does, is someone with an interesting approach to literature.

Cahan, Abraham
The Rise of David Levinsky. Smith, $12 hc; Harper & Row, 1976, $7.95 pb.

First published in 1917, *David Levinsky* is the story of a Jewish immigrant who becomes a wealthy cloak manufacturer by exploiting other Jews. Eventually he becomes aware of the emptiness of his life, realizing that his early life, when he was still part of the Jewish moral tradition, was more meaningful and satisfying. Cahan was an important figure in American Jewish life who deserves to be better known today. A founder of the Yiddish-language *Jewish Daily Forward* in 1897, he was its editor for nearly fifty years. An ardent advocate of socialism, he worked with astonishing energy to improve the life of his fellow immigrants. His desire to help Jews become a part of American life could be seen in the advice he gave his readers in the letters-to-the-editor column (see Metzker's anthology of them, *A Bintel Brief,* in MEDIEVAL AND MODERN HISTORY). In 1909 he even presented "The Fundamentals of Baseball Explained for Non-Sports," including a three-column diagram of the Polo Grounds. As an editor, he was instrumental in launching the careers of Sholem Asch, I. J. Singer, and I. B. Singer. His story "Yekl"

was the basis for the movie *Hester Street.*

Cohen, Arthur A.
An Admirable Woman. Godine, 1983, $14.95.

Set in New York City, this novel is loosely based on the life of Hannah Arendt. It provides an insightful portrait of a strong-willed woman of great intellectual powers and of the European and American intellectual milieu of the 1930s and 1940s in which she moved. Among its accomplishments are its vivid portrayal of the sense of dislocation experienced by European intellectuals attempting to make the transition to life in America and the difficulties they faced in the process. The author does an impressive job of putting himself into the mind of a woman character. It won a National Jewish Book Award in 1984.

Feuchtwanger, Lion
The Oppermans. Translated from the German by Willa and Edwin Muir. Carroll & Graf, 1983, $8.95 pb.

This story describes a sophisticated, assimilated German-Jewish family during the time of Hitler's accession to power. It shows how Nazi anti-Semitism penetrates the lives of people who had seen themselves as totally German, slowly isolating them from their friends, business associates, and neighbors. Written in 1933, it is a gripping work, considered by some to be the first book about the Holocaust. Despite the grim subject matter, it is suitable for younger readers. Feuchtwanger, the author of many other books, is best known for *Jew Suss* (Carroll & Graf, 1984, $18.95 hc, $8.95 pb), a novel about Joseph Suess Oppenheimer, an eighteenth-century court Jew, that was later the basis of the virulently anti-Semitic film made by the Nazis. "Court Jew" is a term that was used to refer to Jews who served as advisers to European rulers. Their access to the court enabled them to represent the interests of the Jewish community.

Gold, Michael

Jews Without Money. Carroll & Graf, 1984, $7.95; Avon Books, $2.50 pb.

This unrelentingly grim novel describes Jewish immigrant life on New York's Lower East Side. The Carroll & Graf edition is a facsimile of the original 1930 Liveright edition and includes the woodcuts from it. Suitable for young adult readers.

Goldreich, Gloria

The author of a number of popular novels, Goldreich infuses all her work with a strong positive feeling toward Judaism and Jewish values. She worked in the office of Hadassah's director of Jewish Education and pursued graduate studies in Jewish history at Hebrew University in Jerusalem. She is a good storyteller who is obviously fond of her

characters and who respects her readers' intelligence. In addition to her work for adults, she has written two novels for young adults.

Four Days. Fawcett Books, 1983, $3.50 pb.

The four days of the title are those that Ina Friedman spends in a hospital recovering from minor surgery—and struggling to decide whether or not to have an abortion. The mother of two grown children who is embarking on a new career of her own, Ina is also the child of Holocaust survivors. The people she talks with during the four days include her sister-in-law, who has been unable to bear children, and her roommate, an Orthodox Jewish woman whose newborn child is desperately ill. It is Goldreich's talent that her story is both one of intense human drama and one that raises serious moral and emotional issues.

Leah's Journey. Berkley Books, 1985, $3.95 pb.

Leah Goldfeder's life takes her from the Russian Revolution to the Holocaust, to New York's Lower East Side, and finally to the birth of the State of Israel. In addition to being an action-filled novel loaded with emotional moments, this story is an entertaining introduction to the major events of modern Jewish history. Winner of a 1979 National Jewish Book Award. A sequel, *Leah's Children* (Macmillan, 1985,

$16.95), carries the story forward through the lives of Leah's three children, all of whom become involved in the great events of our time, from a rescue mission during the Hungarian uprising of 1956 to the American civil rights struggle to the difficulties of life in an Israeli kibbutz.

Greenfield, Robert
Temple. Summit Books, 1983, $15.95; Dell, $4.95 pb.

Winner of a National Jewish Book Award for fiction, *Temple* is a loving look at Paulie Bindel and Ahavath Mizrach, an Orthodox synagogue that is at the center of the community where Paulie lives. It is also the story of Paulie's relationship with his grandfather Mendel—an old man seen by many as a relic of the past but seen by Paulie as a link to the future.

Hobson, Laura Z.
Gentleman's Agreement. Arbor House, 1983, $8.95 pb.

The basis of a movie starring Gregory Peck, *Gentleman's Agreement* is of interest as a social document, but it is also a readable and emotionally engaging novel. It is the story of Phil Green, a non-Jew who is assigned to write an article on anti-Semitism by the newsweekly for which he works. He pretends to be Jewish and, once he is treated as a Jew, learns to see the prejudice and patronization with which Jews are treated by many gentiles. Hobson was the daughter of Yiddish writer Michael Zametkin and had extensive journalistic experience before becoming a novelist.

Kemelman, Harry
Friday the Rabbi Slept Late. Hall, 1983, $13.95 (large print); Fawcett, $2.50 pb.

Friday was the first in a series of mysteries by Rabbi Kemelman, all of which are entertaining and enjoyable introductions to Jewish values. *(Conversations with Rabbi Small*, which came after all the days of the week were used, is not a mystery, is a bit heavy-handed in its didacticism, and isn't especially entertaining.)* All the mysteries feature Rabbi David Small, and in all of them he solves a mystery using talmudic logic and copes with synagogue politics by using Jewish tradition and wisdom. The entire series is suitable for younger readers.

The other titles in the series are, in chronological order,
Saturday the Rabbi Went Hungry
Sunday the Rabbi Stayed Home
Monday the Rabbi Took Off
Tuesday the Rabbi Saw Red
Wednesday the Rabbi Got Wet
Thursday the Rabbi Walked Out

Lewisohn, Ludwig
The Island Within. Ayer, 1975, $30 hc; Behrman House, $5.95 pb.

Lewisohn came from an assimilated background, but rediscovered his Jewish heritage and wrote several books, fiction and nonfiction, in which he called on American Jews to repudiate assimilation and return to a more Jewish way of life. Published in 1928, this soul-searching novel focuses on Arthur Levy, the child of a successful immigrant businessman. Levy faces both overt and more subtle forms of anti-Semitism, and only when he is able to define and accept his being both a Jew and an American can the many crises in his life begin to be resolved. Well suited to young adult readers, but its attitudes toward women are dated.

Malamud, Bernard

The Fixer. Farrar, Straus & Giroux, $17.50 hc, $7.95 pb; Washington Square Press, $3.95 pb.

The Beiliss Case of 1911 was one of the most extreme manifestations of anti-Semitism in tsarist Russia—a twentieth-century example of the "blood libel." Mendel Beiliss was accused of the ritual murder of a young Christian boy and, despite the obvious falsity of the charge, brought to trial. The charges were meant to justify the persecution of all Jews as government policy, but Beiliss was acquitted by a jury of Russians. Based on that case, this novel is about political persecution and personal suffering and how they affect one man's sense of his own Jewishness.

The Stories of Bernard Malamud. Farrar, Straus & Giroux, 1983, $17.95 hc; New American Library, $7.95 pb.

Twenty-five stories selected from Malamud's three previous collections—*The Magic Barrel, Idiots First,* and *Rembrandt's Hat*—plus two previously uncollected stories. Unlike his novels, Malamud's short stories give play to his often brilliant sense of humor, and they are probably the best—and certainly the most enjoyable—way to become acquainted with his work.

Michener, James A.

The Source. Random House, 1965, $22.95 hc; Fawcett, $3.95 pb.

Michener puts his storytelling skills and prodigious research to work in this fictionalized retelling of Jewish history, from prehistoric times to modern Israel. It's a massive book, more than nine hundred pages, but for readers who find history books dry, this is one way to make Jewish history come to life.

Ozick, Cynthia

Cynthia Ozick is a distinguished author, a writer of brilliance who is as much a thinker as a creator of fictional characters. Her prose can be opaque and difficult, but her thinking is sharp and subtle.

The Cannibal Galaxy. Knopf, 1983, $11.95 hc; Dutton, $7.95 pb.

This masterly portrait shows Joseph Brill, a middle-aged, middle-of-the-road man presiding over a Midwestern Jewish middle school "beleaguered by middling parents and their middling offspring." When Brill meets Hester Lilt, the brilliant mother of one of his least promising students, he is forced to examine himself, his assumptions, and his life. It is a mark of Ozick's talent that a novel about the failed aspirations of a small-minded principal can be so engaging and disturbing. Among Ozick's other works are *Bloodshed and Three Novellas* (Dutton, 1983, $6.95 pb) and *The Pagan Rabbi* (Dutton, 1983, $6.95 pb).

Potok, Chaim

One of the best-known figures of modern American Jewish literature, Chaim Potok has written a series of novels that deal with the tensions between faith and doubt, between tradition and modernism. At his best, his works are compelling and provocative; at his worst, they are schematic and lacking in characters who come to life. He is always intelligent, literate, and interesting.

The Chosen. Fawcett, 1978, $2.95 pb.

Set in the world of the Orthodox and Hasidic Jews of Brooklyn, this intense and powerful story revolves around the son of a noted rabbi and his conflict with his father over religion and his choice of a career. It deals with the importance of compassion and love and provides an interesting view of the world of Jewish scholarship.

Davita's Harp. Knopf, 1985, $16.95 hc; Fawcett, $4.50 pb.

Potok's most recent book is also one of his best. Ilana Davita Chandal is the daughter of a Christian father and a Jewish mother, both committed leftists in the tradition of the 1930s. What works for her parents doesn't work for her, though, and Davita turns to traditional Judaism—only to find a world that relegates her to second best because she is a woman. The conflicts are many and, as always with Potok, no simple answers are offered.

My Name Is Asher Lev. Knopf, 1972, $13.95 hc; Fawcett, $2.95 pb.

Set against the backdrop of World War II, in this novel the conflict is between a young artist's commitment to his religious tradition and his drive to paint. Historically there has been a strong aversion within Judaism to visual representation, which makes the main character's ambitions a particular source of disagreement and conflict.

The Promise. Knopf, 1969, $15.95 hc; Fawcett, $2.95 pb.

A continuation of the story begun in *The Chosen*, this book continues that novel's study of the tensions between fathers and sons and the conflict between traditional religion and the modern world.

Rosten, Leo (Leo Q. Ross)

The Education of H*y*m*a*n K*a*p*l*a*n. Harcourt Brace Jovanovich, 1968, $2.95 pb.

Leo Rosten is a natural storyteller, warm and always funny.

These stories are set in an adult education class of immigrants to America, all struggling to learn English—and alien new ways. The star of the class is Hyman Kaplan, and what he does to the English language cannot easily be described, it must be read.

Roth, Henry
Call It Sleep. Cooper Square, reprint of 1934 edition, $20 hc; Avon Books, $3.95 pb.

First published in 1934, *Call It Sleep* fell into obscurity for many years despite favorable reviews, only to be revived to great acclaim in the 1960s. Roth's only published novel, it is about childhood in the immigrant Jewish community of New York's Lower East Side. It is a work of almost suffocating emotional intensity whose great psychological force makes it unusually rewarding reading. Roth has a sensitive ear to the language of immigrants and depicts the often depressing world of poverty with realism and acuity.

Roth, Philip
Goodbye Columbus. Modern Library, 1966, $5.95 hc.

An often scathing portrayal of middle-class American Jewish life. Brenda Patimkin is the beautiful, sexy daughter of a rich suburban family. She is seen by Neil Klugman as the ultimate in desirability—who cannot see her shallowness and hardheaded practicality. In addition to this novella, the book includes several short stories.

Zuckerman Bound: A Trilogy and Epilogue. Farrar, Straus & Giroux, 1985, $22.50 hc, $9.95 pb.

Zuckerman consists of three novels originally published separately (*The Ghost Writer, Zuckerman Unbound,* and *The Anatomy Lesson*), plus a new epilogue, *The Prague Orgy.* All deal with the career and loves of a celebrated Jewish writer, Nathan Zuckerman, and what he calls "the unreckoned consequences of art." The work is one of biting wit and, ultimately, great pain. By putting the three novels together and by adding the epilogue, Roth makes clear that what were first seen as independent novels of varying quality are in fact a unified and powerful work.

Schwartz, Howard
Elijah's Violin: And Other Jewish Fairy Tales. Illustrated by Linda Heller. Harper & Row, 1983, $14.95 hc, $8.95 pb.

"Once upon a time . . . " are the most magic words in English. The fairytales in this book have been collected from a wide range of sources and retold by Howard Schwartz. They are distinguished from other fairytales by their emphasis on Jewish spiritual values and morality, their reaffirmation of Jewish faith and longing. But, like all fairytales, they are filled with kings and princesses, golden mountains and magic birds, sorcerers and enchanted forests. The illustrations by Linda Heller are charming. (See also Moses Gaster's *Ma'aseh Book* in YIDDISH LITERATURE.)

Schwartz, Howard, ed.

Gates to the New City: A Treasury of Modern Jewish Tales. Avon Books, 1983, $12.95 pb.

An anthology of more than a hundred stories, all drawing their inspiration from Jewish tradition. The book is best enjoyed by sampling, rather than by reading it straight through, as the repetition of themes can undermine the sense of uniqueness of each story. Among those whose work is included are Rabbi Nahman of Bratslav, Francine Prose, Franz Kafka, Stefan Zweig, Aharon Appelfeld, Theodor Herzl, Der Nister, S. Y. Agnon, Elie Wiesel, I. L. Peretz, Sholem Asch, Cynthia Ozick, Mendele Mokher Seforim, Isaac Goldemberg, Bernard Malamud, and Isaac Bashevis Singer. A glossary, notes on the authors, a bibliography, and an index add to the value.

Schwartz, Howard, and Anthony Rudolf, eds.

Voices Within the Ark: The Modern Jewish Poets. Pushcart Press, 1980, $50; Avon, $15.95 pb.

This is the most comprehensive anthology of modern Jewish poetry available, including more than 350 poets translated from more than twenty different languages, including Hebrew, Yiddish, Judezmo, German, Amharic, Turkish, and French, and coming from such diverse places as England, Israel, Sri Lanka, and the United States. Among the most recognizable names are Yehuda Amichai, Hayyim Nachman Bialik, Allen Ginsberg, Abraham Sutskever, and Chaim Grade. While the quality of the work is uneven, there is much first-rate material in its 1,200-plus pages, and the opportunity of sampling the work of many little-known poets adds to the value of the collection.

Steinberg, Milton

As a Driven Leaf. Behrman House, 1939, $7.95 pb.

Based on real people and events, this novel set in ancient Israel is the story of Rabbi Elisha ben Abuyah and his obsessive search for faith. It is thoughtful and disturbing and gives abstract issues a powerful emotional urgency. Suitable for young adult readers. Rabbi Steinberg was also the author of *Basic Judaism* (described in HOW-TO).

Tax, Meredith

Rivington Street. Jove, 1983, $3.95 pb.

A well-written popular novel about Jewish immigrants living on the Lower East Side of New York at the turn of the century. The novel focuses on four women, interweaving the battles for women's rights and for union recognition with their personal stories. The characters have vitality and emotional complexity. Not great literature, but entertaining, readable, and an enjoyable way to learn about immigrant life.

Uris, Leon

Exodus. Doubleday, 1958, $19.95 hc; Bantam Books, $4.50 pb.

This popular, fictionalized

narrative describes the creation of the State of Israel in the aftermath of World War II. By focusing on the hardships of individual immigrants to what was then Palestine, it makes the hunger of Jews everywhere for a homeland vivid and exciting. The basis of a big-budget Hollywood movie, *Exodus* has achieved something of the status of a modern classic.

Viertel, Joseph
Lifelines. Pocket Books, 1983, $3.95 pb.

An effective novel about Soviet Jewish life. Part thriller, part social portrait, it gives an emotional reality to a current issue that can all too easily seem remote and unconnected to our lives.

Walden, Daniel, ed.
Studies in American Jewish Literature. State University of New York Press, $12.95 each for individuals, $25 each for institutions.

Each volume in this excellent series of commentaries on American Jewish writing contains a variety of articles and essays on a single topic. Scholarly and aimed for academia rather than the general public. The titles available:
Vol. 1: *Isaac Bashevis Singer*
Vol. 2: *A Mosaic of Jewish Writers*
Vol. 3: *Jewish Women Writers*
Vol. 4: *The World of Chaim Potok*

Wallant, Edward Lewis
The Pawnbroker. Harcourt Brace Jovanovich, 1978, $4.95 pb.

The basis of a powerful movie with Rod Steiger, *The Pawnbroker* tells of a Jewish pawnbroker in Harlem who has built a wall around his emotions to save himself from his memories of imprisonment in a Nazi concentration camp.

Wiesel, Elie
Wiesel is a Holocaust survivor whose many works—*Night* being perhaps the best-known—often deal with this awful event. (See the HOLOCAUST section for additional information.)

Wouk, Herman
Marjorie Morningstar. Doubleday, 1955, $15.95; Pocket Books, $5.95 pb.

Marjorie Morningstar (née Morgenstern) is a young New York Jewish woman whose fantasies of life as an actress clash with her immigrant parents' hopes that she become respectably middle class. Eventually, disillusioned in both love and career, she becomes very much the wife and mother her parents wanted her to be. *The City Boy* (Pocket Books, 1980, $4.95 pb) is the story of ten-year-old Herbie Bookbinder, and is one of Wouk's most endearing books.

Yezierska, Anzia
The popular and critical success of *Hungry Hearts* in the 1920s led to an unhappy Hollywood career for its author. Having fallen into obscurity, in recent years Yezierska has been experiencing something of a revival. Yezierska writes with great skill and fire and is particularly sensitive to the problems faced by women.

Bread Givers. Persea Books, 1975, $6.95 pb.

First published in 1925, and one of Yezierska's most autobiographical works, *Bread Givers* is the story of Sara Smolinsky, a woman who breaks away from her meddlesome father and the restrictive life that is available to a woman. She eventually goes to college and studies to be a teacher, but she is unable to achieve a reconciliation between herself and her family, and learns that she has won her freedom at a high price. The portrait of tenement life is grim and effective.

Hungry Hearts: And Other Stories. Ayer, reprint of 1920 edition, $24.50 hc; Persea Books, 1985, $9.95 pb.

The stories in this book, first published in 1920, are of immigrant Jewish life, and the hearts referred to in its title are hungry for a better life, for freedom from poverty and toil.

Zinberg, Israel

A History of Jewish Literature. Translated from the Yiddish by Bernard Martin. Ktav, 1974, 12 vols., $22.50 each.

Zinberg's study is scholarly, readable, massive, and as close to being the standard work as anyone can come. It covers Jewish literature from the Spanish period (tenth century) through the Enlightenment in Russia (nineteenth century). In addition to poetry, fiction, and drama, it includes virtually every other form of Jewish literary endeavor, from philosophy and biblical exegesis to folklore and memoirs. The typography and production of the volumes are particularly good. Zinberg was a chemical engineer by profession and spent more than twenty years preparing the *History.* He died in 1939, a year after being exiled to Vladivostok. The titles in the series are

Vol. 1: *The Arabic-Spanish Period*
Vol. 2: *French and German Jewry in the Early Middle Ages, and The Jewish Community of Medieval Italy*
Vol. 3: *The Struggle of Mysticism and Tradition Against Philosophical Rationalism*
Vol. 4: *Italian Jewry in the Renaissance Era*
Vol. 5: *The Jewish Center of Culture in the Ottoman Empire*
Vol. 6: *The German-Polish Cultural Center*
Vol. 7: *Old Yiddish Literature from Its Origins to the Haskalah Period*
Vol. 8: *The Berlin Haskalah*
Vol. 9: *Hasidism and Enlightenment (1780–1820)*
Vol. 10: *The Science of Judaism and Galician Haskalah*
Vol. 11: *The Haskalah Movement in Russia*
Vol. 12: *Haskalah at Its Zenith*

The Modern Jewish Experience in Hebrew and Yiddish Literature

Jacob Kabakoff

Modern Hebrew literature had its beginnings in Europe long before the rise of the Jewish center in Palestine and the establishment of the State of Israel. By the end of the nineteenth century, it reached a high level of creativity under the influence of Jewish nationalism and the age-old longing for Zion.

Among the chief exponents of the Hebrew literary revival was the poet Hayyim Nachman Bialik (1878–1934), who has been universally recognized as the central figure in modern Hebrew literature. He gave poetic expression to the inner struggles of Jews as they stood at the crossroads of the modern era. In his effort to conserve the best elements of the past in order to fashion a creative future, Bialik developed a whole gamut of poetic symbols and drew on all levels of Hebrew literary style, beginning with the Bible.

In prose writing, Mordechai Zev Feierberg (1874–1899) vividly depicted the quest of the Jews who sought to enter the modern world while struggling to maintain their attachment to the declining traditional values of Judaism and Jewish culture.

The use of Hebrew as an everyday language in Palestine gave impetus to the development of a many-faceted literature. By the time of World War II, Palestine emerged as the leading

Dr. Jacob Kabakoff is professor emeritus of Hebrew and Jewish studies, Lehman College of the City University of New York, and editor of the *Jewish Book Annual.*

center of Hebrew writing. The contributions of scores of native-born writers in Israel have helped to create an indigenous Israeli literature, particularly in poetry and in the novel and short story.

The Hebrew writers in Europe had been concerned largely with the problems of Jewish existence and with strivings for a new life. In Palestine, their writings mirrored the new society that was arising in the cities and the communal settlements. Many gave expression to the theme of redemption and the attachment of a pioneering generation to the soil. The poets especially were drawn to the new landscape, which they described in a style rich in biblical overtones and allusions.

Many of these writings are included in the anthologies that appear in our listing. Several authors, like the Nobel Prize Laureate Samuel Y. Agnon (1888–1970) and the contemporary prose writers Moshe Shamir (1921–   ), Aharon Appelfeld (1932–   ), Amos Oz (1939–   ), and Abraham B. Yehoshua (1936–   ), are among those whose works have attracted wide attention in translation. They have succeeded in evoking a sense of their world that transcends particularist interests and goes to the heart of human experience.

Agnon has combined past and present in depicting the saintliness of traditional Jewish life and the epic of rebirth in Israel. Both in his symbol-charged novels and short stories and in his modernist tales he has depicted the spiritual malaise and restlessness of modern humanity. Moshe Shamir has dealt not only with life in the communal settlements and with war themes but has also written perceptive historical novels.

Aharon Appelfeld has depicted sensitively the effects of the Holocaust on the survivors and has described the travails of their adjustment to the new life of Israel. Both Amos Oz and Abraham B. Yehoshua are representative of the generation of authors who came to the fore during the 1960s and who have employed a refined symbolist technique in their novels and short stories to stress the problems of the individual and his self-realization. They are among the most widely translated authors in Israeli literature.

The most widely translated Israeli poet is Yehuda Amichai (1924–   ), who has been called the "Father of Young Israeli

Poetry." His verse is characteristically modern in imagery and it conveys the sense of loneliness and bereavement that is the lot of his generation.

In the novellas of Nathan Shaham (1925–   ), who like Amichai is a member of the Palmach generation, we gain a glimpse into the world of the kibbutz and its inhabitants. Writers such as Yoram Kaniuk (1930–   ) blend realism and fantasy in depicting characters who are often exposed to extreme challenges.

Few could have dreamt that modern Hebrew literature, born in Europe, fostered by small bands of dedicated writers, and transferred from one literary center to another, would come to occupy an honored position among the significant literatures of the world. Not the least of the accomplishments of the State of Israel is to be seen in its profound contributions to the development of this literature in all its forms.

Modern Yiddish literature reached a high point in its development at the end of the nineteenth century. It was then that there began its classic period, as exemplified by the works of the three leading authors, Mendele Mokher Seforim, Isaac Leib Peretz, and Sholom Aleichem. Yiddish was the spoken language of millions of Jews and its literature remains invaluable for an understanding of the world of the *shtetl* and of East European Jewry. That it became a refined instrument of literary expression is attested to by the fact that many Yiddish writers, such as Sholem Asch, achieved wide renown in translation and that Isaac Bashevis Singer was awarded the Nobel Prize for his contributions.

The Yiddish stage served as an important vehicle for the dissemination of Yiddish literary and Jewish values. Probably the most widely known play is *The Dybbuk,* by S. Anski (1863–1920). The play, which has been often translated and produced, has had a profound appeal because of its union of the natural and supernatural and its ability to convey the depth of Hasidism.

The stories of Isaac Leib Peretz (1852–1915), who stood at the center of the Jewish cultural renaissance in Eastern Europe at the turn of the century, are characterized by a new emphasis on the inner life of the individual. Drawing on folk material and Hasidic themes, Peretz was responsive also to the new esthetic trends in European letters.

Essentially a humorist of universal appeal, Sholom Aleichem (1859–1916) has served as a constant source of edification and entertainment. At the same time, he has presented his readers with an unparalleled authentic portrait of Jewish life in Eastern Europe. His unforgettable gallery of types continues to arouse the sympathy of all.

The superb poet and novelist Chaim Grade (1910–1982) saw it as his historic obligation to describe the human tragedy and spiritual values of European Jewish life before its uprooting. His attachment to the ethical movement known as Musar, and particularly to the city of Vilna, is seen in his novels and short stories of the rich world of Lithuanian Jewry.

The awarding of the Nobel Prize to Isaac Bashevis Singer (1904–   ) served to focus attention on the seminal contributions of Yiddish literature to the treasury of world letters. Through his realistic epic novels, as well as his innovative short stories, Singer established himself as a vivid storyteller. His deep familiarity with Jewish folklore and his penchant for the grotesque and erotic have contributed to his world fame as an interpreter of Jewish life.

The prisms of both Modern Hebrew and Yiddish literatures show the emergence of the Jews into the modern world and reflect the influence of the great social and political movements on their development. Both literatures depict universal themes as mirrored by the struggles of a historical people and its adjustments to new trends and ideologies.

BOOKS OF HEBREW LITERATURE

The quality and impact of Hebrew literature is out of all proportion to the number of people who can read it in the original. The books listed in this chapter are only a superficial introduction to the great body of work that lies waiting for the reader who wishes to pursue it. As with Yiddish literature, it is misleading to assemble one group of books and label them

"Hebrew literature." In addition to the books listed here, many others must be read to understand the full breadth of the field.

To begin with, there is the Bible, a book that is an entire library of Hebrew literature. There are also writers such as I. L. Peretz and Mendele Mokher Seforim, listed in the YIDDISH LITERATURE section, who were also important contributors to Hebrew literature. And the vast body of religious works written in Hebrew is only touched on in this guide.

Of the books that are listed in this chapter, three anthologies together form an excellent introduction to Hebrew literature. Robert Alter's *Modern Hebrew Literature* samples many of the important writings, both fiction and nonfiction, of nineteenth- and twentieth-century figures. Joel Blocker's *Israeli Stories* focuses on contemporary Israeli fiction. Finally, T. Carmi's *Penguin Book of Hebrew Verse* is a comprehensive and authoritative selection of poetry that ranges from the Bible to modern Israel.

If you wish to delve into the works of specific writers, you probably ought to start with S. Y. Agnon and Hayyim Nachman Bialik. Agnon's work incorporated many strands of Hebrew literature, both ancient and modern. *The Bridal Canopy* is one of his best-known works and a good first choice. Bialik worked in a variety of literary forms, but his principal renown is as a poet. His *Selected Poems* (Union of American Hebrew Congregations) is, regrettably, out of print.

Among contemporary writers, Yehuda Amichai, Amos Oz, and A. B. Yehoshua are all important. Oz is probably the most accessible, but all three are rewarding to read.

—R. S. F. & W. W.

Agnon, S. Y.

Shmuel Yosef Agnon (1888–1970) is one of the masters of modern Hebrew literature. He lived in Jerusalem for many years and his works draw inspiration from its people and places as well as from centuries of Hebrew literature. They incorporate pietistic folk tales and Hasidic tales, and modern psychological insights and existentialist philosophy. His voluminous output includes stories and novels that vary from realistic to experimental, and are often dreamlike and haunting. Agnon received a Nobel Prize for Literature in 1966.

His works continue to be translated into English, with his far-from-simple *A Simple Story* (Schocken Books, 1985, $14.95) being the most recent. In addition to his fiction, *Days of Awe,* Agnon's book about the High Holy Days is very worth reading. (See the section on HOLIDAYS.)

The Bridal Canopy. Translated from the Hebrew by I. M. Lask. Schocken Books, 1967, $8.95 pb.

A novel using parables and folk tales to depict the wanderings of Reb Yudel, a poor Jew in nineteenth-century Galicia who faces the world strengthened by his traditional values and faith. There are stories within stories, and the folk themes reflect both an older world and more modern symbolic meanings.

Twenty-One Stories. Edited by Nahum N. Glatzer. Schocken Books, 1970, $8.95 pb.

This representative selection of Agnon's short fiction includes stories written over a period of more than forty years. One of the stories, "Agunot," was written in 1908 and considered to be Agnon's first major work. **Agunot** (the plural of **agunah**) is Hebrew for "deserted wives," and is a word with many complicated aspects. An *agunah* is a wife whose husband has disappeared and who has neither proof of his death nor a bill of divorce. Jewish law prohibits her to remarry. "A Whole Loaf," another of Agnon's

important tales, is also included. Glatzer's brief postscripts to each story are informative and helpful.

In the Heart of the Seas. Translated from the Hebrew by I. M. Lask; illustrated by T. Herzl Rome. Schocken Books, 1975, $4.95 pb.

One of Agnon's most accessible and moving tales, *In the Heart of the Seas* tells of the journey of a group of Hasidic Jews to the land of Israel in the nineteenth century. It combines elements of the supernatural and mystic with the story of their travels. The story is deeply spiritual and imbued with religious intensity.

Alter, Robert, ed.
Modern Hebrew Literature. Behrman House, 1975, $15.95 hc, $9.95 pb.

A first-rate selection of nineteenth- and twentieth-century Hebrew writing including both essays and fiction. An introduction by Alter traces the history of Hebrew literature over the past two centuries, and each selection is preceded by a preface discussing the author's place in Hebrew literature and providing some background on the work. Many of the most important literary figures are included, among them Mendele Mokher Seforim, Ahad Ha-am, Bialik, Agnon, Hazaz, Amichai, and Oz. The quality and range of the selections make this an excellent choice for someone who wishes to become acquainted with Hebrew literature.

Amichai, Yehuda

The World Is a Room. Jewish Publication Society, 1984, $13.95.

A dominant figure in contemporary Israeli poetry, Amichai is also an important prose writer who blends colloquial language with a metaphoric and philosophic style. The ten short stories in this collection were written in the 1950s but have just recently been translated into English. They deal with the tensions of life in a country constantly torn by war. Filled with allusions to Jewish texts and celebrations, they are notable for their rich, sensuous prose. They are not action-filled. The various translators include Elinor Grumet, who has written a preface, and Hillel Halkin, and they have done an especially noteworthy job, as has the designer Adrianne Onderdunk Dudden.

Appelfeld, Aharon

A Holocaust survivor now living in Israel, Appelfeld writes mostly of the Holocaust and its emotional consequences. He does not write stories of horror and atrocity, but of psychological trauma and human weakness. His novels *Tzili* and *Badenheim 1939* are described in the HOLOCAUST section of this book. The novels described here are not directly about the Holocaust, but they could easily have been listed in that section.

The Age of Wonders. Translated from the Hebrew by Dalya Bilu. Godine, 1981, $12.95; Pocket Books, 1983, $3.95 pb.

As in *Badenheim 1939* and *The Retreat* (described next), Appelfeld deals in this novel with the disintegration of an apparently secure middle-class Jewish world. The first part of the story is about an Austrian town before World War II as seen by a thirteen-year-old boy. Thirty years later, that boy, now a man living in Jerusalem, visits his old home. The writing is vivid and very effective.

The Retreat. Translated from the Hebrew by Dalya Bilu. Dutton, 1984, $12.95.

Located on a remote hilltop outside of Vienna, the Retreat is a hotel where Jews are taught to look and act like gentiles. Set in the years immediately before World War II, this novel is a parable about the failure of assimilation.

Bargad, Warren, and Stanley F. Chyet, trans. and eds.

Israeli Poetry: A Contemporary Anthology. Indiana University Press, 1986, $29.95.

An excellent anthology of Israeli poetry written during the past forty years. The work of ten poets is presented, and both the "big names"—Amichai, Gilboa, Kovner—and many important though less well-known writers—David Avidan, Haim Gouri, Dahlia Ravikovitch, Natan Zach—are included. The translations are good, there is generous selection for each poet, and the brief biographical introductions are informative. One particularly nice touch is the inclusion of the original Hebrew title and source for each poem. A paperback edition of this book would be very welcome.

Bialik, Hayyim Nachman
Selected Poems. Union of American Hebrew Congregations, out of print.

Not only the greatest of modern Hebrew poets, Bialik was also an editor, storyteller, translator, and essayist. His command of the language was unsurpassed, taking all the elements of Hebrew writing and forging them into a new and influential style. The rebirth of Hebrew as a living language, not a captive of archaic biblical styles, was very much a result of his work. His poetry is complex and rich. Although the major theme of his work is the tension between the old, sheltered religious way of life of Jewish Eastern Europe and the modern secular world, he also wrote of the Jewish quest for national identity, of love, and of nature. He also wrote poems for children. Bialik's importance cannot be overestimated and, more than fifty years after his death, his imprint on Hebrew literature remains strong. He has been called *the* national poet of Israel. It is greatly to be regretted that no comprehensive collection of Bialik's poetry is in

print. See also *And It Came to Pass: Legends and Stories about King David and King Solomon* in BIBLE, and *Knight of Onions and Knight of Garlic* in CHILDREN'S BOOKS, AGES TWELVE AND UP.

Blocker, Joel, ed.
Israeli Stories: A Selection of the Best Writing in Israel Today. Schocken Books, 1965, $6.95 pb.

An intelligently edited anthology of contemporary Israeli fiction, all of high quality. Included are two stories by Agnon, and one each by Haim Hazaz, Aharon Megged, Yoram Kaniuk, Benjamin Tammuz, S. Yizhar, Moshe Shamir, and Yehuda Amichai. Only the Hazaz and Yizhar stories overlap with the Alter anthology described earlier, and between the two volumes the reader can get an excellent introduction to modern Hebrew prose.

Burnshaw, Stanley, T. Carmi, and Ezra Spicehandler, eds. and trans.
The Modern Hebrew Poem Itself. Holt, Rinehart & Winston, out of print.

This anthology collects poems by a number of major Hebrew poets, including Bialik, Saul Tchernichovsky, Nathan Alterman, Gabriel Preil, Amir Gilboa, Abba Kovner, Amichai, and Carmi. Each poem is presented in Hebrew, in transliteration, and in a line-by-line literal translation, along with a discussion of its contents and themes, making this a good tool for readers wishing to study the original Hebrew.

Carmi, T., ed.
The Penguin Book of Hebrew Verse. Viking/Penguin, 1981, $25 hc, $9.95 pb.

A comprehensive anthology of Hebrew verse, this book covers the Bible to modern Israeli poetry. The poems, many available only in this volume, are given in both Hebrew and English on facing pages, and are accompanied by brief and informative commentaries. Both secular and religious poems are included, and the reader might be surprised by how much of it is not of Israeli origin—throughout the ages, Jewish poets from many countries have turned to Hebrew to express themselves. Nearly 600 pages long, very thorough and complete, this is *the* anthology of Hebrew poetry. The editor is an important Hebrew poet in his own right. Another Hebrew-English poetry collection of merit is Ruth Finer Mintz's *Modern Hebrew Poetry: A Bilingual Anthology* (University of California Press, 1966, $3.95 pb), which includes both nineteenth- and twentieth-century poets.

Lelchuk, Alan, and Gershon Shaked, eds.
Eight Great Hebrew Short Novels. New American Library, 1983, $7.95 pb.

The works in this collection come both from well-known Israeli writers (Amos Oz and A. B. Yehoshua) and from such modernist European writers as Uri N. Gnessin and David Vogel. Lelchuk's introduction places the writers within the mainstream of world literature, pointing to the parallels between their work and the work of writers in other languages. The stories have a wide range of subject matter, and the translations are uniformly excellent, reading well and reflecting the diverse styles of the original Hebrew texts.

Oz, Amos

With A. B. Yehoshua, Oz is one of the leaders of the generation of writers who grew up in the State of Israel. His work frequently deals with political themes, especially the tensions between Arab and Israeli, and the ways in which politics reflects the inner emotional life of modern Israelis. (See *In the Land of Israel,* in the ISRAEL AND ZIONISM section.)

The Hill of Evil Counsel. Translated from the Hebrew by Nicholas de Lange. Harcourt Brace Jovanovich, 1978, $7.95.

These three stories, written in the 1970s, are set in the Jerusalem of 1946. That period, which saw the British Mandate in Palestine drawing to a close and the onset of the Arab-Israeli war and Israeli independence, was one of tension and turmoil. These stories effectively capture the spirit and mood of the times.

A Perfect Peace. Translated from the Hebrew by Hillel Halkin. Harcourt Brace Jovanovich, 1985, $16.95.

This novel about kibbutz life in the 1960s focuses on the tensions existing between the founders of Israel, the pioneer generation of Zionists who built the country, and their native-born children for whom the existence of Israel is not a moral triumph, merely a fact of life, and who have grown up in a world of endless armed conflict and tension.

Where the Jackals Howl: And Other Stories. Translated from the Hebrew by Nicholas de Lange and Philip Simpson. Harcourt Brace Jovanovich, 1981, $12.95.

A collection of short stories, most of which deal with kibbutz life. Oz doesn't deny the ideals that lie behind the kibbutz movement, but he also sees the emotional and sexual conflicts that exist beneath the surface. This volume is a good starting point for a reader new to Oz's work.

Shaham, Nathan

The Other Side of the Wall: Three Novellas. Translated from the Hebrew by Leonard Gold. Jewish Publication Society, 1983, $13.95.

Shaham draws on his experiences as a member of Kibbutz Bet-Alpha in these stories of Israeli life from World War II to the present. His characters tend to be outsiders, troubled and unhappy people. The title story is about a spinster, a newcomer to kibbutz life, who hears an illicit love affair being carried out on the other side of the wall dividing her from her neighbors. Another story, "Salt of the Earth," is based in part on Shaham's time spent as an Israeli cultural attaché in New York City, and it offers some telling criticisms of American Jewish life. The translation is particularly fluent.

Shamir, Moshe

The Hittite Must Die. Translated from the Hebrew by Margaret Benaya. Hebrew Publishing, 1978, $5.95 pb.

The author of several collections of short stories as well as many plays, Shamir is best known for his historical fiction. *The Hittite Must Die* is a retelling of the murder of Uriah by King David, who wished to claim Uriah's wife, Bathsheba, for himself. The story is mostly told by Uriah, who speaks of his many years as a soldier fighting for David, his own pursuit of Bathsheba, and his despair and confusion resulting from David's attempts to kill him. Shamir's works have been very popular in Israel although they are not well known abroad. Another of his historical novels, *A King of Flesh and Blood,* is also available from Hebrew Publishing ($5.95 pb). It is about Yannai, one of the Hasmonean kings in ancient Judah.

Yehoshua, A. B.

One of the major figures of contemporary Israeli literature, Yehoshua uses his fiction to explore the tensions of a society caught up in unending conflict with its neighbors. Like Amos Oz, he has spoken frequently of the need for reconciliation with the Arabs.

A Late Divorce. Translated from the Hebrew by Hillel Halkin. Doubleday, 1984, $16.95; Dutton, $9.95 pb.

In this story of a family torn by internal divisions, Yehuda Kaminka has returned from America to divorce his wife, who has been hospitalized for schizophrenia. There are three grown children from the marriage, two of them in troubled marriages themselves, the third a homosexual. Yehoshua uses the members of the family and their various problems to comment on life in Israel today. It is a powerfully written, unhappy novel.

The Lover. Translated from Hebrew by Philip Simpson. Dutton, 1985, $9.95 pb.

Yehoshua's first novel, *The Lover* depicts Arab-Jewish relations and their effect on a family during the Yom Kippur War. The relations between the characters are tangled and frustrated. Yehoshua uses allegory and modern fictional techniques in telling his story.

BOOKS OF YIDDISH LITERATURE

The title of this section is in a sense misleading. Yiddish was the principal language of European Jews for much of the past thousand years. It is based largely on a dialect of German, with elements of Hebrew and other languages blended in. To take a sampling of "literary" works and label them as Yiddish literature is to ignore the major part of what was written in the language. Going no farther than the limits of this book, you can find biographies (*Gluckel of Hameln,* in the section on WOMEN), music (multiple entries in ARTS), movies (Eric Goldman's *Visions, Images and Dreams,* in ARTS), the Bible (Jacob ben Isaac Ashkenazi's seventeenth-century Yiddish version, in BIBLE), and religious parables (Rabbi Nachman's cryptic Hasidic tales, in MODERN JEWISH THOUGHT).

Other works that you need to consult in order to grasp the breadth of Yiddish culture—and it really is a culture, not just a language—include Lucy Dawidowicz's *The Golden Tradition,* a notable anthology of documents about Eastern European Jewish life (MODERN HISTORY), and Leo Rosten's entertaining *Joys of Yiddish* (REFERENCE BOOKS).

Now that you have been sent off in all directions to other parts of this guide, you might wonder what to start with in this chapter. If you were to read only one book, it would have to be *The Best of Sholom Aleichem,* edited by Irving Howe and Ruth Wisse. No Yiddish writer is more accessible or captivating. To get a broader sampling of Yiddish, the anthologies edited by Howe and Greenberg, encompassing fiction, poetry, essays, and memoirs, are a good second step. Neugroschel's anthology *The Shtetl* has selections about Eastern European Jewish life, including some stories that are biting and strong. It is, unfortunately, out of print. *Selected Stories,* by I. L. Peretz, will introduce you to a writer who is not as famous—or charming—as Aleichem, but who is also a figure of importance to world literature. *Pushcarts and Dreamers,* edited by Max Rosenfeld, is a good choice for readers interested in Jewish immigrant life in America. Among the modern writers, Isaac Bashevis Singer is of special interest. His *The Slave* is a masterpiece.

The *Ma'aseh Book,* edited by Moses Gaster is a good source of Jewish tales and legends, and serves to communicate the religious fervor and piety of generations of Jews. And for a survey of the entire scope of Yiddish literature, Sol Liptzin's *History of Yiddish Literature* is the place to turn.

One last comment. As far as we can ascertain, the two major works by Chaim Grade, *The Agunah* and *The Yeshiva,* are not currently in print, the company that published the most recent editions of them having gone out of business. Grade is too good an author for this to be an acceptable state of affairs. Some publisher should acquire the rights to these books and bring them back to press.   —R. S. F. & W. W.

Aleichem, Sholom
See Sholom Aleichem

Anski, S.
The Dybbuk. Included in *Twenty Best European Plays on the*

American Stage, edited by John Gassner. Crown, 1957, $22.50.

In Jewish folklore, a *dybbuk* is an evil spirit, frequently the spirit of a dead sinner, that has entered the body of a living person. The spirit talks through the person's mouth and causes mental illness. Anski's dramatization of this legend is considered to be the classic version. Written in Yiddish, it was translated into Hebrew by Hayyim Nachman Bialik. When the original Yiddish manuscript was lost, Anski retranslated it into Yiddish from Bialik's Hebrew. In addition to his work as a playwright, Anski (his real name was Solomon Zanwil Rapaport) was also a professional ethnographer who gathered folk material from Eastern European villagers in the early years of this century. Also contained in this anthology is "Jacobowsky and the Colonel" by Franz Werfel, plus several non-Jewish works. The best collection of Yiddish drama, *The Dybbuk and Other Great Yiddish Plays*, edited by Joseph C. Landis, is out of print. Somebody ought to reissue it.

Asch, Sholem
Three Cities. Translated from the Yiddish by Willa and Edwin Muir. Carroll & Graf, 1983, $10.50 pb.

This trilogy offers a look at Jewish life in the cities of St. Petersburg, Warsaw, and Moscow during the first decades of the twentieth century. It combines a realistic style with an idealistic world view, and is grand storytelling. Asch (1880–1957) had a long and productive career, and by the 1950s was the best-known Yiddish writer in the world. His popularity in the Jewish community was badly damaged when he wrote a series of Christological novels, beginning with *The Nazarene*, which told the story of Jesus. Asch said he was reclaiming Jesus and his followers for the Jews; his opponents felt he had betrayed the Jews. Controversy aside, Asch is a novelist worth reading. Unfortunately, *Salvation* (Putnam, 1934), which may be his best work, is not currently in print. It is an epic of nineteenth-century Polish Jewry, and looks specifically at the world of the Hasidim.

Blinken, Meir
Stories by Meir Blinken. Translated from the Yiddish by Max Rosenfeld. State University of New York Press, 1983, $10.95.

Blinken was part of a Yiddish literary movement in early twentieth-century America that sought to break from what it saw as overly ideological and political fiction aimed at an overly sentimental readership. The stories collected here were written between 1909 and 1914, and they portray the inner life and feelings of their characters. Blinken was especially aware of the obsessive sexual passions that can drive people's actions. He was also unusually sensitive to the feelings of women. Most of the stories depict immigrant life in America, with the others set in Eastern Europe. They are touching and provide an interesting glimpse into a world now gone.

Rosenfeld's translations are outstanding.

Gaster, Moses, ed. and trans.

Ma'aseh Book: Book of Jewish Tales and Legends. Jewish Publication Society, 1981, $10.95 pb.

The more than 250 stories in this collection were first compiled and published in 1602. The stories came from the Talmud, from oral traditions, and the surrounding cultures, and all were adapted to convey a moral point—the value of charity, judging others charitably, the importance of piety and modesty. Included are stories about Moses, Isaac, King David, Akiba, Elijah, Maimonides, and Rashi, the legend of the "Jewish pope," and even a Jewish version of "Androcles and the Lion." The language of the translation is, appropriately, archaic in tone. While not a book you would want to read from cover to cover, this is a rich collection that can be dipped into many times.

Grade, Chaim

Although he lived for many years in the United States, Grade's creativity was rooted in the world of Eastern Europe where he grew up—specifically the city of Vilna, Lithuania where his family had lived for generations. His fiction attempted to blend Yiddish culture with elements of modern European literature. He is one of the few modern writers to present a detailed look at the world of talmudic study in the *yeshiva*. The theme of conflict—within an individual, between individuals, and between world views—is central to his work.

The Agunah. Twayne, 1974, out of print.

The *agunah* of the title is an "abandoned wife," a woman whose husband disappeared in action during World War I fifteen years earlier but who cannot remarry because she never received a divorce and there is no firm proof that her husband is dead. The rabbinic authorities split over whether she should be allowed to remarry and when she does, she, her new husband, and the rabbi who granted permission all become social outcasts. Eventually, she commits suicide, but even her death does not end the dispute, which continues without compromise or common ground. This novel is one of stunning force.

Rabbis and Wives. Translated from the Yiddish by Harold Rabinowitz and Ina Hecker Grade. Knopf, 1982, $15.95; Random House, $5.95 pb.

This collection of three novellas, set in Lithuania, deals with a variety of characters—a reclusive rabbi, a dying wheat merchant, a scheming woman. The stories do not have the sustained power of Grade's longer works, but they do have the same psychological insight, the same realistic depiction of daily life.

The Yeshiva. Bobbs-Merrill, 1977, out of print.

The Yeshiva is Grade's longest and most ambitious novel. The story is set in a Lithuanian *yeshiva* in the period between the World Wars. Tsemakh Atlas, a teacher there, is a tormented man, perpetually haunted by self-doubt and fear that he might slip into moral impurity. His own self-doubts lead him to mistrust not only himself, but also everyone around him. Chaikl Vilner, a student (and a semi-autobiographical figure) is torn between Atlas and the more humane Reb Avraham-Shaye Kosover, a man of faith and inner peace. The irony of people whose goals are so idealistic being involved in such endless, and ultimately fruitless, discord and hostility gives the novel much of its impact.

Howe, Irving, and Eliezer Greenberg, eds.

Irving Howe, author of *World of Our Fathers*, has also edited some fine anthologies of Yiddish literature in conjunction with Eliezer Greenberg. All three following books provide a good selection of materials.

A Treasury of Yiddish Poetry. Schocken Books, 1976, $10.95 pb.

This book has English translations of work by the pioneers of Yiddish poetry and by the second generation, known as *Die Yunge* (the Young Ones). It also includes poems by writers from the Soviet Union, Europe before World War II, the United States, and Israel. Each of the sections is introduced by a lengthy discussion of the major figures and their use of language. Among the writers included are Abraham Reiser, Morris Rosenfeld, and Mani Leib.

A Treasury of Yiddish Stories. Schocken Books, 1973, $11.95 pb.

Arranged into such thematic sections as "Portrait of a World," "Jewish Children," and "New Worlds," this anthology includes stories by Sholom Aleichem, I. L. Peretz, I. J. Singer, and I. B. Singer, among others. An introduction on the culture of Eastern Europe discusses the major themes and most important writers.

Voices from the Yiddish: Essays, Memoirs, and Diaries. Schocken Books, 1975, $5.95 pb.

This collection includes literary essays, scholarly studies, autobiographical memoirs, and excerpts from historical works. The writers include I. L. Peretz, Max Weinreich, Jacob Glatstein, Abraham Heschel, and others. The rise of Yiddish literature in nineteenth-century fiction, poetry, and other literary forms is discussed in the introduction.

Jaffe, Marie B.

Gut Yuntif, Gut Yohr. Citadel Press/Lyle Stuart, 1969, $10 hc, $5.95 pb.

We cannot pretend that this is a work of serious literature. What it is, is great fun. Jaffe has taken many well-known English poems and translated them, quite skill-fully, into Yiddish, with the Yiddish given in transliteration. Included are "The Village Blacksmith," "Hiawatha's Childhood," "The Rubyiat of Omar Khayyam," plus some Shakespeare sonnets, the Gettysburg Address, and more. "A Visit from St. Nicholas"—the poem that begins "Twas the night before Christmas"—appears here as *"Erev Krismes,"* and its closing line is now *"Gut yuntif, mishpocheh, und zeits mir gesindt!"* You don't need to know much Yiddish to enjoy this book.

Liptzin, Sol
A History of Yiddish Literature.
David, 1985, $12.95 pb.

A comprehensive survey providing a good introduction to Yiddish literature from its earliest origins to the present. Liptzin traces the development of the Yiddish language and describes early works such as the *Tz'enah Ur'enah,* a combination of Bible stories and commentaries in Yiddish. He covers all the major movements and writers, providing capsulized plot summaries and evaluating each author's work. He also covers some of the less well known corners of Yiddish literature, including authors from Australia, Latin America, South Africa, and Israel. The size of the subject makes in-depth analysis impossible, but Liptzin's survey is wide-ranging and thorough, and his judgments informed and sensible. This is a

reissue of a book first published in 1972.

Mendele Mokher Seforim
Travels and Adventures of Benjamin III. Translated from the Yiddish by Moshe Spiegel. Schocken Books, 1985, $5.50 pb.

Like Peretz, Mendele Mokher Seforim (the pen name of Shalom Jacob Abramowich) wrote in both Hebrew and Yiddish with skill and imagination. He is considered to be the first serious modern writer in Yiddish, with more sophisticated characterizations and structure than his predecessors. This story (which is also anthologized in Neugroschel's *The Shtetl* described later) is a Jewish variant of the Don Quixote story, which mocks its main character for pursuing romantic dreams even though he cannot put bread on the family's table. But Mendele also displays an obvious love for Benjamin and his ability to remain goodhearted and not be brutalized by an often brutal world.

Neugroschel, Joachim, ed. and trans.
The Great Works of Jewish Fantasy and Occult. Overlook Press, 1986, $27.95.

Originally published in 1976 as *Yenne Velt: The Great Writings of Jewish Fantasy,* this 709-page anthology contains thirty-one short stories and novellas, dating from the seventeenth through the twentieth centuries. It includes stories about demonic possession, about a rabbi who turns into a werewolf, about the famous Golem of Prague, and other fantastical doings. Among the authors are S. Anski, Mendele Mokher Seforim, Der Nister, I. L. Peretz, and Rabbi Nachman of Bratslav. An anthology by Neugroschel that is in some ways superior, *The Shtetl* (Putnam, 1979) is now regrettably out of print. It includes fiction by many of the most important Yiddish writers and provides an outstanding portrait of the world of the *shtetl*—the small Jewish towns of Eastern Europe. The stories have some of the conventional piety and nostalgia, but there is also privation, emotional claustrophobia, violence, and horror. A good nonfiction profile of *shtetl* life can be found in Mark Zborowski and Elizabeth Herzog's *Life Is with People,* described in the MODERN AND MEDIEVAL HISTORY section.

Peretz, I. L.

Selected Stories. Edited by Irving Howe and Eliezer Greenberg. Schocken Books, 1975, $4.95 pb.

Peretz occupies an important place in both Hebrew and Yiddish literature, writing plays, essays, and stories. It is generally felt that his major accomplishment was as a short story writer in Yiddish, although he is still read extensively in Hebrew. The stories frequently use old tales from the Jewish folk heritage, putting them into more modern—

and more complex—forms. He is, perhaps, closer to Franz Kafka than he is to Sholom Aleichem. Among the eighteen stories in this collection, "Bontsche Schweig" is the most famous. It is touching and folkloric, but also deeply skeptical and ironic. "The Magician," one of his best stories, is also included. It is a folktale in which Elijah the Prophet appears to provide a Passover *seder* for a poor, pious family.

Rosenfeld, Max, ed. and trans.

Pushcarts and Dreamers: Stories of Jewish Life in America. Illustrated by Everett H. Solovitz and Edward Moskow. Sholom Aleichem Club Press, 1967, $4.95 pb.

The stories in this anthology are about the great wave of Jewish immigration to America between 1890 and 1910. Writing from personal experience, their authors describe appalling physical conditions, long hours of sweatshop labor, the difficulties of breaking with an old way of life and building a new one, and the constant debates about how best to improve the standard of life. Few of the writers are well known today, Sholem Asch being the only name familiar to many modern readers. Among the others included are Abraham Reisin, Joseph Opatoshu, and Leon Kobrin. The work is varied, with elements of humor and irony that keep the mood from being too somber. The result is an anthology that is good reading and is also a good way to understand the lives of an entire generation of American Jews. (See Irving Howe's *World of Our Fathers* in MODERN HISTORY for a book that fills in the background of this world).

Sholom Aleichem (Sholom Rabinovitz)

Seventy years after his death, Sholom Aleichem remains a writer of enormous popularity and appeal. His gentle and warm humor, his compassion, and his literary skill combined to create and populate a world that still lives and breathes. Born Sholom Rabinovitz, he took a pen name because, among other reasons, writing in Yiddish was not seen as a respectable occupation. ("Sholom Aleichem" is a Hebrew greeting, meaning "Peace to you.") He was prolific, partly because he was a terrible businessman and had to produce endlessly to make a living. His works include plays, reviews, poems, and, most importantly, novels and stories. The musical based on his stories of Tevye the Dairyman, "Fiddler on the Roof," has helped keep his work in the public eye. There has been a revival of interest in his work, and several of his books are now appearing in English for the first time. These include *Marienbad* and *The Nightingale*.

Although known primarily as a humorist, Sholom Aleichem dealt with the very serious theme of a Jewish world in transition from its old, religious ways to a more modern and secular life. Generally, the "big issues" form the background of his stories. Sometimes, as in *In the Storm* (Putnam's, 1983, $15.95), which describes the impact of the 1905 pogroms in Russia, the political issues are central. A collection of his nonfiction Zionist writings was published in 1984 by Herzl Press/ Cornwall Books under the title *Why Do the Jews Need a Land of Their Own?* (See also *Holiday Tales of Sholom Aleichem* in CHILDREN'S BOOKS, AGE EIGHT TO TWELVE.)

The Best of Sholom Aleichem. Edited by Irving Howe and Ruth R. Wisse. Pocket Books, 1983, $3.95 pb.

It is especially difficult to do full justice to Aleichem's rich and colorful style in translation. The stories in this collection, a good representative selection, are as well translated as could be hoped. Among the tales included here are some about the famous village of Kasrilevke, one of Aleichem's greatest and most enduring fictional creations.

From the Fair: The Autobiography of Sholom Aleichem. Edited and translated by Curt Leviant. Viking/Penguin, 1985, $20 hc, $7.95 pb.

At the age of forty-nine, Sholom Aleichem began writing his autobiography, a project he continued working on until his death in 1916. Much of the material was produced for newspaper serialization, and it has been gathered together here in English for the first time. The book covers his early life, through his days as a student and his beginning years as a writer.

Singer, Isaac Bashevis

A winner of the Nobel Prize, Singer is unquestionably the most famous modern Yiddish writer. He continues to be an active writer for both Yiddish- and English-speaking audiences, with stories appearing regularly in the *Jewish Daily Forward* and *The New Yorker.* He is a superbly gifted storyteller. His output includes many novels and short stories. Within the Yiddish-speaking community in particular, there is some resentment that a writer not considered to present Jews in a favorable light should be the Yiddish writer best-known by Americans. His portrayal of *shtetl* life is often harsh. Some critics feel he is preoccupied with sex and with the supernatural. Yiddish novelist Cahanan Ayalti said that Singer's work "derives from second-rate Polish and French romances." Sol Liptzin, in his history of Yiddish literature (described earlier), says that Singer has an "infatuation" with the horrible and that he abuses his talent by "straining far too often for sensational effects." We do not agree with that assessment, finding in Singer's work an intense love for Jewish life and an ability

to communicate that love to his readers. His stories for children are a special treat, for adults as well as children (see CHILDREN'S BOOKS). His memoir, *In My Father's Court,* described in MODERN AND MEDIEVAL HISTORY, is also rewarding.

The Family Moskat. Translated by A. H. Gross. Farrar, Straus & Giroux, 1965, $15 hc, $7.95 pb.

Singer's most ambitious novel, *The Family Moskat* is a realistic portrait of a patrician Jewish family in pre-World War II Poland. It traces the family's decline, especially following the death of the family's patriarch, after which its level of religious observance and standards of conduct weaken. The novel is long and loosely structured, and it is filled with sharp characterizations. It is not Singer's easiest work to read, but it is among his best.

Gimpel the Fool. Translated from the Yiddish by Saul Bellow, Isaac Rosenfield, Norbert Guterman, et al. Fawcett Books, 1985, $2.95.

The short story is Singer's forte. The title story of this collection is one of his finest. Gimpel is a *schlemiel,* a simpleton who believes everything he is told, who assumes that everyone else is as honest as he is. On her deathbed, his wife, whom he had always believed to be faithful, tells him that all six of her children were fathered by other men. After her death, he wanders the world aimlessly, facing the prospect of his own death with relief: "When the time comes I will go joyfully. Whatever may be there, it will be real, without complication, without deceit, without ridicule, without deception."

The Magician of Lublin. Translated from the Yiddish by Elaine Gottlieb and Joseph Singer. Fawcett Books, 1979, $2.50.

In this dazzling, passionate, and lyrical story, the magician is Yasha Mazur, a touring acrobat and magician who has cast off religious ways and who has many mistresses. Recruited by gangsters to crack an old man's safe, he fails, and becomes a fugitive, betrayed by his mistress. On the run, he rediscovers his religion and is transformed into a saintly hermit. His internal struggle with evil is riveting.

The Slave. Translated from the Yiddish by the author and Cecil Hemley. Farrar, Straus & Giroux, 1962, $4.95 pb; Fawcett Books, $2.50 pb.

This is our personal favorite from all of Singer's work. Set in seventeenth-century Poland following the pogroms known as the Chmielnicki Massacres, its hero is Jacob, a young Jew living in slavery. He falls in love with Wanda, the daughter of his master, and she converts to Judaism. The story is about the power of love to transcend barriers between people, and it is rich in descriptions of Jewish life and customs.

Singer, I. J.

The Brothers Ashkenazi. Translated from the Yiddish by Joseph Singer. Carroll & Graf, 1985, $9.95 pb.

Israel Joshua Singer (1893–1944) was Isaac Bashevis Singer's older brother. Their writing styles are quite different, with I. J. using a plainer and more economical prose. *The Brothers Ashkenazi* is representative of I. J. Singer's work in its emphasis on family and its broad historic sweep. At the heart of the novel are two brothers, the twins Max and Jacob Ashekenazi, their bitter feuds, and occasional reconciliations. Their story is set against a panoramic view of the city of Lodz, Poland: its rise from backwater to flourishing textile manufacturing center, and then gradual decline following the Russian Revolution in 1917. The story is powerfully told, with an intense energy.

Renaissance in the Arts
Esther Nussbaum

"Jewish Art" as a category has eluded definition. Do Jewish artists create Jewish art? Is a picture of a woman lighting candles Jewish art by virtue of its subject matter? Is a silver wine cup used for the *Kiddush* (the blessing over the wine) an object of Jewish art? Is an antique sugar container to which an inscription in Hebrew has been added to designate it an **etrog** container considered Jewish art? These questions continue to be debated in the open forum just as books dealing with the esthetic aspects of the Jewish cultural heritage are being published in increasing numbers.

Not surprising is the fact that the focus of most books is the ceremonies associated with holiday celebrations and life cycle occasions. Ritual objects integral to those ceremonies may draw on many disciplines and be executed in a variety of media. The works of artisans in precious metals and other crafts as well as those of fiber artists as applied to Judaic themes have been examined and written about more in the decades following World War II than ever before. Undoubtedly, there was creative enterprise in the desire to adorn and beautify the Jewish experience both in the home and the synagogue throughout the ages, but the requisite scholarship and readership is a contemporary phenomenon.

What has coincided is the knowledge gained from historical, ethnographic, archeologic, and anthropologic disciplines with Jewish scholarship and the freedom to express and proclaim enthusiastically both the ancient tradition and its modern manifestations. Heretofore, the study of Jewish art was the province

---

Esther Nussbaum is a library media specialist at Ramaz Upper School in New York City with special interest in the Jewish arts, on which she has written extensively.

of academics. Its popularization paralleled the revival of interest in national and folk traditions that has flourished in recent years. The State of Israel and the earlier years of Zionist revitalization gave impetus to artistic endeavors by organizing art schools, funding archaeological projects, and encouraging the study of art as an important part of the cultural functions of the nation. The establishment of Jewish museums, another twentieth-century phenomenon (due, in part, to the decimation of artifacts during the Nazi era), reflects the pride of heritage as well as involvement in the inspiration for Jewish creativity.

How has the book world recorded artistic achievement? Exhibition catalogues, executed for and by galleries, museums, or auction houses remain the largely inaccessible printed record of these important but temporary events. Such catalogues seldom reach the marketplace and do not have the channels of distribution to the retail market available to large press publishers. (Similarly, interest in ethnic theater has inspired studies of the Yiddish and Hebrew stage. The revival of interest in Jewish music has also resulted in publications devoted to the musical heritage, with small presses often taking the lead in collecting and printing Jewish music, including the instrumental notation, thus preserving the folk and liturgical traditions.)

The study of visual arts necessitates photographic reproduction, and quality printing of illustrations and photographs is so costly as to deter publication. When such a book is published, the price of the book often inhibits wide distribution, or it may be in so limited a printing as to become unavailable in a relatively short time. Regrettably, some of the best books on Jewish art, architecture, ceremonial objects, and so on have been out of print for many years, while others are threatened with the same fate. It remains for the demand for such books to be strengthened so that publishers will be motivated to keep the titles in print, or to bring out new or revised editions of titles long unavailable.

The dearth of books in the area of the arts is due also, in part, to the breadth of expertise necessary to give accurate historical and religious context. Jewish life has been experienced in so many different locations, influenced by so many factors that ultimately affected the design and decoration of religious implements used in the home and synagogue. Likewise, various interpretations of biblical dicta resulted in inhibiting decorative motifs acceptable to the Jewish community. (Most so-called biblical art is found in churches and Christian religious illustration.) One must be versed in the history of design as well as the history of the Jewish people, knowledge of Hebrew, possibly Aramaic, Yiddish, and Ladino if one wishes to study original texts, before attempting to explore a topic competently. Cecil Roth's monumental work *Jewish Art* (now out of print) is seminal to the field. Most works do not aim at such comprehensiveness, but it is important that such a work be extant in order to proceed from there into more indepth studies.

It is interesting to note that among the many Jewish publishing entrepreneurs, Harry N. Abrams started the first commercial firm devoted solely to art books. (He named it after himself.) The firm has continued to excel in the field but its only connection with Jewish art is its books dealing with artists who happen to be Jewish. Marc Chagall and Chaim Gross are two examples whose works have been treated to the firm's special expertise.

The archival record of Jewish life in pre-World War II Europe has become a major contribution in visual arts publication. Rivaling their importance as historical documents, as visual testaments, they captivate readers. The popularity of books whose titles begin with such phrases as "Illustrated history of . . . " or "Picture book of . . . " has brought about a spate of publishing of often demeaning textual and pictorial quality. The photographic essay, on the contrary, is a dimension of publishing that is just beginning to be explored in areas of Jewish life. It promises to be a popular format, and a book such as Gail Rubin's *Psalmist with a Camera: Photographs of a Biblical Safari* (Abbeville) sets high standards.

The Holocaust brought about the creation of "art in exile" and in concentration camps, where the horrific experience was depicted, usually with makeshift supplies and under dire conditions. Artists who otherwise might not have been concerned with Jewish life were forced to confront their Jewishness because of the anti-Jewish oppression. Several books and exhibition catalogues have focused on the surviving artistic output of the Nazi years.

The bibliography reveals that the thrust of most studies of Jewish creative arts is to place them in a historical context and to trace their varied developments through the ages. Although proportionately small relative to books on other aspects of Jewish life, works that emphasize the esthetic dimension are but another means to understand and enjoy the many facets of Jewish life.

BOOKS ON MUSIC AND THE ARTS

It is unfortunate that there is no readily available book providing a good introduction to Jewish art. Roth's *Jewish Art* is out of print. Wigoder's *Jewish Art and Civilization* is available in the form of an inexpensive reprint that is not widely distributed. Altshuler's *The Precious Legacy* is a beautiful book showing many examples of Jewish ritual art. It also includes several informative articles. For readers interested in synagogue design and architecture, Kampf's *Contemporary Synagogue Art* is a useful survey. Krinsky's *Synagogues of Europe* is both an art book and a serious scholarly study. A touching photographic reminder of the Eastern European life destroyed by the Nazis can be found in Vishniac's *A Vanished World*.

A good survey of Jewish music is available, Idelsohn's *Jewish Music in Its Historical Development,* and an abundance of Jewish music is also in print. The books by Coopersmith and by Pasternak described later are collections that fill virtually every possible need. The theater is not as well covered. One of the best-known Yiddish plays, Anski's *The Dybbuk,* is available as part of Gassner's *Twenty Great European Plays on the American Stage* (YIDDISH LITERATURE). Goldman's *Visions, Images and Dreams* is a solid and readable history of Yiddish film in Europe and America. Readers should also consult ARCHEOLOGY AND ANCIENT HISTORY for books on the design of ancient synagogues. —R. S. F. & W. W.

Aber, Ita

The Art of Judaic Needlework: Traditional and Contemporary Designs. Scribner, $3.95 pb.

In addition to many suggestions for projects appropriate to home and synagogue based on Jewish life and ritual, the author offers detailed information on proper techniques for finishing a piece and on textile conservation. The projects are suitable for a variety of skill levels, from beginner to advanced.

Altshuler, David

The Precious Legacy: Judaic Treasures from the Czechoslovak State Collections. Summit Books, $40 hc, $17.50 pb.

The Czechoslovak State Jewish Museum of Prague houses one of the largest Judaica collections in the world. This enormous assemblage of material was amassed by the Nazis, who were planning to establish a "museum to an extinct race." In 1983 the Smithsonian organized a traveling exhibit of nearly three hundred objects from the collection, and this book is that exhibit's catalogue. It is a beautiful and poignant book, and the articles it includes make it even more worth owning. (See Chaya Burstein's *Joseph and Anna's Time Capsule* in CHILDREN'S BOOKS, AGES EIGHT TO TWELVE.)

Anonymous

Great Jewish Classics. Tara, 1973, 4 vols., $11.95 each, pb.

Earlier this century, a Yiddish theatrical district flourished on New York's Lower East Side. In 1918, Henry Lefkowitch founded the Metro Music Shop in the middle of that district, a company that was active as a publisher and seller of music for many decades. The back of "Songs for Young Folks" offered Metro's "complete catalogue of high class Jewish Music." The four volumes in this series are reprints of material originally published by Metro, including Yiddish folk, art, and liturgical songs, arranged for voice and piano. For the most part, the Yiddish lyrics are presented only in transliteration, not in English translation. Volume 3 has some interesting oddities: music by Franz Schubert and Jules Massenet with Yiddish and Hebrew texts, and a work written for the eightieth birthday of Emperor Franz Joseph I that contains a Hebrew chorus written to the melody of "Deutschland Über Alles." (!) For more about the Yiddish theater, try *Bright Star of Exile* by Lulla Rosenfeld. A biography of Jacob Adler, it also includes a good history of the Yiddish theater. It is now out of print.

Blatter, Janet, and Sybil Milton, eds.

Art of the Holocaust. Routledge Press, 1981, $29.95.

This powerful and grim book reproduces more than three hundred works of art created in, and depicting life in, the Nazi death camps. It includes information on the historical background of the Holocaust, a perceptive analysis of the works of art, and information on how the works were preserved after the war in museums and archives. Biographical information is given on the artists and the names and addresses of research centers and museums dealing with Holocaust art are included. Winner of a 1982 National Jewish Book Award.

Coopersmith, Harry, ed.
The New Jewish Song Book. Behrman House, 1965.

An anthology of songs especially appropriate for children, this book includes both liturgical and secular music, with songs for the holidays and the Sabbath, songs from Europe and Israel translated from Yiddish and Hebrew, and a section of rounds. Chords are given.

The Songs We Sing. Illustrated by K. Oeschli. United Synagogue Commission on Jewish Education, 1950, $22.50.

This book is an attractive and sturdily bound collection of songs, including music for the Sabbath and holidays, **z'mirot** (Sabbath and holiday "table" songs), songs and dances from Israel, biblical cantillation, prayer motifs, Yiddish songs, and more. Full piano scores are included, and many of the songs are translated into English. (The rest include English summaries.)

More of the Songs We Sing. Illustrated by K. Oeschli. United Synagogue Commission on Jewish Education, 1971, $9.50.

As the title says, this book offers more songs for the various occasions of the Jewish year, plus some part songs and rounds. Unlike the first volume, piano accompaniments are not included, only chords. Both collections are fun and entertaining.

Davidovitch, David
The Ketuba: Jewish Marriage Contracts Through the Ages. Adama Books, 1985, $29.95.

The *ketubah* is the Jewish marriage contract, a document with roots in antiquity—possibly as far back as the Babylonian Exile. It spells out in considerable detail the obligations, largely financial, that a husband has toward his wife, and was a great step forward in the protection of women's rights. In part because marriage is a joyous occasion, in part because it is seen as a "woman's document," the *ketubah* became elaborately ornamented, with different countries developing different traditional designs. This book includes a brief but thorough introduction to the history and form of the *ketubah,* and eighteen spectacularly beautiful tipped-in color plates, plus several black-and-white illustrations. The results are dazzling.

Erens, Patricia
The Jew in American Cinema. Indiana University Press, 1985, $27.50.

A historical survey of more than eight hundred feature films with Jewish characters and themes. Erens begins in 1903 and proceeds decade by decade up to 1983, discussing genres, themes, and Jewish stereotypes. The sheer number of films covered precludes any detailed analysis, but this is a useful and comprehensive study.

Fine, Jo Renee (photographs), and Gerald R. Wolfe (text)
The Synagogues of New York's Lower East Side. Washington Mews Books/New York University Press, 1978, $12.95 pb.

Early in this century, New York's Lower East Side may well have had the highest concentration of synagogues anywhere in the world. There were grand, soaring buildings, and tiny *stieblach*—congregations located in storefronts, apartments, and cellars. This fine book includes an introductory essay on the origin and development of these synagogues, and then surveys some of the most interesting of them. For each, there are photographs and discussion of the building's history, architecture, and current status.

Goldman, Eric A.
Visions, Images and Dreams: Yiddish Film Past and Present. UMI Research Press, $39.95.

This profusely illustrated history of Yiddish film, with detailed and interesting discussions of the major directors, performers, and films, is scholarly but readable. It's unfortunate that a more affordable paperback edition hasn't been published.

Idelsohn, A. Z.
Jewish Music in Its Historical Development. Greenwood, 1981, $35 hc; Schocken Books, $12.50 pb.

Originally published in 1929, this remains the best one-volume survey of the history of Jewish music. Idelsohn describes and analyzes Jewish music from its earliest origins, discussing the ways in which it expresses and reflects Judaism and Jewish life. He also examines the influence exerted by the music of surrounding cultures and how some foreign elements have become part of Jewish music. The range is wide—secular and religious music, folk music, Hasidic music, *klezmer* bands, synagogue music, and Jews in general music. Many samples of music are included, and some technical grounding is useful, although not essential, for a reader to get the full benefit of the discussion. The section on the style and work of famous cantors is especially interesting.

Jochsberger, Tzipora H., and Velvel Pasternak, eds.
A Harvest of Jewish Song. Tara, 1980, $14.95 pb.

Seventy-three songs from Israel, some predating the establishment of the state, including religious and secular music. Most of the songs are in Hebrew, with both the transliterated text and vocalized Hebrew text supplied. There are also some songs in Yiddish and Ladino. All have piano accompaniment and guitar chords.

Kalisch, Shoshana, and Barbara Meister
Yes, We Sang! Songs of the Ghettos and Concentration Camps. Harper & Row, 1985, $22.95 hc, $12.95 pb.

As a child, Kalisch was imprisoned in Auschwitz. For many years after the war, she repressed her memories of the experience, but eventually the songs she had heard began coming back to her. This collection of those songs presents them with piano accompaniment, English translations, and additional verses. Each song is given with information about the circumstances under which it was created and a story relating it to a particular person or event. The stories are often heartbreaking; the songs are often inspiring.

Kampf, Avram
Contemporary Synagogue Art: Developments in the United States, 1945–1965. Union of American Hebrew Congregations, 1966, $15.

This critical survey of synagogue art and architecture in America includes 275 black-and-white photographs and discussions of work by such noted figures as Ben Shahn, Frank Lloyd Wright, and Walter Gropius. Kampf deals with the work in terms of its esthetic value and in terms of the synagogue's cultural and religious functions. He includes a discussion of the biblical prohibition against graven images. The absence of color photographs and the mediocre layout and printing make the book of value primarily for utilitarian, not esthetic purposes.

Jewish Experience in the Art of the Twentieth Century. Bergin & Garvey, 1984, $49.50.

Based on an exhibit held at the Jewish Museum in New York in 1975–1976, this work is not a study of "Jewish art"—in fact, Kampf denies there is any such thing. It is a study of how major Jewish subjects such as the Diaspora, the Holocaust, the anxiety of assimilation, and Israel have been incorporated as motifs by twentieth-century artists. The work of more than fifty artists, not all of them Jewish, is covered. Although a pioneering study, the book suffers from the lack of color illustrations (only sixteen out of more than 200), and from unevenness in the quality of the chapters. Kampf assumes his readers have a good knowledge of art history.

Krinsky, Carol Herselle

Synagogues of Europe: Architecture, History, Meaning. MIT Press, 1985, $50.

What a terrific book! The first part of this oversize volume is a history of synagogue architecture and an analysis of the ways in which it differs from the architecture of churches and mosques. The second part describes approximately a hundred synagogues in detail, most from Central and Western Europe, with information on their history and design. Krinsky provides much more than dry architectural analysis—she tells a moving human story of congregations determined to build and maintain houses of worship despite legal and social obstacles. The many illustrations (unfortunately all in black and white) include photos, floor plans, and drawings. The notes are extensive and informative. The number of synagogues that have been destroyed or fallen into disrepair makes this a work with sad overtones. Two other books on synagogue architecture, now out of print, are definitely worth looking for. They are *Synagogue Architecture in the United States* (1955) and *The Architecture of the European Synagogue* (1964), both by Rachel Wischnitzer.

Leaf, Reuben

Hebrew Alphabets: 400 B.C.E. to Our Day. Bloch, 1976, $20.

A sampling of more than sixty Hebrew alphabets from over the centuries, including examples from Canaan, medieval Spain, "Rashi script," and modern Hebrew. Background on the alphabet, an example of Aramaic, and other information are included. A particularly useful book for calligraphers and designers.

Levin, Neil, ed.

Songs of the American Jewish Experience. Tara, 1976, $12.95 spiral binding.

Prepared in commemoration of the American Bicentennial celebration, this collection presents an overview of American Jewish music from colonial times to the present. It does not include cantorial or modern synagogue choral music, but those are the only major omissions. Included are the anthems of the ILGWU (International Ladies and Garment Workers Union) and Workman's Circle, songs for children, sentimental Yiddish classics like *A Brivele Der Mamen* ("A Letter to Mama"), Yiddish art songs, and Irving Berlin's "God Bless America." English summaries of the lyrics are provided. Someone should tell the editor, though, that Castle Garden and Ellis Island are not the same place.

Levin, Neil, and Velvel Pasternak, eds.

Z'mirot Anthology: Traditional Sabbath Songs for the Home. Tara, 1981, $24.95 hc, $16.95 pb.

It is a long-standing Jewish custom for families to sing

songs known as *z'mirot shel Shabbat* around the table during Sabbath. *Z'mirot*—literally "songs" or "hymns," but generally translated as "table songs"— are mostly settings of religious poems written between the tenth and seventeenth centuries. This anthology has an introductory essay discussing their history, themes, forms, and sources. It includes an extensive selection of songs, all presented with Hebrew text, transliterated text, English translation, and background information.

Mlotek, Eleanor
Mir Trogen a Gezang: The New Book of Yiddish Songs. Workman's Circle, 1984, $10.95 pb.

More than a hundred Yiddish songs are given here, with transliterated texts, English summaries, and background information. The songs are all of recent vintage.

Pasternak, Velvel

Easily one of the most energetic and active figures in Jewish music today, Pasternak is a cantor, accompanist, arranger, teacher, composer, author, and, as the head of Tara Publications, a major publisher. He has compiled many volumes of Jewish music, and the next several titles are his work.

The Best of Hasidic Song. Tara, 1984, $9.95 pb.

An anthology of Hasidic music compiled from seven previous books published by Tara, including *Songs of the Chassidim*, Volumes 1 and 2 listed later. The music has been selected as being especially appropriate for occasions such as weddings, Bar Mitzvahs, and other celebrations.

Favorite Songs of Israel. Tara, 1985, $19.95.

This comprehensive and varied collection of Israeli music has a good selection of songs of **Sephardic**, Ladino, and Oriental heritage. A section of dances is included.

Holidays in Song. Tara, 1985, $11.95 spiral binding.

More than a hundred songs are given here for the Sabbath, High Holy Days, Sukkot, **Simchat Torah**, Hanukkah, Tu bi-Shevat, Purim, Passover, Shavuot, Tisha B'av, and Yom Ha-shoah. The songs have transliterated Hebrew lyrics, and brief English translations are given.

Israel in Song. Compiled with Richard Neumann. Tara, 1974, $12.95 spiral binding.

Originally prepared in conjunction with the Board of Jewish Education, this anthology was produced to help bring Israeli songs to Jewish schools and teachers. There are brief notes for each song, giving some information about its writer or history. Both secular and liturgical music is included, as are rounds and choral settings. Among the better-known pieces are "Hatikvah" (the Israel national anthem), "Hava Negila," "Jersusalem the Golden," "Dodi Li," and "Tsena, Tsena," a song the Weavers turned into a surprise hit recording in the 1950s. A companion volume, *Great Songs of Israel* (Tara, 1976, $12.95 spiral binding), is also available and includes an additional ninety Israeli songs.

Jewish Wedding Music. Tara, 1985, $9.95 pb.

Selected from other Tara books, among them *Israel in Song*, this anthology has processionals, recessionals, and dances, including Hasidic and Israeli music.

The New Children's Songbook. Tara, 1981, $10.95 spiral binding.

More than a hundred Hebrew songs for children, some with singable English-language versions, are collected here. The categories include songs for *Shabbat*, the holidays, Israel Independence Day, prayer, and songs about animals, the seasons, etc. Suggested activities are also included.

Songs of the Chassidim, Vol. 1, Tara, 1968, $24.95; Vol. 2, Tara, 1971, $28.95.

Volume 1 of this set includes 170 Hasidic songs, about half arranged so that they can be sung by a two-part chorus. An introduction discusses the origins of Hasidic music; there is a section of texts and translations, and a discography. Included is liturgical music, *z'mirot*, wedding songs and dances, and music for the festivals and High Holy Days. Volume 2 has an additional 210 songs, covering the same categories plus a section of Psalms and another drawn from the Passover Haggadah. For many of the songs, there is a one-paragraph background description. The two volumes are available as a set for $49.95.

Podwal, Mark
A Book of Hebrew Letters. Jewish Publication Society, 1978, $5.95.

This delicate and fanciful collection of black-and-white drawings is based on the twenty-two letters of the Hebrew alphabet. Each letter illustrates a Hebrew word, beginning with "aleph-bet" and ending with "Torah." The illustrations reflect the richness of Jewish life and tradition. Notes on the drawings include historical, literary, and midrash information. A slender volume with a great deal in it. You can see some of Podwal's work in this book.

Rivkin, Nacha, and Ella Shurin
Come Sing with Me. Arranged by Velvel Pasternak. Tara, 1984, $10.95.

These sixty-five simple children's songs, many with singable English versions, were all originally recorded as part of the Shiru Li series of children's records. They have lyrics that emphasize teaching about the joys of *Shabbat*, the holidays, ethical values, and such practical matters as crossing on the green light or washing behind your ears.

Roth, Cecil
Jewish Art: An Illustrated History. McGraw-Hill, 1961, out of print.

This authoritative and readable history of Jewish art was written by a noted Jewish historian. It covers Jewish art from antiquity to modern times, synagogue architecture, Hebrew illuminated manuscripts and the first printed books, and includes a section on Jewish sculptors. Several important architects, critics, and art historians contributed to the volume, among them M. Avi-Yonah, Rachel Wischnitzer, and Franz Landsberger. There are many black-and-white illustrations, but not as many in color as could be wished.

Rozin, Albert
Favorite Hebrew Songs for Piano. Tara, 1984, $7.95 pb.

A selection of Hebrew songs with easy-to-play piano arrangements that ranges over Israeli, Hasidic, and liturgical materials, and songs for the Sabbath and festivals. Among the songs are "Hatikvah," "Kol Nidre," and "Dayenu." The omission of English translations is a drawback.

Vishniac, Roman
A Vanished World. Farrar, Straus & Giroux, 1983, $65.

A masterpiece and a wonderful gift. In the late 1930s, Vishniac traveled with a camera, recording the world of Eastern European Jewry about to be destroyed in the Holocaust. Of some 16,000 photographs taken, about 2,000

survived, many hidden in a village in France and rescued after the war. This beautifully printed book reproduces 179 of them. The faces are haunting. Some of the same photographs are reproduced, although much less impressively, in *Polish Jews: A Pictorial Record* (Schocken Books, 1965, $7.95 pb), which also includes an introductory essay by Abraham Joshua Heschel on the inner world of the Polish Jews.

Wigoder, Geoffrey, ed.
Jewish Art and Civilization. Chartwell, 1984, $22.98.

A thorough survey of Jewish art, covering the Ancient Near East, Byzantium, Moslem lands, Spain, Portugal and the Conversos, Italy, France, Germany, England, the Netherlands, Poland and Russia, the United States, South and Central America, and the State of Israel. The chapters are by noted authorities and deal with religion, social and economic factors, history, and Jews as portrayed by non-Jewish artists. All forms of art—painting, ritual objects, synagogue architecture, books, and photography—are discussed. This is an inexpensive edition of a two-volume work originally published by Walker in 1972, and now out of print.

Zim, Sol
The Joy of Jewish Memories. Tara, 1984, $9.95 spiral binding.

This selection of twentieth-century Yiddish songs is presented in singable English versions. In addition to songs from the Yiddish theater, there are songs about the Old Country, the Holocaust, and Israel. Such classics of schmaltz as "Yiddishe Mame" are included. The Yiddish texts are given, and there is a brief glossary.

IX

<u>Periodicals</u>

Periodicals

There is a pleasing richness and variety in Jewish magazine publishing today. There is virtually no aspect of Jewish life that isn't covered, no approach that isn't taken. There are magazines with an editorial staff of dozens, and magazines with a staff of one; there are magazines speaking for large organizations and espousing establishment positions, and magazines speaking for no one but themselves and taking stands guaranteed to get on your nerves. Virtually every narrow niche is filled. One area in particular that is especially well served is coverage of Israel and Israeli affairs. The general media in the United States do not do a good job—and sometimes do a disturbingly bad one—when it comes to writing about Israel. But several magazines that focus on Israel help make up for that lack.

The publications described in this chapter are a representative sampling of the best Jewish periodicals.

—R. S. F. & W. W.

Ariel. Published by Jerusalem Post Publications, P.O. Box 3349, Jerusalem, 91002 Israel. Subscriptions: $22 for four issues, via seamail. Editor: Asher Weill.

This digest-size review of Israeli arts and letters includes fiction, poetry, reviews, and articles on such topics as Israeli art and museums, the development of modern Hebrew, architecture, and movies. Editions are published in English, French, German, and Spanish. Color and black-and-white photographs add to the appeal of the magazine.

Biblical Archeology Review. Published every other month by the Biblical Archeology Society, Connecticut Avenue N.W., Washington, DC 20008. Subscriptions: P.O. Box 10757, Des Moines, IA 50347. $23.70 per year. Editor: Hershel Shanks.

This review prints articles on all aspects of biblical archeology. The contents are aimed at the general reader, and there are many color photographs and pictures. Recent articles include discussions of the route and the dates of the Exodus from Egypt, Champollion's decipherment of the Rosetta Stone, the excavation of Shiloh, and a debate over the identification of an archeological site as Joshua's altar. The occasional disagreement between the Bible's text and the findings of archeology is an issue hotly debated in letters to the editor. Articles on New Testament sites are included.

Bible Review. Published quarterly by the Biblical Archeology Society, Connecticut Avenue N.W., Washington, DC 20008. Subscriptions: P.O. Box 601, Holmes, PA 19043. $15 per year. Editor: Hershel Shanks.

Like its sister publication, *Biblical Archaeology Review*, this is a glossy magazine with articles written for the nonexpert, and filled with color pictures. Its approach is that of secular Bible scholarship and both the Hebrew and Christian Bibles are covered. Among the topics covered are the biblical basis for the kosher prohibition against mixing meat and milk, the implications of the Dead Sea Scrolls on our understanding of the Bible, technical aspects of epigraphy, and whether the Documentary Hypothesis and its theory of multiple authorship of the Bible is accurate. There are also book reviews and a Bible quiz in each issue.

Commentary. Published monthly by the American Jewish Committee, 165 East 56th Street, New York, NY 10022. Subscriptions:

$33 per year, $89 for three years. Editor: Norman Podhoretz.

Possibly the most overtly political of all Jewish magazines, *Commentary* is a leading voice of the "Neo-Conservative" movement, providing an outlet for such writers as Norman Podhoretz and Midge Decter. In addition to specifically Jewish issues—and even those tend to be politically oriented, such as patterns of Jewish voting—it ranges over such issues as the Khmer Rouge, and religion and the conservatives. The book reviews also frequently deal with such political topics as human rights or contemporary affairs. The intellectual level is high, and the writing is generally excellent.

Conservative Judaism. Published quarterly by the Rabbinical Assembly and the Jewish Theological Seminary of America,. 3080 Broadway, New York, NY 10027. Subscriptions: Human Sciences Press, Circulation, 72 Fifth Avenue, New York, NY 10011. $26 per year for individuals; $66 for institutions. Editor: David Wolf Silverman.

In its own words, *Conservative Judaism:* "publishes articles which express a serious critical inquiry of Jewish texts and traditions, legacy, and law; further the quest for a Conservative theology and ideology; and explore today's changing Jewish community." It is intellectually rigorous, frequently dry, and deals both with theological and practical matters. One recent issue included a discussion of how rabbis should minister to the terminally ill and a lengthy article on the rationale behind the Conservative **siddur** (prayer book). This periodical is of value whether or not you are a member of the Conservative movement.

Face to Face. Published three times a year by the Anti-Defamation League of B'nai B'rith, 838 United Nations Plaza, New York, NY 10017. Subscriptions: $12 per year. Executive Editor: Theodore Freedman.

This specialized publication deals exclusively with relations between Judaism and other religions. It has a distinguished, interreligious editorial advisory board. Among the topics it has covered are the twentieth anniversary of *Nostra Aetate*, the Vatican's declaration on Catholic-Jewish relations; rabbinic Judaism and early Christianity; Martin Luther and the Jews; and the Oberammergau Passion Play as an example of Christian folk religion and anti-Judaism. Scholarly and valuable.

Forum. Published quarterly by the World Zionist Organization, 515 Park Avenue, New York, NY 10022. Subscriptions: $15 per year. Editor: Amnon Hadary.

Although *Forum* covers the entire range of Jewish life, including world Jewry, history, religion and philosophy, Jewish identity,

personalities, literature, and education, as you would expect, the focus is on Israel and Zionism. It has strong pro-Israel leanings.

Hadassah Magazine. Published ten times a year by Hadassah, 50 West 58th Street, New York, NY 10019. Subscriptions: $15 per year. Executive Editor: Alan M. Tigay.

You'd expect a magazine published by a women's Zionist organization to have articles on Israel and subjects of interest to women, and this one does, plus a lot of ads for cottage cheese and breakfast cereal. But the articles on Israel are more than mere boosterism; they are thoughtful and well written. And there are also articles on family life, the arts, and religion. The book reviews are current and particularly good.

Israel Scene. Published monthly by the World Zionist Organization, 515 Park Avenue, New York, NY 10022. Subscriptions: $15 per year. Editor: Asher Weill.

News, analysis, opinion, and features on Israeli life. Despite being published by the WZO, *Israel Scene* is not a puff piece for Israel. Its articles are frequently critical of specific aspects of Israeli life and politics, although the basic outlook is pro-Israel. Virtually every part of Israeli life is covered—the peace process and why there is resistance to it in Israel, Meir Kahane, relations between Israeli Arabs and Jews, the settlements in Judea and Samaria, kibbutzim, sports, terrorism, nature and environmental concerns, and the arts and media, including dance, movies, theater, and music. The articles are generally readable and short, occasionally provocative, and almost always informative.

The Jerusalem Post International Edition. Published weekly by Jerusalem Post Publications, 120 East 56th Street, New York, NY 10022. Subscriptions: P.O. Box 5200, Patterson, NY 12563. $25 for six months; $44.95 for one year. Editors: Ari Rath and Erwin Frenkel.

This weekly English-language newspaper is published in Israel for distribution abroad. It provides extensive coverage of Israeli politics, religion, business, diplomacy, military affairs, and culture. There is also some coverage of Jewish life outside of Israel. Among its regular columnists are Daniel Gavron on Israeli life, Wolf Blitzer on American-Israeli relations, and Pinchas H. Peli on Torah.

Jewish Book World. Published quarterly by JWB Jewish Book Council, 15 East 26th Street, New York, NY 10010. Subscriptions: Free. Editor: William Wollheim.

News about books of Jewish interest and about the activities of the JWB Jewish Book Council. Each issue contains book reviews and brief descriptions of more than 150 new books, including fiction, nonfiction, and children's books. There are also occasional articles about authors, publishers, and others involved in Jewish literary activities. Nothing fancy, but useful and an excellent value. The Jewish Book Council also publishes the *Jewish Book Annual* (see REFERENCE) and specialized bibliographies.

The Jewish Spectator. Published quarterly by the Jewish Spectator, P.O. Box 2016, Santa Monica, CA 90406. Subscriptions: $15 per year. Editor: Trude Weiss-Rosmarin.

The single best thing about this publication is "The Editor's Quarter," in which Weiss-Rosmarin expresses her opinions. She is iconoclastic, unpredictable, and doesn't hesitate to say just what she means. When she writes of the plight of Ethiopian Jews, she also mentions the difficulties they face in being absorbed into Israeli society—and rakes the United Jewish Appeal over the coals for using their problems as a "ploy" to raise funds. She disagrees with the call for women's prayer groups, not because it's halakhically wrong but because she believes in integration, not separation, of the sexes. The second best part of the magazine are the many varied articles: fiction by Aharon Megged; Balfour Brickner on black-Jewish relations; and discussions of Jewish law, subway "vigilante" Bernard Goetz, Jewish terrorism and Israel, and of being female and single in Israel. The worst part? Too many congratulatory letters from readers scattered throughout the pages.

Journal of Reform of Judaism. Published quarterly by the Central Conference of American Rabbis, 21 East 40th Street, New York, NY 10016. Subscriptions: $12 per year; $20 for two years. Editor: Samuel M. Stahl.

The journal of the organization of Reform rabbis prints articles on and discussion of practical and spiritual aspects of the rabbinate, liturgy, Reform perspectives on Jewish law, and modern Jewish life. There are also usually book reviews, letters, and often poetry. The intellectual level is generally high, and most of the material is understandable by the general reader.

Judaica Book News. Published twice a year by Book News, 303 West 10th Street, New York, NY 10014. Subscriptions: $8 per year. Editor: Ernest Weiss.

Somewhat similar in content to *Jewish Book World, Judaica Book News* includes many more reviews in each issue plus several articles related to Jewish books or literature. Some of the reviews are quite lengthy, although most are fairly short. Brief descriptions of new and forthcoming books are included.

Judaica Librarianship. Published twice a year by the Association of Judaica Libraries, (AJL), 19 Brookfield Road, New Hyde Park, NY 11040. Subscriptions: $25 per year, includes membership in the association and four issues a year of the AJL newsletter. Editors: Marcia Posner and Bella Hass Weinberg.

This new magazine is intended for use by professional librarians although also valuable to anyone responsible for a Judaica library. Each issue includes material specifically related to Jewish books, with sections on children's books, reference books, and Israeli libraries. Articles on the use of computers, classification, and other aspects of librarianship in general are also included.

Judaism. Published quarterly by the American Jewish Congress, 15 East 84th Street, New York, NY 10028. Subscriptions: $12 for one year, $20 for two years. Editor: Robert Gordis.

Its statement of purpose declares that *Judaism* is published to encourage "creative discussion and exposition of the religious, moral and philosophical concepts of Judaism and their relevance to the problems of modern society." That's an accurate description, and it also conveys some of the flavor of the magazine—frequently abstract and theoretical, but not unconnected to "the real world." Among the recent articles were discussions of Martin Buber's influence on twentieth-century religious thought, whether rabbis should also be social activists, how the prayer book developed, Maimonides on the best life for humanity, and how a convert views Jewish ethics. Each issue usually includes several reviews of scholarly books on Jewish subjects.

Lilith. Published four times a year by Lilith, 250 West 57th Street, New York, NY 10107. Subscriptions: $14 for four issues; $26 for eight issues. Editors: Susan Weidman Schneider and Aviva Cantor.

This is a pioneering publication whose devotion to both feminism and Judaism—and concern over the tensions that can arise between the two—is intense, impassioned, and thoughtful. It has included fiction by Cynthia Ozick, articles on the way Jewish humor stereotypes Jewish women, on women who wield power in the Jewish community, and on Jewish women in the Old West. *Lilith* is indispensable for anyone interested in the role of women in modern Judaism.

Midstream. Published ten times a year by the Theodor Herzl Foundation, 515 Park Avenue, New York, NY 10022. Subscriptions: $15 a year. Editor: Joel Carmichael.

Essays, articles, fiction, poetry, memoirs, reviews, and letters, with Israel as the focus but not the exclusive subject. Within the context of a deep Zionist commitment, the contents of *Midstream* are freewheeling and varied.

Modern Hebrew Literature. Published quarterly by the Institute for the Translation of Hebrew Literature Ltd., P.O. Box 11210, 61111 Tel Aviv, Israel. Subscriptions: $6 a year. Editor: Anat Feinberg.

Here are published poems, book and theater reviews, excerpts from works in progress by Israeli writers, and other articles about Hebrew literature, all in English translation. A good value for readers interested in following Israeli writing. There are many photographs and the magazine is attractively designed.

Modern Judaism. Published three times a year by Johns Hopkins University Press, Journals Division, 701 West 40th Street, Suite 275, Baltimore, MD 21211. Subscriptions: $17 per year for individuals, $31 per year for institutions.

A scholarly journal with articles on modern Jewish thought and religion. Its quality is high, and its audience is very definitely an academic one—people who are interested in articles such as "Gershom Scholem's Ten Unhistorical Aphorisms on Kabbalah" or "Buber's Critique of Heidegger."

Moment. Published ten times a year by Jewish Educational Ventures, Boylston Street, Suite 301, Boston, MA 02116. Subscriptions: P.O. Box 922, Farmingdale, NY 11737. $27 for one year;

$45 for two years. Editor: Leonard Fein.

The contributing editors of this periodical include Bernard Avishai, Thomas J. Cottle, Mae Rockland, Danny Siegel, Bill Aron, Yehuda Amichai, Abba Eban. It ranges from (sometimes strained) humor, and articles on Jewish dating services, to fiction, analysis of Jerry Falwell and the relationship between Jews and fundamentalist Christians, and personal ads. Accessible, entertaining, and graphically much livelier than most Jewish magazines.

Present Tense. Published quarterly by the American Jewish Committee, 165 East 56th Street, New York, NY 10022. Subscriptions: $14 per year. Editor: Murray Polner.

The emphasis of *Present Tense,* as its name implies, is current events in the Jewish world. Its articles deal with the situations of Jews in all countries, with particular attention paid to Israel. It covers such topics as Jewish terrorism in Israel, intermarriage, Jewish relations with blacks and with Christians, and the impact of right-wing politician Meir Kahane. Each issue also includes book reviews, both in-depth and short reviews.

Prooftexts. Published three times a year by Johns Hopkins University Press, Journals Division, 701 West 40th Street, Suite 275, Baltimore, MD 21211. Subscriptions: $16 per year for

individuals, $29.50 per year for institutions. Editors: Alan Mintz and David G. Roskies.

A scholarly journal with articles on Jewish literature, including traditional and modern writing, in English, Hebrew, Yiddish, and other languages. Meant more for the specialist than for the general reader, it is well edited and accessible, if somewhat dry.

Shdemot. Published by the Federation of Kibbutz Movements, Beit Takam, 10 Dubnov Street, Tel Aviv, Israel. Subscriptions: Kibbutz Aliya Desk, 27 West 20th Street, 9th floor, New York, NY 10011. $12 for three issues. Editor: Shelly Lilker.

The "cultural forum" of the kibbutz movement, *Shdemot* covers every facet of kibbutz life and culture: philosophy, art, religion, politics, current events, education, ideology, history, and personal and family life. In addition to articles, there are reviews, poems, stories, interviews, and art.

Sh'ma. Published biweekly except June, July, and August, by Sh'ma, 735 Port Washington Boulevard, Port Washington, NY 11050. Subscriptions: $22 for two years; half price for retired or handicapped people of restricted means. Editor: Eugene B. Borowitz.

If you like intelligent debate and disputation, this is the publication for you. The usual format is eight pages crammed full of articles, responses to those articles, letters about earlier articles, and calls for more articles. It ranges over virtually every aspect of modern Jewish life—women's *minyanim*, Holocaust art, teaching *kabbalah*, the Jewish Defense League, nuclear war and the ethics of arms control, conversion to Judaism—and from Judaism, theology, and the propriety of debating halakhic issues in English. There are also innumerable short, and occasional long, book reviews. Many of the issues it deals with are similar to those in the *Jewish Spectator*, but the tighter format leads to somewhat tighter arguments. A stimulating and provocative publication.

Shofar. Published eight times a year by Senior Publications, 43 Northcote Drive, Melville, NY 11747. Subscriptions: *Shofar*, P.O. Box 852, Wheatly Heights, NY 11798. $14.50 per year. Editor: Alan A. Kay.

This magazine is for grade-school pupils, with an emphasis on Jewish stars, sports figures, astronauts, and other positive role models. Also included are games, puzzles, cartoons, poems, stories, crafts, and activities. The layout and writing are generally lively, especially for a publication with education as a principal goal. A teacher's guide is available.

Tradition. Published quarterly by the Rabbinical Council of America, 275 Seventh Avenue, New York, NY 10001. Subscriptions: $20 per year for individuals; $12 per year for students; $25 per year for libraries. Editor: Walter Wurzburger.

Produced by the national organization of Orthodox rabbis, *Tradition* is essential to anyone wishing to keep up to date with current Orthodox thought. It includes articles on such subjects as Reform Jewish marriages, the implications of the approach of the classical Jewish exegetes for modern Bible study, and whether it is permissible for an Orthodox Jew to vacation at Club Med. It also offers translations of responsa on subjects such as whether Israeli *yeshiva* students ought to be subject to the draft in Israel. (The conclusion was that they should.) Each issue features J. David Bleich discussing halakhic issues, ranging from physicians' strikes to the implications of crossing the international dateline. There are also book reviews, mostly dealing with theological or halakhic issues. The viewpoint is consistently and strictly Orthodox, and there is frequent criticism of Reform and Conservative Jewish practices and beliefs.

X

Prayer Books

"The Prayer." A traditional Jew at morning prayer, phylacteries on his head and arm, wrapped in a prayer shawl. Silk screen print by Avrum Ashery, graphic designer, Rockville, MD, © 1966.

Prayer Books

It is not possible to evaluate and compare prayer books in the same way one does books of history or fiction. Instead, we will provide a little background on Jewish prayer books and present brief descriptions of some of them from each of the four major branches of modern Judaism—Conservative, Orthodox, Reconstructionist, and Reform.

The prayer book is the most popular, most used book in Jewish life—the principal way in which the basics of Jewish belief have been conveyed to the people. It is an anthology of selections from the Bible, including the Psalms, the Song of Songs, and excerpts from all five books of the Torah, plus material from the Mishnah, post-talmudic literature, and a few prayers—the mourner's *kaddish* being best known—that are in Aramaic rather than Hebrew. Over the centuries variations developed in the way Ashkenazic and Sephardic Jews arranged and used the material. The arrangement is called **nusach**, the versions being called *Nusach Ashkenaz* and *Nusach Sepharad*. Despite the differences in some specifics, most of the contents are the same. The *siddur* is the one sacred book of the Jews that remained open to change; it was never closed as were the Bible and Talmud. While the Orthodox *siddur* has remained essentially unchanged for several centuries, there are substantial differences in the prayer books produced by the other branches of Judaism.

There are two basic prayer books used in synagogues. The book used for daily and sabbath services is generally referred to as a *siddur*. This name derives from a Hebrew word meaning "order"—that is the order in which the prayers are to be recited. It is related to the word *seder*. The second type of prayer book has additional material added specifically for the High Holy Days (Rosh Hashanah and Yom Kippur) and is called a **machzor**, derived from a Hebrew word referring to the yearly cycle. Many prayer books come in more than one edition—compact editions, deluxe editions, and so on. We have not made any attempt to list all these variations.

—R. S. F. & W. W.

GENERAL

Cohen, Jeffrey M.
Understanding the High Holyday Services. Routledge & Kegan Paul; distributed by Hebrew Publishing, 1983, $12.50.

A commentary on the *machzor*, covering each of the Rosh Hashanah and Yom Kippur services, explaining what is done and why. Cohen mostly offers traditional interpretations, but is willing to express his own ideas when they seem relevant. He also discusses the Jewish doctrine of repentance. Since the text of all the prayers is not included, you need a *machzor* to read along with this book.

Donin, Hayim Halevy
To Pray as a Jew: A Guide to the Prayer Book and the Synagogue Service. Basic Books, 1980, $16.50.

Donin was one of the clearest expounders of traditional Jewish thought and practice of the last several decades. *To Pray as a Jew* was his last book, and it maintained the high standards set by his earlier work. (See HOW-TO.) It is a guide to Jewish prayer and what might be called "synagogue skills," filled with details about the daily, Sabbath, festival, and High Holy Day services. In addition, Donin discusses such practical matters as putting on a prayer shawl, proper dress when attending a synagogue, and finding your way around the prayer book. No other book covers this material in such detail. The writing is clear and unpretentious and while it deals only with the services held in an Orthodox synagogue, it is filled with useful information for anyone interested in prayer. Blessings and prayers for the home are also included.

Martin, Bernard
Prayer in Judaism. Basic Books, 1968, out of print.

Following an introduction on the importance of the prayer book in Judaism, and the history and forms of Jewish prayer, Martin presents a sampling of prayers with helpful commentaries on their background and meaning. He includes selections from the Psalms, plus daily and Sabbath prayers, prayer for the High Holy Days, and modern prayers that reflect the creation of the State of Israel, the Holocaust, and other concerns of our times. Although out of print, this is a book worth looking for.

Millgram, Abraham
Jewish Worship. Jewish Publication Society, 1975, $13.95.

A comprehensive, nontechnical survey of Jewish worship with an emphasis on the development of the *siddur*. This is a good complement to the books by Donin and Martin listed earlier. Unlike Donin, it is not a guide to Jewish worship, nor does it deal with the laws and rules governing synagogue worship. And, unlike Martin, it does not include the text of many prayers with specific comments on their history and content. What it does cover is just about everything else related to Jewish worship: its foundations, prayer in the Bible and Temple periods, the organization and content of the *siddur*, the liturgy of the major festivals and High Holy Days, private and home worship, the theology of the *siddur*, the expansion of the *siddur* during the Middle Ages, the impact of the development of printing, Hasidic liturgy, the impact of mysticism, modern developments, and considerably more. Its over six hundred pages and great detail make this a book more suited for use as a reference than for reading from cover to cover.

CONSERVATIVE

Harlow, Jules, ed.
Siddur Sim Shalom. Rabbinical Assembly, 1985, $18.

This is a *siddur* for daily, Sabbath, and festival use, with commentaries that are helpful and informative. The Conservative *siddur* is quite similar to the Orthodox, but there are some rewordings to bring it into accordance with Conservative beliefs. An example of this is the elimination of the pledge to restore the sacrificial cult as part of Jewish worship. Some new material has also been added; for instance, a prayer in commemoration of Israel Independence Day. This *siddur* has replaced the Morris Silverman *Sabbath and Festival siddur* first published in 1947 and still in use by many Conservative congregations. The Silverman *siddur* is available from United Synagogue Book Service in a regular edition for $14, and a large-type edition for $30.

Machzor for Rosh Hashanah and Yom Kippur.
Rabbinical Assembly, 1972, $12.

In addition to the traditional High Holy Day services, this *machzor* includes materials, among them some very moving reflections on the Holocaust. A large-type edition is available for $50.

ORTHODOX
Unlike Conservative, Reconstructionist, and Reform Judaism, there is no one official body issuing prayer books for Orthodox Jews. Each of the first three groups has just one organization representing its rabbis and one organization representing its congregations; Orthodoxy is considerably more diverse. It would not be possible, therefore, to list all of the many Orthodox prayer books published. Those listed here are representative, but hardly inclusive.

Birnbaum, Philip, ed.
Daily Prayer Book (Ha-Siddur Ha-Shalem). Hebrew Publishing, 1977, $9.

Possibly the most popular traditional *siddur*, used by both Orthodox and some Conservative Jews. The Hebrew and English texts are on facing pages, in easily readable type. There are some commentaries and explanatory notes; however, they are very brief. The directions are also quite brief, although explicit and clear. Birnbaum's English translation is occasionally free, and is fairly modern in tone while preserving some of the archaic flavor of older translations. Birnbaum also edited a *High Holyday Prayer Book* (Hebrew Publishing, 1964, $17).

Davis, Avrohom, ed.
The Metsudah Siddur. Metsudah Publications; distributed by ZionTalis/Book Division, 1981, $9.95.

This *siddur* is particularly useful for people who can read Hebrew but not fluently. Instead of blocks of Hebrew and English text on facing pages, each Hebrew phrase is placed on the same line on the same page as its English translation. The translation reflects the classic Jewish commentaries and emphasizes accuracy over poetic qualities. It is modern in tone and does not use "thee" and "thou." Footnores explain confusing or obscure points, and each prayer is prefaced with a sentence or two explaining its origins and any special laws or procedures involved in reciting it. None of the Hebrew is transliterated. Also available in the same format are a *Sabbath and Festivals* prayerbook (1982, $13.95) and the two-volume *Metsudah Machzor* (1985, $27.50).

Mangel, Nissen, ed.
Siddur Tehillat Hashem. Merkos L'inyonei Chinuch, 1982, $10.95.

In its Hebrew version, this *siddur* is the one used by the Lubavitch Hasidim. It follows the *Nusach Ha-Ari*, an arrangement composed by Rabbi Isaac Luria, a sixteenth-century kabbalist and founder of a mystical system, known for his ascetic and saintly character. He is the author of "*L'cha dodi*," a prayer welcoming the Sabbath that is recited by observant Jews every Friday evening. A prayer book based on his *nusach* (arrangement) was produced in 1803 by Rabbi Shneur Zalman of Liadi, called the *Alter Rebbe* by Lubavitch Hasidim. This edition includes the Hebrew text of that prayer book, a new English translation, and extensive excerpts from the *Shulkhan Arukh* and the rulings of the *Alter Rebbe* on the laws pertaining to prayer and ritual. This is a very complete prayer book, even including the section of the Mishnah to be studied by mourners. Aside from the instructions and laws, the commentaries are very sparse. The type is quite large. A *Machzor for Rosh Hashanah* (1983, $11) and a *Machzor for Yom Kippur* (1983, $12) are available. These machzors, like the *siddur*, are based on the *Nusach Ha-Ari* as arranged by Rabbi Shneur Zalman of Liadi.

Scherman, Nosson, ed.
The Complete ArtScroll Siddur. Mesorah, 1984, $15.95.

Like the Lubavitch prayer books, the ArtScroll *siddur* is very complete. What sets it apart are the extensive commentaries, based on traditional sources and serving to explain difficult passages and involve the reader emotionally and spiritually in the prayers. Packing all of this in has resulted in smaller type than some other prayer books. The instructions on what to do and when are frequent and clear. With the exception of the Torah readings, all the Hebrew is translated. The translations follow a strictly Orthodox understanding of the text, an example being the Song of Songs, which is translated according to its allegorical meaning. None of the recent prayers for the State of Israel are included. Editions following *Nusach Ashkenaz* and *Nusach Sepharad* are available. A large-type edition is available for $29.95. Mesorah has also published *The Complete ArtScroll Machzor* (1985, $14.95), a Rosh Hashanah *machzor* very much in the mold of the ArtScroll *siddur*. It is quite comprehensive, and includes extensive commentaries and frequent, explicit instructions.

RECONSTRUCTIONIST

Kaplan, Mordecai M., and Eugene Kohn, eds.
Sabbath Prayer Book. Reconstructionist Press, 1979, $8.50.

Originally published in 1945, this prayer book is scheduled to be replaced by a new edition soon. It follows Reconstructionist belief in omitting all reference to an individual Messiah, rejecting corporeal resurrection, and eliminating prayers for the restoration of animal sacrifice at a rebuilt Temple. It includes a supplement with prayers for various personal occasions such as sickness, or the birth of a child, and for civic festivals such as July 4th, Labor Day, and Thanksgiving. Hebrew and English text is on facing pages.

Festival Prayerbook. Reconstructionist Press, 1958, $8.50.

This book offers prayers, Torah readings, hymns, and meditations for the three Pilgrimage festivals—Passover, Shavuot, and Sukkot. Hebrew and English text are on facing pages.

Kaplan, Mordecai M., Eugene Kohn, and Ira Eisenstein, eds.
High Holiday Prayerbook. Vol. 1: **Rosh Hashanah.** 1948, $6.00. Vol. 2: **Yom Kippur.** 1948, $8.50. Two-vol. set, $12.50.

Like the Reconstructionist *siddur*, a new edition of this *machzor* is scheduled to be published soon. It reflects Reconstructionist practice, modifying the text to bring it into accord with what are seen as the "spiritual needs of our day." Supplemental readings are drawn from ancient, medieval, and modern sources, with some new prayers added. The type is large and readable. Hebrew and English text are on facing pages.

REFORM

Stern, Chaim, ed.
Gates of Prayer (Shaarei Tefillah): The New Union Prayerbook. Central Conference of American Rabbis, 1975, $15.

Gates of Prayer includes services for weekdays, Sabbaths, festivals, and modern holidays such as Israel Independence Day. The services are supplemented with readings, meditations, and a section of prayers on such "special themes" as nature, righteousness, justice, peace, Israel's mission, and doubt. Following the Reform approach of allowing individual latitude, several different services are offered from which a congregation can choose. These services range from the fairly traditional to one that does not even mention God. Except for a section of songs, most of the text is not transliterated. The Hebrew and English texts appear in alternating paragraphs on the same page. A large-type edition is available for $20.

Gates of the House (Shaarei Habayit): The New Union Home Prayerbook. Central Conference of American Rabbis, 1977, $9.

Prayers and meditations for private devotions and for family and communal occasions. In addition to prayers for life cycle events such as marriage, retirement, a *bris*, or the adoption of a child, there are prayers for the Sabbath, for festivals, and for weekday services. More of the Hebrew is transliterated than in *Gates of Prayer*, but there is not much in the way of instructions. The Hebrew and English texts appear in alternating passages on the same page.

Gates of Repentance (Shaarei Teshuvah): The New Union Prayerbook for the Days of Awe. Central Conference of American Rabbis, 1978, $15.

This *machzor* for Rosh Hashanah and Yom Kippur includes two services for Rosh Hashanah, and additional prayers and meditations. Like the other Reform prayer books, latitude is allowed in structuring the service. The English text is freely translated from the Hebrew, and some passages appear only in English. The layout of Hebrew and English is the same as in the Reform *siddurs*.

XI

References and Resources

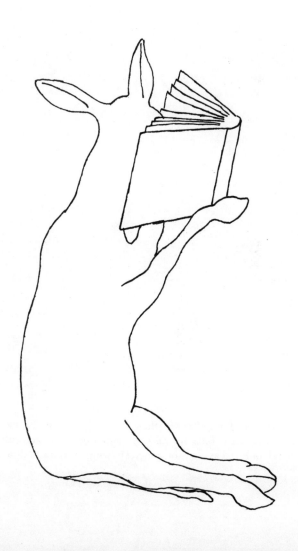

"The Ass." The Talmud states that the ass is one of the most stupid creatures. But when Balaam was confronted by the angel with a sword in his hand, only the ass saw the angel. Drawing by Mark Podwal, © 1984.

Reference Books

This chapter includes encyclopedias, dictionaries, atlases, bibliographies, travel books, and a few books that didn't quite fit in any place else. They are all useful and belong in both personal collections and libraries. Travel books about Israel are in ISRAEL AND ZIONISM.

Aharoni, Yohanan, and Michael Avi-Yonah
The Macmillan Bible Atlas. Macmillan, 1977, $25.95.

This authoritative atlas, covering the Hebrew Bible and the New Testament, shows the historical development and changes of the lands of the Bible. The maps are printed in green and black and vary in size from small to full-page. Each map is accompanied by explanatory notes, up to a page in length. The more than two hundred maps covering the period of the Jewish Scriptures begin with the Canaanite period and continue to the time of King Herod.

Alcaly, Reuben
The Complete English-Hebrew Dictionary. Massada, 1981, 2 vols.

The Complete Hebrew-English Dictionary. Massada, 1981, 3 vols., $69.

Published in Israel, this authoritative dictionary should be available at many Jewish bookstores. It is comprehensive, including colloquialisms, derivations, phrases, idioms, and quotations from the Bible. All the Hebrew is vocalized (meaning that the vowels are indicated), and the definitions have an American slant.

Baron, Joseph L., ed.
A Treasury of Jewish Quotations. Aronson, $25.

A compilation of 18,000 aphorisms, maxims, proverbs, and comments of Jewish authorship or on Jewish themes, arranged by subject. The quotations are selected from more than 2,500 years of Jewish history, with an emphasis on such traditional sources as Talmud, Mishnah, and Bible. A glossary, bibliography, and subject and author indexes add to the book's usefulness. *Leo Rosten's Treasury of Jewish Quotations* is smaller, also useful, and unfortunately out of print.

Birnbaum, Philip
Encyclopedia of Jewish Concepts. Hebrew Publishing, 1979, $19.50 hc, $11.95 pb.

In his usual clear and easy-to-understand manner, Birnbaum defines more than 1,600 concepts and terms related to the essential teachings of Judaism—its ideals and practices. Birnbaum presupposes some degree of Jewish knowledge. That, combined with the fact that the terms appear in alphabetical order according to their Hebrew spelling, makes the book not completely suitable for total beginners. The three indexes—Hebrew, English, and topical—do make it somewhat easier to find your way around the book and to locate the information you want. The entries fall into such major categories as Bible, Torah, synagogue worship, the Jewish calendar, death and mourning, Talmud, law, Hebrew language, and *kabbalah* and mysticism.

Buttrick, George, and Keith A. Crim, eds.

The Interpreter's Dictionary of the Bible. Abingdon Press, 1976, 5 vols., $112.

Covering both the Hebrew Bible and the Christian New Testament, this is not a "Jewish" book. It is, however, a major reference work of value to serious Bible students. The entries vary from the terse to the lengthy—the article on David runs more than ten pages—and there are many black-and-white and color photos and maps. In addition to covering the major books and characters of the Bible, it also discusses important words and phrases, concepts, and apocryphal works.

Cutter, Charles, and Micha Falk Oppenheim

Jewish Reference Sources: A Selective, Annotated Bibliographic Guide. Garland, 1982, $24.

Including both references such as dictionaries and bibliographies, and monographs that the editors consider basic, this bibliography contains brief descriptions of more than 360 works. The titles are subdivided into more than thirty subjects, including anti-Semitism, Bible studies, crafts, genealogy, history, Jewish law, Ladino language, music, women, and Zionism. The majority of titles have been published since 1970. The authors are professional Judaica librarians, Cutter at Brandeis University and Oppenheim at the Jewish Theological Seminary in New York. The book includes both author and title indexes.

Davis, Enid

Comprehensive Guide to Children's Literature with a Jewish Theme. Schocken Books, 1981, $18.95.

This reference gives more than four hundred reviews, listings of resources, a directory of book publishers and distributors, and guidelines on selecting books for children. Age levels are given for all the books. The *Guide* is indexed by author, title, and subject, adding greatly to its value. It is a useful book that would be even more useful if an updated edition were to be published—its judgments are sensible but too many new books have been published and too many of the old ones have gone out of print since it was first published. Despite that, it remains an essential reference for any parent or children's librarian.

de Lange, Nicholas
Atlas of the Jewish World. Facts on File, 1984, $35.

This is a cross between a reference book and a coffee table book, and not totally successful as either. Using maps, photographs, and extensive text, it has three major sections: "The Historical Background," from antiquity to the present; "The Cultural Background," which surveys Jewish culture and religion in different times and places; and "The Jewish World Today," which presents a geographical survey of world Jewry by regions and countries. Also included are a chronological table, glossary, bibliography, gazetteer, and index.

Freedman, Warren
World Guide for the Jewish Traveler. Dutton, 1984, $8.95 pb.

Covering virtually every part of the world—from Aden to Zimbabwe—Freedman offers information on synagogues, Jewish museums and memorials, kosher restaurants, embassies and consulates, educational facilities, and just about anything else a Jewish traveler might want to know.

Granted, he doesn't have *much* to say about Jewish sites and sights in Pakistan, but it's probably more than you knew. The lack of photos and maps is a drawback.

Gilbert, Martin
Atlas of Jewish History. Dorset Press/Barnes & Noble, 1985, $5.95.

More than 120 maps are presented here, covering Jewish history from antiquity to the present. The maps show major events and minor ones, giving both the facts and the flavor of Jewish history. Included are the biblical Exodus from Egypt and the twentieth-century exodus from Ethiopia, the wars against Rome, the Khazar Jewish kingdom, false messiahs, the travels of Benjamin of Tudela, the Chmielnicki Massacres, the Arab-Israeli conflict, and Soviet Jews denied visas. This atlas is a revised edition of a book originally published under the title of *Jewish History Atlas.* A very valuable reference work at a good price.

Gurock, Jeffrey S.
American Jewish History: A Bibliographical Guide. Anti-Defamation League of B'nai B'rith, 1983, $6.95 pb.

Extended bibliographic essays are collected here, on specific aspects of American Jewish history—the colonial period, the era of German migration, Jewish voting patterns, and so on. The essays are followed by a comprehensive bibliography. This book concentrates on English-language works almost exclusively, paying comparatively little attention to Hebrew and Yiddish books. Author and title indexes are included. Gurock is a specialist in American Jewish history and wrote the introduction to that section of our book.

Heller, Abraham Mayer

The Vocabulary of Jewish Life. Hebrew Publishing, 1967, $8.95.

Designed for use by adult study groups or children preparing for a Bar or Bat Mitzvah, this useful book is a compilation of about a thousand Hebrew words of significance in Jewish spiritual life. The words, arranged in categories such as "The Jewish Home," "The Synagogue," "Human Virtues and Failings," and "Jewish Learning," are given in Hebrew and in English transliteration, and they are defined and explained. Both Sephardic and Ashkenazic pronunciations are given.

Himmelfarb, Milton, and David Singer, eds.

American Jewish Year Book, 1985. American Jewish Committee and Jewish Publication Society, 1985, $25.95.

Published annually, the population statistics, lists of national Jewish organizations and Jewish Federations, a directory of Jewish periodicals, a necrology, and informative articles included in the *Yearbook* make it a valuable reference. The articles, which cover such topics as demographics, and political, communal, and religious developments, make even old copies worth owning.

Israelowitz, Asher

Guide to Jewish Europe: Western Europe Edition. Available from the author, P.O. Box 228, Brooklyn, NY 11229, $9.95 pb.

For each city covered in this guide, there is information on kosher restaurants, butchers, bakeries, and hotels; Jewish historic landmarks, synagogues, cemeteries, and **mikvehs**; telephone numbers of Jewish community centers; youth hostels; Sabbath candle-lighting times; and historical background.

Kabakoff, Jacob, ed.

Jewish Book Annual, Vol. 43: 1985–1986. JWB Jewish Book Council, 1985, $18.

A treasure for bibliophiles, this annual offers annotated bibliographies of new American books of Jewish interest in seven categories, including fiction and non-fiction in English, Hebrew, and Yiddish. Selected lists of books published in England and Israel are also included. Published annually, each year's edition includes articles on Jewish literature and scholarship.

Kaganoff, Benzion C.

A Dictionary of Jewish Names and Their History. Schocken Books, 1977, $10.95 hc, $8.95 pb.

The first part of this book discusses how names are created and evolve over a period of centuries.

It then explains how to use this information in tracing the background of any particular name. The second part is a dictionary of the most common Jewish first and last names. Although not the most essential of reference works, it is one of the most enjoyable. If, after you have traced your family name, you wish to trace your family history, see Arthur Kurzweil's *From Generation to Generation* (in HOW-TO).

Klagsbrun, Francine
Voices of Wisdom: Jewish Ideals and Ethics for Everyday Living. Pantheon Books, 1980, $17.95.

Something of a cross between Bartlett's *Familiar Quotations* and a guide to living, this anthology contains material on the values, wisdom, and moral teachings of Jewish tradition. It draws from a wide range of sources—for example, the section on love, sex, and marriage includes material from both the Bible and Isaac Bashevis Singer. The quotations are organized around themes and issues such as education, work, family, health, scholarship, government, relationships, faith, and death. There are brief introductory and explanatory remarks whenever they are needed.

Kolatch, Alfred J.
The Complete Dictionary of English and Hebrew First Names. Jonathan David, 1984, $19.95.

An enlarged edition of a 1967 work, this dictionary has 11,000 entries of English and Hebrew first names, giving their origin, meaning, and variant spellings. It includes many names from the Bible or commonly used in Israel. An introduction discusses the types of names, the naming process, names to be avoided, and naming customs. Compared to the Kaganoff book described earlier, it is less a book to read and more a book to refer to. Unlike the Kaganoff book, it does not discuss last names.

The Jewish Book of Why. Jonathan David, 1981, $12.95.
The Second Jewish Book of Why. Jonathan David, 1985, $13.95.

Admittedly these are not exactly reference books but they don't fit anywhere else in this book and since they are useful references, we put them here. The first *Book of Why* looks at the how and why of hundreds of Jewish practices—from why a glass is broken at weddings and why it takes ten men to form a *minyan* to why Yom Kippur really isn't the most sacred day of the Jewish year. It describes Orthodox, Conservative, and Reform traditions, and concentrates on the basics of Jewish life—life cycle events, holidays, prayer, dietary laws, and so on. The second book takes the same question-and-answer approach to more controversial issues, including the role of women, conversion, intermarriage, organ transplants, and birth control. Both books are fascinating reading. Suitable for younger readers.

Levenston, Edward A., and Reuven Sivan
The New Bantam-Megiddo Hebrew and English Dictionary. Bantam Books, 1975, $3.95 pb.

A handy and affordable Hebrew-English, English-Hebrew dictionary, with information on the declension of nouns, conjugation of verbs, and other grammatical matters. The compact size means that the definitions are short, with few synonyms or etymologies.

Lightman, Sidney, ed.
The Jewish Travel Guide. Sepher-Hermon Press, 1985, $9.25 pb.

This travel guide gives information on kosher restaurants, synagogues, hotels, places of historic interest, and Jewish organizations around the world, including Europe, America, the Far East, Israel, and Soviet bloc countries.

Lubetski, Edith, and Meir Lubetski
Building a Judaica Library Collection: A Resource Guide. Libraries Unlimited, 1983, $30.

This handbook is valuable for librarians, teachers, or anyone else working in the field of Jewish books whether at a small synagogue library or a major academic institution. It covers, in addition to books, magazines, microfilm, archives, dissertations, publishers, booksellers in the United States and abroad, antiquarian bookdealers, and library- and book-related organizations.

Mendes-Flohr, Paul, and Arthur A. Cohen, eds.
Contemporary Jewish Religious Thought. Scribner, 1986, $75.

Just as we were getting ready to go to press, we had the chance to see page proofs of this book, and based on that preliminary look, we have included it here. It has nearly 150 alphabetically arranged essays, running from five to ten pages, virtually all of them specially commissioned. The essays, written by some of the most important and best-known modern Jewish scholars, are somewhat academic in approach and language. They cover both specifically religious topics—conversion, dogma, liturgy, prayer, sin—and the Jewish view of such other topics as esthetics, education, science, and sex. It's a big book, with more than a thousand pages, and, unfortunately, it also carries a big price. It is, nonetheless, a valuable reference.

Patai, Raphael, ed.
Encyclopedia of Zionism and Israel. Herzl Press/World Zionist Organization, 1971, 2 vols., $39.50.

This attractively produced encyclopedia has nearly three thousand articles, many black-and-white photos, and an impressive roster of contributors. In its coverage of Israel it confines itself largely to events since the mid-nineteenth century, although there is one survey article covering Israel's history since antiquity. The articles on Israel include information on major towns and natural features, as well as Israeli government and social, cultural, economic, religious, political, and agricultural developments. There are also many articles on Zionist leaders and thought. As valuable as this encyclopedia is, so much has happened since it first came out that a new edition is sorely needed. Even with that limitation, the comprehensive coverage of Zionism makes this an excellent choice for synagogue and school libraries.

Postal, Bernard, and Lionel Koppman

American Jewish Landmarks: A Travel Guide and History. Fleet Press.
Vol. 1: *New England.* 1977, $15 hc, $12.50 pb.
Vol. 2: *The South and Southwest.* 1979, $20.95 hc, $10.95 pb.
Vol. 3: *The Middle West.* 1984, $20.95 hc, $10.95 pb.

If you want to find major landmarks such as synagogues, memorials, and museums, they are all in these books—as are *matzah* factories, hospitals, educational institutions, and the addresses of all the *mikvehs* in Heightstown, New Jersey. For each state, there is a brief Jewish history, followed by a listing of areas and sites of interest. Filled with interesting information. A fourth volume,

covering the American West, is scheduled to be published soon.

Rosten, Leo

The Joys of Yiddish. McGraw-Hill, $19.95 hc; Pocket Books, $3.95 pb.

Rosten describes this as a "relaxed lexicon" with "excursions into Jewish humor, habits, holidays, history, religion, ceremonies, folklore, and cuisine." Who are we to argue? It defines and explains a variety of Yiddish words, making it a useful reference. It also contains some of the funniest stories you'll ever read, which is the real reason to buy it. See also Leo Rosten, *The Education of H*y*m*a*n K*a*p*l*a*n* (FICTION).

Roth, Cecil, and Geoffrey Wigoder, eds.

The Concise Jewish Encyclopedia. New American Library, 1980, $8.95 pb.

Of value especially for its low price and compactness, this is a competent one-volume reference work.

Encyclopaedia Judaica. Keter, $465.

Published in 1972, the sixteen volumes, over 12,000 pages and 11 million words, and more than 8,000 black-and-white and color illustrations of the *Encyclopaedia Judaica* make it a massive and impressive reference work. It has a distinguished roster of contributing scholars, a thorough index, and is printed in a readable typeface. On topics such as the Bible and where there is a divergence of approach between the various branches of Judaism, the articles present both the traditional and the liberal points of view. It is the major Jewish reference of our time. The *Encyclopaedia* is frequently sold at a substantial discount. Several *Yearbooks* plus one *Decennial Book* have been published since 1972 to keep it up to date.

Szonyi, David M.
The Holocaust: An Annotated Bibliography and Resource Guide. Ktav, 1985, $29.50 hc, $16.95 pb.

This is the most extensive and authoritative bibliographic guide to the Holocaust. Szonyi has also included a filmography, information on Jewish music resources for Holocaust programming, lists of traveling exhibits, a directory of education and research centers, suggestions on Holocaust curricula, Yom Ha-shoah services, and more. The great value of this book is badly undermined though by the absence of any index at all.

Since the books are arranged into approximately thirty different categories, tracking down any one particular book can be difficult. A shorter list edited by Judith Muffs is available from the Anti-Defamation League of B'nai B'rith. It sells for $5 and is called *The Holocaust in Books and Films: A Selected, Annotated List.* As we go to press, a second edition of *The Holocaust: An Annotated Bibliography* by Harry James Cargas has been published (American Library Association, 1986, $27.50). Covering both primary and secondary sources, and including audio-visual materials, Cargas's book is thorough and solid.

Wigoder, Geoffrey, ed.
The New Standard Jewish Encyclopedia. Doubleday, 1977, out of print.

A concise yet comprehensive one-volume encyclopedia. An updated edition would be very welcome because this is a very good book.

BOOKS FOR A BAR/BAT MITZVAH*

Young boys and girls and their families preparing for the Bar/Bat Mitzvah ceremony will find the titles listed here useful. To save space, only those books not described elsewhere in this guide are annotated. Those books that are out of print are available in most synagogue libraries.

---

* Compiled by Rita Frischer, Director of Library Services, Sinai Temple Blumenthal Library, Los Angeles.

BIBLE

Chiel, Arthur A.
A Guide to Sidrot and Haftarot.
Ktav, 1971, out of print.

Summaries of each week's Torah reading plus questions to think about. An excellent introduction and valuable aid for preparing the Bar/Bat Mitzvah's *parashah* (Torah reading) or *haftorah* (reading from the Prophets).

Tanakh. Jewish Publication Society, 1985, $19.95.

Hertz, J. H., ed.
The Pentateuch and Haftorahs.
Soncino Press, 1960, $26.

Feinsilver, Alexander, ed. and trans.
The Talmud for Today. St. Martin's Press, 1980, $14.95.

Excerpts from the Talmud, organized topically, demonstrating its relevance to modern life.

Lipis, Philip L.
Torah for the Family. World Jewish Bible Society, 1977, out of print.

This thoughtful guide for either family or individual study includes questions for three different age groups (4 to 8, 8 to 14, and youth to adult) and answers to be considered and discussed.

Plaut, W. Gunther, and Bernard J. Bamberger, eds.
The Torah: A Modern Commentary. Union of American Hebrew Congregations, 1983, $32.

Union of American Hebrew Congregations
Your Bar/Bat Mitzvah: Haftarot for Special Days. 1984, $3.95 pb.

A 63-page booklet containing Haftarot for special *Shabbats* from *Shabbat Shuvah* through *Tisha b'Av.*

Weinberg, Norbert
The Essential Torah. Bloch Publishing, 1974, $10.95.

Your Bar/Bat Mitzvah: Parashah and Haftarah with Commentary. Union of American Hebrew Congregations, 1983, $3.95 each, pb.

Fully cantillated pamphlets, one for each *parashah,* with the text of the Plaut and Bamberger edition of the Torah.

PRACTICAL GUIDES

Jeiven, Helene
Checklist for a Perfect Bar Mitzvah (and a Bat Mitzvah). Doubleday, 1983, $3.95 pb.

A step-by-step planning book for coping with every detail from choosing a florist to what clothes to wear.

Latner, Helen
The Book of Modern Jewish Etiquette. Schocken Books, 1981, $19.95.

Lewitt, Jan, and Ellen Robinson Epstein
Bar/Bat Mitzvah Planbook. Stein & Day, 1982, $18.95.

A guide to combining "the ethical insights of religion with a meaningful and tasteful event."

Rockland, Mae Shafter
The Jewish Party Book: A Contemporary Guide to Customs, Crafts and Foods. Schocken Books, 1978, out of print.

A little history and a lot of ideas for entertaining, crafts, and gifts.

NONFICTION

Donin, Hayim Halevy
To Be a Jew: A Guide to Jewish Observance in Contemporary Life. Basic Books, 1972, $15.95.

Drucker, Malka
Celebrating Life: Jewish Rites of Passage. Holiday House, 1984, $11.95.

Efron, Benjamin
Coming of Age: Your Bar or Bat Mitzvah. Union of American Hebrew Congregations, 1977, $5.

This book, published by the U.A.H.C. under the auspices of the Reform Movement, speaks directly to the Bar/Bat Mitzvah candidate about the ritual's history and significance.

Frieman, Donald G.
Milestones in the Life of a Jew. Bloch Publishing, 1980, $3.95 pb.

Included are the history and meaning of Bar Mitzvah, with biblical and talmudic sources, and some discussion of Bat Mitzvah.

Greenfield, Howard
Bar Mitzvah. Holt, Rinehart & Winston, 1981, $7.95.

A handsome book which explains the significance of becoming Bar/Bat Mitzvah in the Jewish community.

Kellerman, Eli
Jewish Ceremonial: A Guide to Jewish Prayer. Hippocrene, 1983, $9.95.

Originally published in Israel, this book contains explanations and prayers (in Hebrew and English) connected with important life cycle events.

Kolatch, Alfred J.
The Jewish Book of Why. David, 1981, $12.95.

Marcus, Audrey Friedman
Bar and Bat Mitzvah: A Family Education Unit. Alternatives in Jewish Education, n.d., 20 student manuals and a teacher's guide, $30; additional manuals $1.50 each.

A complete fourteen- to eighteen-hour course for pre-Bar/Bat Mitzvah students and their families.

Metter, Bert
Bar Mitzvah, Bat Mitzvah: How Jewish Boys and Girls Come of Age. Ticknor and Fields, 1984, $10.95 hc, $4.95 pb.

Neusner, Jacob
Mitzvah. Rossel Books, 1982, $3.95 pb.

Prager, Dennis, and Joseph Telushkin
Nine Questions People Ask About Judaism. Simon & Schuster, 1981, $16.95 hc, $7.95 pb.

Well-reasoned answers to questions about Judaism and God.

Strassfeld, Michael, and Sharon Strassfeld
The Second Jewish Catalog. Jewish Publication Society, 1976, $8.95 pb.

Swartz, Sarah Silberstein
Bar Mitzvah. Doubleday, 1985, $50.

Excerpts from memoirs, biographies, novels, short stories, and religious, ethical, and psychological literature, combined with visual art to provide the Bar Mitzvah boy with examples from his Jewish heritage.

Trepp, Leo
The Complete Book of Jewish Observance: A Practical Manual for the Modern Jew. Behrman House, 1980, $16.95.

BUILDING YOUR HOME JEWISH LIBRARY: A BEGINNER'S LIST

The books on this list represent a selection of some of the best titles for the nonexpert reader. They are not necessarily easy to read but they are all understandable to people who do not have a formal Jewish education and who are eager to learn. All the books listed here are described in this guide. The categories that are used here are not exact duplicates of the categories into which the book is divided, but the index will help you find the appropriate place.

BIBLE

Tanakh. Jewish Publication Society, 1985.

J. H. Hertz, ed.
The Pentateuch & Haftorahs: Hebrew Text, English Translation & Commentary. Soncino Press, 1960.

W. Gunther Plaut and Bernard J. Bamberger, eds.
The Torah: A Modern Commentary. Union of American Hebrew Congregations, 1981.

Louis Ginzberg.
Legends of the Bible. Jewish Publication Society, 1956.

Samuel Sandmel
The Enjoyment of Scripture. Oxford University Press, 1978.

PRAYER BOOKS

(Conservative) Jules Harlow
Siddur Sim Shalom. Rabbinical Assembly, 1985.

(Orthodox) Philip Birnbaum, ed.
The Daily Prayerbook: Ha-Siddur Ha-Shalem. Hebrew Publishing, 1964.

(Reconstructionist) Mordecai M. Kaplan and Eugene Kohn, eds.
Sabbath Prayer Book. Reconstructionist Press, 1979.

(Reform) Chaim Stern, ed.
Gates of Prayer: The Union Prayerbook. Central Conference of American Rabbis, 1975.

FICTION AND LITERATURE

Nathan Ausubel, ed.
A Treasury of Jewish Folklore. Crown Publishers, 1948.

Joel Blocker, ed.
Israeli Stories: A Selection of the Best Writing in Israel Today. Schocken Books, 1965, pb.

Irving Howe and Ruth Wisse, eds.
The Best of Sholom Aleichem. Pocket Books, 1983, pb.

Julia Wolf Mazow, ed.
The Woman Who Lost Her Names. Harper & Row, 1981, pb.

James Michener
The Source. Random House, 1965, hc; Fawcett, pb.

Howard Schwartz, ed.
Gates to the New City. Avon, 1983, pb.

Isaac Bashevis Singer
The Slave. Farrar, Straus & Giroux, 1962, pb.

Milton Steinberg
As a Driven Leaf. Behrman House, 1939. pb.

Leon Uris
Exodus. Doubleday, 1958; Bantam, pb.

FOR YOUNGER READERS

Nathan Ausubel and David C. Gross, eds.
Pictorial History of the Jewish People. Crown, 1984. Ages 12 and up.

Naomi Ben-Asher and Hayim Leaf, eds.
The Junior Jewish Encyclopedia: 10th Edition. Shengold, 1984. Ages 12–16.

Chaya Burstein
Jewish Kids Catalog. Jewish Publication Society, 1983, $10.95 pb. Ages 8 and up.

Malka Drucker.
Jewish Holiday Series. Holiday House. Ages 10 and up.
Hanukkah: Eight Nights, Eight Lights. 1980.
Passover: A Season of Freedom. 1981.
Rosh Hashanah and Yom Kippur: Sweet Beginnings. 1981.
Shabbat: A Peaceful Island. 1983.
Sukkot: A Time to Rejoice. 1982.

Deborah Pessin
The Aleph-Bet Storybook. Jewish Publication Society. 1946. Ages 6–10.

Judyth Saypol and Madeline Wikler
My Very Own Jewish Library. (8 titles.) Kar-Ben Copies. Ages 4–8.

Sydney Taylor
All-of-a-Kind Family. Dell, 1951, pb. Ages 8–12.

Isaac Bashevis Singer.
Zlateh the Goat and Other Stories. Illustrated by Maurice Sendak. Harper & Row, 1966. Ages 9–12.

Hella Taubes
The Bible Speaks. 3 vol. Soncino, 1965. Ages 6–10.

Sadie Rose Weilerstein.
The Best of K'tonton. Jewish Publication Society/Women's League for Conservative Judaism, 1980, pb. Ages 4–8.

HOW-TO BOOKS

Hayim Halevy Donin.
To Be a Jew: A Guide to Jewish Observance in Contemporary Life. Basic Books, 1972.

To Pray as a Jew: A Guide to the Prayer Book and the Synagogue Service. Basic Books, 1980.

To Raise a Jewish Child: A Guide for Parents. Basic Books, 1977.

Blu Greenberg
How to Run a Traditional Jewish Household. Simon & Schuster, 1984, hc and pb.

Simeon J. Maslin, ed.
Gates of Mitzvah: A Guide to the Jewish Life Cycle. Central Conference of American Rabbis, 1979.

Joan Nathan
The Jewish Holiday Kitchen. Schocken Books, 1979, hc and pb.

Richard Siegel, Michael Strassfeld, and Sharon Strassfeld
The Jewish Catalogs. Jewish Publication Society.
The (First) Jewish Catalog: A Do-It-Yourself Kit. 1973, pb.
The Second Jewish Catalog: Sources and Resources. 1976, pb.
The Third Jewish Catalog: Creating Community. 1980, pb.

HISTORY

Lucy S. Dawidowicz
The War Against the Jews 1933–1945. Bantam Books, 1976.

Irving Howe
World of Our Fathers. Harcourt Brace Jovanovich, 1976, hc; Simon & Schuster, 1977, pb.

Arthur Hertzberg, ed.
The Zionist Idea. Atheneum, 1969, pb.

Cecil Roth
A History of the Jews. Schocken Books, 1970, pb.

Leo W. Schwartz, ed.
Great Ages and Ideas of the Jewish People. Random House, 1956.

Elie Wiesel.
Night. Bantam Books, 1982.

JEWISH THOUGHT

Nahum N. Glatzer
The Judaic Tradition. Behrman House, 1969, pb.

Abraham J. Heschel
Between God and Man: An Interpretation of Judaism. Free Press, 1965, pb.

Francine Klagsbrun, ed.
Voices of Wisdom: Jewish Ideals and Ethics for Everyday Living. Pantheon, 1980.

Milton Steinberg
Basic Judaism. Harcourt Brace Jovanovich, 1965, pb.

Adin Steinsaltz
The Essential Talmud. Basic Books, 1976, hc and pb.

Elie Wiesel
Souls on Fire. Summit Books, 1982, pb.

REFERENCE

Philip Birnbaum, ed.
The Birnbaum Haggadah. Hebrew Publishing, 1976, pb.

Cecil Roth and Geoffrey Wigoder, eds.
Encyclopaedia Judaica. Keter, 1972.

Philip Birnbaum, ed.
Encyclopedia of Jewish Concepts. Hebrew Publishing, 1983, hc and pb.

Edward A. Levenston and Reuven Sivan, eds.
The New Bantam Megiddo Hebrew and English Dictionary. Bantam Books, 1975, pb.

BOOKSTORES AND OTHER PLACES TO FIND JEWISH BOOKS

JEWISH BOOKSTORES

BEHRMAN HOUSE INC.
235 Watching Avenue
West Orange, NJ 07050
(800) 221-2755

BOB AND BOB
Fine Jewish Gifts, Crafts and Books
151 Forest Avenue
Palo Alto, CA 94301
(415) 329-9050

CENTERSTORE JUDAIC BOOKS AND GIFTS
1718 W. Maryland
Phoenix, AZ 85015
(602) 249-9090

7119 E. Shea Boulevard
Scottsdale, AZ 85253
(602) 998-4206

1965 East Hermosa
Tempe, AZ 85282
(602) 894-0588

THEODORE S. CINNAMON LTD.
420 Jerusalem Avenue
Hicksville, L.I., NY 11801
(516) WE 5-7480

EICHLER'S BOOKS
1429 Coney Island Avenue
Brooklyn, NY 11230
(718) 258-7643

5004 13th Avenue
Brooklyn, NY 11219
(718) 633-1505

S. GOLDMAN, OTZAR HASEFARIM
33 Canal Street
New York, NY 10002
(212) 674-1707

ISRAEL BOOK SHOP, INC.
410 Harvard Street
Brookline, MA 02146
(617) 566-7113-4   566-8255

ISRAEL'S . . . THE JUDAICA CENTRE
973 Eglinton Avenue West
Toronto, Ont. M6C 2C4 Canada
(416) 789-2169

JEWISH BOOK STORE OF GREATER WASHINGTON
11250 Georgia Avenue
Wheaton, MD 20902
(301) 942-2237

THE JEWISH DEVELOPMENT COMPANY
18331-C Irvine Boulevard
Tustin, CA 92680
(714) 730-1419

JEWISH MEMORIAL COUNCIL
Woburn House
Upper Woburn Place
London, WC1H OEP England

THE JEWISH MUSEUM BOOKSHOP
1109 Fifth Avenue
New York, NY 10028
(212) 860-1860

THE JUDAICA HOUSE, LTD.
412 Cedar Lane
Teaneck, NJ 07666
(201) 836-5264

JUDAIC SPECIALTIES
45 Broad Street
Carlstadt, NJ 07002
(201) 939-4522

J. LEVINE COMPANY
58 Eldridge Street
New York, NY 10002
(212) WO 6-4460

THE MUSEUM STORE SPERTUS COLLEGE OF JUDAICA
618 South Michigan Avenue
Chicago, IL 60605
(312) 922-9012

NEGEV IMPORTING CO., LTD.
3509 Bathurst Street
Toronto, Ontario M6A 2C5, Canada
(416) 781-0071/3664

PINSKER'S
2028 Murray Avenue
Pittsburgh, PA 15217
(412) 421-3033

J. ROTH/BOOKSELLER
9427 W. Pico Boulevard
Los Angeles, CA 90035
(213) 557-1848

SHALOM BOOKS & GIFTS GALORE
3712 Oak Street
Vancouver, B.C., V6H 2M3 Canada
(604) 734-1106

THE SOURCE
110 Longwood Avenue
Altamonte Springs, FL 32701
(305) 830-1948

SPITZER'S HEBREW BOOK AND GIFT CENTER
21770 West Eleven Mile Road
Southfield, MI 48076
(313) 356-6080/1

STAVSKY HEBREW BOOK STORE
147 Essex Street
New York, NY 10002
(212) 674-1289

STEIMATZKY BOOKS OF NORTH AMERICA
56 East 11th Street
New York, NY 10003
(212) 505-2505

WEST SIDE JUDAICA
2404 Broadway (at 88th Street)
New York, NY 10024
(212) 362-7846

ZUCKER'S BOOKS
3453 Bathurst Street
Toronto, Ontario M5A 2C5, Canada
(416) 781-2133

OUT-OF-PRINT BOOK SEARCHERS

The companies listed below will search for out-of-print books of Jewish interest; the names with the asterisk have indicated there is no search charge or obligation.

OUT-OF-STATE BOOK
SERVICE
Box 3252
San Clemente, CA 9267-1053

*Marion F. Adler
OUT-OF-PRINT CHILDREN'S
BOOKS
Box 744
Stockbridge, MA 01262

*CHICAGO BOOK MART
Box 636
Chicago Heights, IL 60411

BOOKFINDER
WORLD-WIDE BOOKSEARCH
3600 Landis Avenue
P.O. Box 623
Sea Isle City, NJ 08234
(609) 263-1435

*BOOK TRACERS
Box 114
Fords, NJ 08863

PAST HISTORY
ANTIQUARIAN BOOKS
136 Parkview Terrace
Lincroft, NJ 07738
(201) 842-4545

TRANSATLANTIC BOOKS
Box 44
Matawan, NJ 07747
(William H. Groeman)

RELIABLE BOOK SERVICE
Post Office Box 2033
Paterson, NJ 07509

*AVONLEA BOOKS
Box 74, Main Station
White Plains, NY 10602

DONAN BOOKS, INC.
235 East 53rd Street
New York, NY 10022

THE BOOK RANGER
105 Charles Street
New York, NY 10014

BRENNAN BOOKS
Rare and Out-of-Print Books
P.O. Box 9002
Salt Lake City, UT 84109-0002

BOOK CLUBS

B'nai B'rith Jewish Book Club
230 Livingston Street
P.O. Box 941
Northvale, NJ 07647

Enjoy-a-Book (children's books)
25 Lawrence Avenue
Lawrence, NY 11559

Jewish Publication Society
1930 Chestnut Street
Philadelphia, PA 19103

Judaica Book Club
Jonathan David
68-22 Eliot Avenue
Middle Village, NY 11379

The Steimatzky Jewish-Book-of-
the-Month Club
56 East 11th Street
New York, NY 10003

BOOK-RELATED ORGANIZATIONS AND MAJOR JEWISH LIBRARIES

We have listed here some organizations that are involved with Jewish books, and some of the larger Jewish libraries. Some of them are specialized—YIVO has books on Yiddish and Eastern European Jewish life—while others are general. We have not listed the libraries at universities with Jewish studies departments, many of which have extensive collections of Jewish books.

Anti-Defamation League of
B'nai B'rith
823 United Nations Plaza
New York, NY 10017

Association of Jewish Libraries
c/o National Foundation for Jewish Culture
122 East 42nd Street, #1512
New York, NY 10068

American Jewish Archives
3101 Clifton Avenue
Cincinnati, OH 45220

American Jewish Historical
Society
2 Thornton Road
Waltham, MA 02154

Leo Baeck Institute
129 East 73rd Street
New York, NY 10021

Dropsie University
Broad and York Streets
Philadelphia, PA 19066

Hebrew Union College–Jewish
Institute of Religion
3101 Clifton Avenue
Cincinnati, OH 45220

Hebrew Union College–Jewish
Institute of Religion
1 West Fourth Street
New York, NY 10012

Jewish Braille Institute of
America
110 East 30th Street
New York, NY 10010

Jewish Division, New York Public
Library
42nd Street and Fifth Avenue
New York, NY 10018

Jewish Guild for the Blind
15 West 65th Street
New York, NY 10023

Jewish Theological Seminary of
America
3080 Broadway
New York, NY 10027

JWB Jewish Book Council
15 East 26th Street
New York, NY 10010

National Yiddish Book Center
Old East Street School
P.O. Box 969
Amherst, MA 01004

Spertus College of Judaica
618 South Michigan Avenue
Chicago, IL 60605

Yeshiva University
500 West 185th Street
New York, NY 10033

YIVO Institute for Jewish
Research
1048 Fifth Avenue
New York, NY 10028

XII

Women

Women and the Jewish Literary Tradition

Roselyn Bell

Women have been an integral part of the Jewish experience ever since Sarah (then Sarai) left Ur of the Chaldees with Abraham (then Abram), but they have played a far less integral role in the Jewish literary tradition. While Jewish men wrote commentaries and philosophical treatises, poetry, and *midrash*, Jewish women left behind few writings during the centuries of Jewish history before the last two. Only the poetry of Miriam and Deborah and Hannah in the Bible, the diary of Gluckel of Hameln, and a few anonymous *tehinnot* (special devotional prayers popular among women) come to mind.

Yet over the past decade there has been a sudden flowering of writing by and about the Jewish woman. All aspects of Jewish women's lives—their history, roles and role models, religious sensibilities, and sociological strengths and difficulties—have become the subject of scholarly and popular examination. This contemporary interest in women's issues is, of course, partially an influence of the general feminist movement, in which Jewish women have played a leading role. But long before "women" became a "hot topic," Jewish law was concerned with the subject of their rights and responsibilities and in fact devoted an order of the Mishnah to them. (The tractate titled "Women" actually deals with marital law and other not exclusively "women's" subjects.)

The interest of Jewish law (*halakhah*) in women, however, is quite different from the contemporary one. *Halakhah* defines

---

Roselyn Bell is senior editor of *Hadassah* magazine and has been active in religious feminist groups.

being a woman as a separate, all-encompassing and unchange-
able status. With this status come privileges, responsibilities,
and exemptions—exemptions from *mitzvot* that today's feminists have charged relegated women to second-class citizenship
with fewer avenues of religious and intellectual expression.

Why, if the biblical account of creation in Genesis 1:27 describes male and female as reciprocal parts of the image of
God, should Jewish law have mandated such different roles for
the two sexes? Quite simply, because Jewish law is status law,
which recognizes different categories of people—Jew and non-
Jew, slave and freeman, man and woman—with differing obligations and derivatively varying rights and privileges in society. Under this kind of law, equality is not a general concept
except among people of a common status, and status definitions shape all relationships among individuals—the goal being
the overall good of society.

The rubric most frequently given by the Talmud for differ-
entiating men's role in *mitzvot* from women's is quoted in *Kid-
dushin 29A*: "All positive commandments limited as to time,
men are liable and women are exempt." Thus, for example,
women are excused from wearing **tallit** and **tefillin**, counting
the *omer* (the eight weeks between Passover and Shavuoth), or
hearing the *shofar* blown. But as a predictor this rule of thumb
is not as foolproof as one might wish: there are lots of positive,
time-bound *mitzvot* that women are required by *halakhah* to do,
such as eating *matzah* on **Pesach** or hearing the Megilla read
on Purim, and two of the three special women's *mitzvot*—
lighting *Shabbos* candles and going to *mikveh*—are very time-
related.

Altogether Maimonides in his *Sefer Hamitzvot* counts only
fourteen *mitzvot* out of sixty positive commandments from which
women are exempt. But the pattern of exemption led to wom-
en's exclusion from counting as persons in the *minyan*, serving
as witnesses in court or engaging in prolonged, systematic
study of the Torah—that is, restriction of access to the devotional, ritual, judicial, and intellectual aspects of Judaism. Rabbi
Saul Berman has suggested that this pattern of exemption was
intended to protect the woman's preferred (but not required)
role in the home, by barring her from mandatory appearances

in the public realm at fixed times. But what does this mean in our day, when even a "traditional homemaker" spends large chunks of her life in the public sphere—in school, in the market, or behind the wheel of a car "chauffering"?

If the public sphere has greatly expanded in our generation, perhaps also the home sphere was not so narrow a place in the past. The "woman of valor" described in Proverbs 31:10–31—the first portrait of a superwoman—had an important economic role outside the home as well as managing the domestic economy of her household. On the historical plane, we know from the lives of Doña Gracia (c. 1510–1569) and Gluckel of Hameln that Jewish women sometimes wielded considerable political and economic clout, often as a result of a power base inherited from husband or father, but expanded under female direction. Further down the economic ladder, it was common for European and first-generation American Jewish women to be major breadwinners in their families. They worked out of necessity because their husbands were engaged in the study of Torah, could not make an adequate living due to adverse conditions or restrictive laws, or had disappeared entirely, leaving the woman to support the family.

It is difficult to get a clear picture of just what the lives, mind sets, and motivations of Jewish women of earlier generations were like, precisely because the literary record is so sparse. Not that Jewish women were illiterate; they could usually read prayer book Hebrew (although not always, as evidenced by the numerous "women's prayer books" translated into Yiddish or the language of the land) and often Yiddish or Ladino and the lingua franca of their gentile neighbors. But through the centuries until our own, they rarely got a formal Jewish education, with Renaissance Italy being a remarkable exception. Of course, there were the occasional rabbis' daughters, such as Beruriah or Rashi's daughters, who became learned in Torah almost by osmosis and could engage in halakhic discourse. But they were certainly the exception.

In the latter part of the nineteenth century, it became customary for Jewish girls from the upper class or comfortable bourgeoisie to attend the secular schools of the country, which gave them a vastly different cultural orientation than that of their *yeshiva*-educated brothers and husbands-to-be. Not until 1917, when Sarah Schenirer founded the first school of the Bais Yaakov movement, were there full-time, formal schools that gave girls both a Jewish education and vocational skills. By today, of course, Jewish women have been formally educated for several generations. But only in the last decade has the spark of the feminist movement been added to the kindling wood of adequate Jewish and secular learning to produce scholarly works on many aspects of the Jewish woman's experience.

It is precisely because of the lack of a Jewish woman's literary tradition that the present outburst of scholarship by and about women is so exciting. Everywhere gaps are being filled: delving into history, Marion Kaplan has studied the Jüdischer Frauenbund, the German Jewish woman's social service network that was the precursor of contemporary Jewish feminism, while Edward Bristow has examined the white slave trade in Jewish girls. Turning to literature, Julia Wolf Mazow has produced an anthology of Jewish women's fiction, while Sonya Michel and Charlotte Baum (in *The Jewish Woman in America*, coauthored with Paula Hyman) have analyzed how American Jewish literature has portrayed Jewish women.

Taking on the core area of *halakhah*, so long exclusively a rabbinical and thus a male preserve, Blu Greenberg and Rachel Biale have written knowledgeable yet committed feminist critiques of the delineations of women's role set down by Jewish law. Greenberg has written that Judaism and feminism should learn from each other, and has predicted that women who become expert in *halakhah*, along with rabbis who are sympathetic to women's needs, will discover a "halakhic way" to resolve women's present disabilities under Jewish law without rending the fabric of tradition. Naturally, strict tradition has its defenders, too, and not a few books have appeared in recent years defending the *halakhah* and the traditional female role against the perceived onslaughts of feminism. Moshe Meiselman's *Jewish Woman in Jewish Law* and Yisroel Miller's *In Search of the Jewish Woman* are two such works.

Another area where controversy—and creativity—can be expected is in the production of new rituals to celebrate the female life cycle and new liturgy expressing women's sensibilities and insights. Some of these innovations have caught on already, as with *simhat bat* (girl baby-naming ceremonies) and Rosh Hodesh (New Moon) celebrations, but others, such as addressing God as "She," still seem to jar. Another avenue of creativity, open to men and women alike, is the creation of new *midrash* that takes a feminine or feminist point of view. Examples of this genre are the *Akeda* (sacrifice of Isaac) as seen by Sarah, or the victory of Deborah and Barak as seen by Sisera's mother.

Even more fundamental a challenge has been Susannah Heschel's call for a theological revision that will "transform women in Judaism from object to subject." This more global task perhaps will be accomplished by building on the groundwork being laid by the present generation of women scholars.

In the coming decade there will probably be an expansion of both research and *midrash* bringing a female perspective to Judaism—and an explosion, too, of polemics on the desirability of this trend. But despite the controversies, one can rejoice that the Jewish woman's voice is at last being heard—and read—on numerous aspects of Jewish life and experience. It is an exciting time to be Jewish and a woman.

BOOKS ON WOMEN AND JUDAISM

There is no book that provides an objective and nonpartisan survey of the issues raised by the conflict between modern feminism and traditional Judaism. The subject has produced much heat and generated intense polemics, but it has produced little solid scholarship. Kaplan's study, *The Jewish Feminist Movement in Germany*, is one of the few exceptions, but it is a very specialized work. *The Jewish Woman*, edited by Koltun, may be the best choice for an introduction to the subject, since it includes essays expressing a balanced range of views. For a study of the issues as Jewish law (*halakhah*) deals with them, *Women and Jewish Law* by Biale is a useful work. It is written by a feminist but it presents the sources objectively.

The strongest and most authoritative statement of the case against feminism is made in Meiselman's *Jewish Woman in Jewish*

Law. His knowledge of the legal issues is unquestioned even by those who disagree with him. On the other side of the issue, Heschel's anthology, *On Being a Jewish Feminist,* states the feminist position forcefully. Schneider's *Jewish and Female* doesn't so much argue the feminist case as take it for granted. Its goal is to provide useful information to Jewish women who agree with the feminist position. Schneider is the editor of *Lilith* (see PERIODICALS), a Jewish feminist magazine essential to any reader who wishes to keep informed on the issues.

In addition to the lack of works of scholarship, there is also a shortage of biographies of Jewish women. The only biography of Golda Meir in print is one for children. (It's by David Adler, and it's a good one.) Her autobiography is out of print. Lillian Wald is also represented only by a biography for younger readers. And there are many other important women waiting for a biographer. Overall, the role of women is still not fairly represented in general historical works. (*Written Out of History* by Henry and Teitz is something of a corrective to this situation. It is described later.) —R. S. F. & W. W.

Brown, Charlotte, Paula Hyman, and Sonya Michael
The Jewish Woman in America. New American Library, 1977, $6.95 pb.

This combination of history, social analysis, and literary criticism covers virtually every aspect of American Jewish life for women. The topics covered include Eastern European Jewish women in America, assimilation, the split between the "uptown lady" and the "downtown woman," and the changing image of Jewish women in literature. Perhaps as a result of its wide-ranging subject matter, the book loses its focus. It remains a valuable study nonetheless.

Biale, Rachel
Women and Jewish Law: An Exploration of Women's Issues in Halakhic Sources. Schocken Books, 1984, $18.95.

While there is no doubt that the author's sympathies are with the feminists, this is an objective, dispassionate, and scholarly survey of the traditional sources as they deal with women. The issues covered include marriage, divorce, birth control, rape, abortion, lesbianism, and participation in congregational worship. Biale argues that rabbinic thinking has been flexible in its development and, therefore, can be flexible today. While disagreeing with aspects of traditional Jewish thought, she attempts to understand its rationale, and she does not oversimplify the beliefs of those with whom she disagrees.

Bristow, Edward J.
Prostitution and Prejudice: The Jewish Fight Against White Slavery, 1870–1939. Schocken Books, 1983, $21.95.

Bristow traces the origins of Jewish prostitution in central and eastern Europe, seeing it as linked to the enormous social and religious upheaval that occurred in the Jewish community during the late nineteenth century. Among the sources Bristow draws on are police reports, government studies, and contemporary newspapers. He also discusses how Jewish communities throughout the world responded to the sudden growth in prostitution, a response that involved some of the most important Jewish leaders and organizations. Some feminists have criticized Bristow for a tendency to sexual stereotyping in his analysis. While the book is filled with statistics and references, they have been consigned to the back—available to those who need them, out of the way of the general reader.

Dash, Joan
Summoned to Jerusalem: The Life of Henrietta Szold. Jewish Publication Society, $15.

The biography of a truly remarkable woman. After visiting Palestine, Szold concluded that massive health and sanitation projects were needed to help build a Jewish homeland. In 1912, to carry out these efforts she founded Hadassah, a women's Zionist organization. She was the first woman to become a member of the Zionist Executive. After Hitler's accession to power, she was active in programs to help European Jewish youth emigrate to Palestine, and she was responsible for saving thousands of lives. In addition, she was an editor at the Jewish Publication Society for 23 years, and translated Ginzberg's monumental *Legends of the Jews.*

Gluckel of Hameln
The Memoirs of Gluckel of Hameln. Translated by Marvin Lowenthal. Schocken Books, 1977, $7.95 pb.

An extraordinary work, these memoirs were written in 1690 by a woman who married at fourteen, was widowed at forty-four after thirty years of marriage, and took on the responsibility of raising her twelve children and running the family business. She began writing in an attempt to combat the melancholy caused by her husband's death. Although world events are reflected in her memoirs—plagues, wars, pogroms, the false messiah Shabbetai Zevi—the focus is on daily life, on intimate and mundane affairs. Gluckel was a natural storyteller and wrote in a lively manner, making use of fables and folktales. Her book is compelling reading as well as an invaluable historical source. The account of her husband's death is especially touching.

Greenberg, Blu

On Women and Judaism: A View from Tradition. Jewish Publication Society, 1982, $5.95 pb.

Many feminists have criticized this book as not being firmly enough committed to the feminist cause. As many or more Orthodox Jews have criticized it for placing a commitment to modern "humanistic" feminism above Jewish law. Greenberg writes as a feminist who is also loyal to traditional Jewish law. She contends that despite the tensions between the demands of *halakhah* and feminism, these need not be contradictory loyalties; that both are essential to Orthodox women. She argues that Jewish law has changed in the past and can change now to reflect new realities and attitudes. Whether or not you agree with her, there is no question that she writes clearly, with warmth and sensitivity. Among the topics she discusses are women's role in the synagogue, divorce, abortion, and the relationship between feminism and Jewish survival.

Henry, Sondra, and Emily Teitz

Written Out of History: Our Jewish Foremothers. Biblio Press, 1983, $12.95 hc, $9.75 pb.

This book gathers in one place a diverse range of references to Jewish women drawn from historical reports, memoirs, court papers, and other documents. It profiles women from the biblical to the modern era, including Sarah, the noted talmudic figure Beruriah, Doña Gracia, and Emma Lazarus. The authors also describe women of the ghetto, Hasidic women, and other less well known figures. The book is a useful supplement to histories that have ignored the role of Jewish women, even if it is sometimes overstated and polemical.

Heschel, Susannah

On Being a Jewish Feminist: A Reader. Schocken Books, 1983, $20 hc, $9.95 pb.

A collection of essays, about half previously published, on the images of Jewish women in literature, myth, and liturgy, and the role of women in modern Jewish life. Among the contributors are Cynthia Ozick, Rachel Adler, Rabbi Laura Geller, Judith Plaskow, and Deborah Lipstadt. The essays are uneven in quality, but the overall level is very high. Particularly noteworthy are Ozick's "Notes Towards Finding the Right Question," originally published in *Lilith* magazine, and Adler's "The Jew Who Wasn't There," one of the first serious studies of the subject. Heschel's introduction, possibly the best thing in the book, excoriates "the failure" of Judaism to respond to the challenges of feminism, saying that it demonstrates "the morbid condition of Judaism" and indicates Judaism's unwillingness to accept women as equals.

Kaplan, Marion
The Jewish Feminist Movement in Germany: The Campaigns of the Jüdischer Frauenbund, 1904–1938. Greenwood Press, 1979, $17.95.

This carefully researched book tells about Bertha Pappenheim (1859–1936) and the *Jüdischer Frauenbund*, the social service organization she founded in 1904 to promote female suffrage and to fight white slavery, prostitution, and illegitimacy. Although specialized and not intended for the general reader, Kaplan's study is important as one of the first major works of scholarship in this field. Three facts about Bertha Pappenheim: She was a descendant of Gluckel of Hameln. She was the woman referred to by Freud as "Anna O.," and her case was considered of central importance to the development of psychoanalysis. She died following an interrogation by the Gestapo.

Koltun, Elizabeth, ed.
The Jewish Woman. Schocken Books, 1976, $7.95 pb.

The basic anthology of texts on women in Judaism, this book contains many important essays reflecting many points of view. Included are an essay by Rabbi Saul Berman, dean of Stern College for Women at Yeshiva University, which affirms the centrality of the domestic role for Jewish women; Marion Kaplan on Bertha Pappenheim; Blu Greenberg on Judaism and feminism. Other essays are on women in Jewish literature, women in Jewish education, life cycle rituals for women, Henrietta Szold (the founder of Hadassah), and creating a new *ketubah* (the traditional Jewish marriage contract). Compared to the Heschel anthology listed earlier, Koltun's book is less issue oriented and more historical.

Mazow, Julia Wolf, ed.
The Woman Who Lost Her Names. Harper & Row, 1980, $6.68 pb.

An anthology of fiction with Jewish feminist themes. The title story is by Nessa Rapoport, and the other writers anthologized include Anzia Yezierska, Emma Goldman, Tillie Olsen, Grace Paley, and Aviva Cantor. Much of the material is not readily available elsewhere.

Meiselman, Moshe
Jewish Woman in Jewish Law. Ktav, 1978, $15.

A strong defense of the traditional role of women in Jewish life, this book was written to rebut feminist arguments. Meiselman argues that feminism is antithetical to Jewish life, that a woman's desire for a career is destructive, and that Jewish law explicitly requires a woman's main goal to be her family's religious well-being. He is very knowledgeable about Jewish law, making this book a useful reference even for those who totally disagree with him. Probably the most extensive antifeminist treatise.

Miller, Yisroel
In Search of the Jewish Woman. Feldheim, 1984, $7.95 hc, $5.95 pb.

Miller makes a concise and straightforward presentation of the traditional viewpoint on the role of Jewish women. He concentrates on a woman's role as mother, housewife, and guardian of the moral and spiritual life of the family. He discusses such topics as child rearing, modesty, and careers, and cites the Bible, *midrash*, and rabbinic sources to support his views.

Roth, Cecil
Doña Gracia of the House of Nasi. Jewish Publication Society, 1978, $4.95 pb.

By any standards, Gracia Nasi was an extraordinary person. Born in the early sixteenth century, she was a Converso—one of the Sephardic Jews who had publicly accepted Christianity while secretly remaining Jewish. She was repeatedly forced to flee from persecution, moving from Portugal to the Low Countries to Italy to Turkey. She worked tirelessly to aid fellow Jews escape the Inquisition. Finally, once settled in the Turkish Empire, she revealed her Jewish identity. She was a political activist and, in addition to her efforts on behalf of refugees, she was an active patron of scholarship who established synagogues and academies, and

founded a *yeshiva*. Roth's biography of her is solidly grounded in his knowledge of the period and is the book to read for anyone interested in learning about her.

Schneider, Susan Weidman
Jewish and Female: Choices and Changes in Our Lives Today. Simon & Schuster, 1984, $19.95 hc, $10.95 pb.

A founder of the feminist magazine *Lilith* (see PERIODICALS), Schneider has written a book that is informative and sympathetic, and less concerned with polemic than with building the foundation for social change. The first part of the book deals with the intellectual, spiritual, emotional, and sexual lives of Jewish women; the second part with marriage, divorce, and children; the third part with power and participation in the community. A "Networking Directory" includes a wide variety of resources—stores, cantorial schools for women, child care services, centers for battered women, *mikvehs*, women rabbis, libraries, and more.

Wagenknecht, Edward
Daughters of the Covenant: Portraits of Six Jewish Women. University of Massachusetts Press, 1983, $17.50.

Wagenknecht profiles six Jewish women, not all of them especially concerned about either Judaism or women's issues, but all notable for their accomplishments. They represent a wide range of personalities, from the genteel and elegant Rebecca Gratz, a founder of the Jewish Sunday School movement in America, and said to be the basis for the character of Rebecca in Scott's *Ivanhoe*, to the fiery revolutionary, Emma Goldman, to Henrietta Szold, founder of Hadassah. Also included are writers Emma Lazarus and Amy Levy, and Lillian Wald, a social reformer and founder of the Henry Street Settlement.

Welch, Susan, and Fred Ullrich
The Political Life of American Jewish Women. Biblio Press, 1984, $5.95 pb.

Drawing on various surveys of public opinion, the authors analyze the ways in which the political views of American Jewish women differ from those of men and from those of Protestant and Catholic women. The issues examined are both those seen as of specific concern to women—abortion, women's rights—and those of general concern, such as defense spending and welfare programs. Profiles of some important American Jewish women in politics are also included. Reproduced from typescript.

Glossary

aggadah. The nonlegal, narrative, and interpretative material in the Talmud is called *aggadah.*

agunah (pl., agunot). A woman whose husband has disappeared and who has neither proof of his death nor a divorce. In Jewish law, she is prohibited from remarrying.

Bar Mitzvah, Bat Mitzvah. The name of the ceremony conferring adult status and obligations on a Jewish child. Bar Mitzvah is the ceremony for boys; Bat Mitzvah is the ceremony for girls. See also: *mitzvah.*

B.C.E. B.C. (Before Christ) has Christological implications; B.C.E. (Before the Common Era), which refers to the same historical period, does not.

Beth Din. A rabbinical court empowered to resolve religious issues such as divorces and to mediate civil disputes between Jews who accept its authority.

bris. The ritual circumcision of Jewish boys, usually performed on their eighth day of life.

C.E. To avoid the Christological implications of A.D. (anno Domini, or Year of Our Lord), C.E. (Common Era) is used.

chesed. A Hebrew word for which there is no exact English equivalent, *chesed* is generally translated as "lovingkindness" or "benevolence."

Chumash. A Hebrew word meaning "five," used to refer to the first five books of the Bible, which are also known as the Torah and the Five Books of Moses.

Diaspora. A term derived from a Greek word meaning "dispersion," it is used to describe collectively those places where Jews live outside of Israel.

etrog. A citron; used ritually during the celebration of the Jewish holiday Sukkot.

The Five Scrolls. Five books of the Bible—Ecclesiastes, Esther, Song of Songs, Ruth, and Lamentations—are referred to collectively as the Five Scrolls.

Gaon. A title meaning "genius" or "great one."

Gemara. The Talmud comprises two major components: the *Mishnah* (q.v.) and the *Gemara,* which is an extended commentary on the Mishnah.

Haftorah (pl., Haftarot). Each week in the synagogue service, a portion of the Torah is read aloud. A specific selection from the Prophets is also read, and that selection is called a *Haftorah.*

Haggadah. Haggadah is a Hebrew word meaning "the telling." When the phrase "the Haggadah" is used, it refers to the text of the service for the Passover *seder,* which tells the story of the Exodus from Egypt.

Halakhah. Jewish law. The Hebrew word literally means "pathway."

Hanukkah. A Jewish holiday commemorating the victory of the Jews over the Syrians in 165 B.C.E. and the rededication of the Temple. Also spelled *Hanukah, Chanukah.*

Hasid, Hasidic. A Hasid, or Hasidic Jew, is one who is a member of any of a number of Orthodox Jewish groups known for their piety and religious fervor. The plural form is Hasidim. Their religious outlook is based on the ideas of Rabbi Israel ben Eliezer (known as the Baal Shem Tov).

Haskalah. The Jewish "Enlightenment" of the eighteenth and nineteenth centuries, a movement that sought to modernize Jewish life and to bring Jews into the mainstream of European culture.

Havdalah. The ceremony marking the end of Shabbat and the beginning of the new week—the passing from the holy to the secular—is called Havdalah. The literal meaning of the word in Hebrew is "separation."

Havurah. A small prayer or study group.

Judenrat (pl., Judenrate). A Jewish council, specifically one formed by the Nazis to help them rule the Jewish ghettos.

kaballah. The term used to describe Jewish mystical teachings.

ketubah (pl., ketubim). A Jewish marriage contract.

Kiddush. The blessing, usually said over a cup of wine, to sanctify the sabbath or a holiday.

klezmer. The Jewish folk music that developed in Eastern Europe is known as *klezmer* music. The musicians who perform it are known as *klezmerim.*

Ladino. Also known as Judeo-Spanish, Ladino is a language that originated during the Middle Ages among Jews of Spanish origin. It blends elements of Spanish and Hebrew.

Maccabees. The name of the family that led the rebellion against Syrian rule now commemorated by the holiday Hanukkah.

Maccabiah Games. The "Jewish Olympics"—an international sports competition for Jewish athletes held every four years in Israel.

machzor. A special prayer book used during the Jewish High Holy Days of Rosh Hashanah and Yom Kippur.

menorah. The word menorah has two distinct meanings. It refers to the seven-branched candelabrum that once stood in the Temple in Jerusalem. It also refers to the nine-branched candelabrum now used during the Hanukkah celebration.

mensch. An admirable, upstanding, first-rate human being. To be considered a *mensch* is a real compliment; to be a *mensch* is a real accomplishment.

mezuzah. A small case containing a parchment scroll on which are written specific verses from the Bible. Traditional Jews attach one to the right side of the door frames of the entrance of their home and of the rooms within it.

midrash (pl., midrashim). Derived from a Hebrew word meaning "exposition," *midrash* refers to homiletic literature—much of it of great antiquity—that explains and expands on the text of the Bible.

mikveh (pl., mikvehs or mikvot). A ritual bath. Jews who are in a state of ritual impurity—such as women following their menstrual period—immerse themselves in the bath to ritually purify themselves.

Mishnah. A body of Jewish law, compiled in the third century C.E., and forming the core of the Talmud.

mitzvah (pl., mitzvot). A divine precept or command. The Torah contains 613 *mitzvot*.

mohel. The man who performs the ritual circumcision known as *bris*.

nusach (pl., nusachot). The arrangement of prayers and tunes used in prayer are referred to as the *nusach*. Over the centuries, different communities of Jews developed different *nusachot*.

Oral Law. According to traditional Jews, when the Torah—the Written Law—was given at Sinai it was accompanied by explanations of its meaning and purpose. These explanations are known as the Oral Law.

Passover. The holiday commemorating Israel's deliverance from slavery in Egypt. The name comes from the Angel of Death passing over Jewish homes, while killing the firstborn sons of the Egyptians.

Pesach. The Hebrew name for Passover.

Purim. The holiday that celebrates the deliverance of the Jews from persecution in ancient Persia. The story is told in the Book of Esther.

responsum (pl., responsa). Rabbinic answers to questions of Jewish law. Responsa have been written and collected into books for centuries.

Rosh Hashanah. The Jewish New Year.

Sacred Writings. The name given to that portion of the Bible known in Hebrew as *Kethuvim*. It encompasses, among other books, the Psalms, Proverbs, and the Five Scrolls.

schlemiel. An inept and foolish bungler.

Seder. The ritual dinner at which Passover is celebrated.

Sephardim. Jews of Oriental or Iberian descent. The adjective to describe them is *Sephardic*.

Shabbat, Shabbos. The Sabbath. *Shabbos* is the way the word is pronounced by Western European Jews; *Shabbat* is the Sephardic and Israeli pronunciation.

Shavuoth. A holiday observed seven weeks after the beginning of Passover. It is both a harvest festival and a commemoration of the giving of the Ten Commandments.

shivah. The formal seven-day period of mourning following the death of a close relative. People who are observing the mourning period are said to be "sitting shivah."

shofar. A ram's horn made into a trumpet. It is blown in the synagogue during prayers on Rosh Hashanah and Yom Kippur.

shtetl. The Yiddish word for a small Jewish town in Eastern Europe.

Shulkhan Arukh. A codification of Jewish law, compiled in the sixteenth century by Rabbi Joseph Karo and, with emendations by later scholars, still accepted as authoritative by Orthodox Jews.

siddur. The prayer book used for daily, sabbath, and holiday prayers. See also: *machzor*.

Simchat Torah. The holiday celebrating the completion of the annual cycle of Torah readings in the synagogue.

sukkah. A small hut or booth in which observant Jews eat their meals during the weeklong celebration of Sukkot. It is symbolic of the huts or tents in which Jews lived during their wanderings in the wilderness following the Exodus from Egypt.

Sukkot. Also called Sukkos, this is a holiday of thanksgiving for the harvest.

tallit. A fringed prayer shawl worn by men during the morning prayers.

Talmud. The Talmud comprises the Mishnah and the Ge-mara—a compilation of Jewish law and a later body of commentary and analysis.

Tanakh. A Hebrew acronym for the Bible. The word comes from the three parts into which Jews divide the Bible: *T*orah, *N*evi'im, and *K*ethuvim (Torah, Prophets, Sacred Writings).

tefillin. Also known as *phylacteries, tefillin* are two small leather boxes containing scrolls on which are written selected verses from the Bible. Men strap them onto their left arm and head during morning prayers.

Torah. The first five books of the Bible, the "Books of Moses."

Tu bi-Shevat. A minor holiday also known as the New Year for Trees, and frequently referred to as "Jewish Arbor Day."

Tz'enah Ur'enah. A seventeenth-century compilation of Torah commentary and lore. Written in Yiddish, its principal readership was women, most of whom did not read Hebrew.

Yad Vashem. The Holocaust memorial and museum in Israel.

yeshiva. A school for the advanced study of the Talmud and other Jewish religious knowledge.

Yiddishkeit. A Yiddish word meaning "Jewishness."

Yom Ha'atzmaut. A modern holiday celebrating Israel Independence Day and the creation of the modern State of Israel.

Yom Ha-shoah. The day on which the victims of the Holocaust are commemorated.

Yom Kippur. The culmination of the High Holy Days, Yom Kippur is a day on which Jews and pray to atone for their sins, and the sins of the Jewish people, during the previous year. It is also known as the Day of Atonement.

Yom Kippur War. The 1973 Arab-Israel War, in which the Arabs launched a surprise attack on Israel on Yom Kippur.

Zohar. The Book of Splendor, a Jewish mystical work attributed to the second-century sage Rabbi Shimon ben Yohai.

z'mirot. Songs sung around the table during Sabbath and holiday meals.

Index of Authors and Titles